Robert A. Evans
and
Alice Frazer Evans

HUMAN RIGHTS

A DIALOGUE BETWEEN
THE FIRST AND THIRD WORLDS

ORBIS BOOKS

Maryknoll, New York 10545

LUTTERWORTH PRESS
Luke House, Farnham Road,
Guildford, Surrey, GU1 4XD

**To the children of God
who benefit from, contribute to, and labor for
"a more just, sustainable,
and peaceful world community"**

Unless otherwise noted, all biblical quotations are from the New English Bible.

Copyright © 1983 by Orbis Books

Published by Orbis Books, Maryknoll, NY 10545 in collaboration with Lutterworth Press, Luke House, Farnham Road, Guildford, Surrey, GU1 4XD, England

All rights reserved

Manufactured in the United States of America

Manuscript Editor: William E. Jerman

Library of Congress Cataloging in Publication Data
Main entry under title:
Human rights.

   Includes bibliographical references.
   1. Civil rights—Religious aspects—
Christianity—Addresses, essays, lectures.
2. Church and underdeveloped areas—Addresses,
essays, lectures.   I. Evans, Robert A., 1937–
II. Evans, Alice F., 1939–   .   III. Title.
BT738.15.H85 1983   261.7   82-18780
ISBN 0-88344-194-2 (pbk.)

Lutterworth ISBN 01-7188-2589-6

CONTENTS

PREFACE

There is an acknowledged and expanding distance between the peoples and nations that have come to be characterized as the "First" and "Third" Worlds. These are disturbing designations, because they point to the polarity and growing tension between the rich and poor, the satisfied and hungry, the powerful and powerless, wherever they live. The added tragedy is that these same divisions exist not only within national and international political and economic structures but also within a worldwide community that the Christian churches claim to be the Body of Christ.

The plea to respect, protect, and promote human rights has been raised repeatedly by the United Nations General Assembly, by individual countries, independent organizations such as Amnesty International, and religious bodies throughout the world, including the Roman Catholic, Orthodox, and Protestant churches. Yet there is an increasing gap between rhetoric and application. There appears to be little agreement on the meaning of human rights, especially on the issue of which rights have priority when claims are in conflict. There seems to be a pattern in this struggle that breaks down along First (capitalist), Second (socialist), and Third (nonaligned) World perspectives.

Global studies show that individuals and nations are increasingly interdependent in a world that is more vulnerable to destruction by environmental deterioration, wars, and other human disruptions with every passing year. However, the global reports also reveal little evidence that nations or significant numbers of individuals are taking the necessary steps to adjust their policies or lifestyles to address the danger. Perhaps most troublesome is the apparent lack of meaningful dialogue about these life-threatening problems in ordinary communities in any region of the globe. The Christian community is international and cross-cultural, but has so far failed to put the issues of human rights or global survival as a universal priority.

Without methods and strategies to bridge these gaps, there is a danger of growing isolation, strengthened by renewed claims to territorial rights of interpretation. In this light a project of research and education was developed to contribute to the bridging of these gaps in the critical area of human rights understood from a global perspective. A previous project, employing factual case studies of contemporary issues followed by commentaries from prominent theologians (*Christian Theology: A Case Method Approach,* Robert A. Evans and Thomas D. Parker, eds. [New York: Harper & Row, 1976]), provided a model. After two years of interviews and field research in countries on six continents, we finally selected eight cases. They were written, revised, disguised, taught (often in the country of origin), revised again, and finally approved and released by the principal parties in each case.

v

There are several types of cases. The eight cases in this volume are not "verbatims," which include all the comments made on a given occasion, nor are they "case histories," which often present an entire range of background material and a broad narrative picture of a situation. Rather, this kind of case study contains selected factual information which focuses on specific issues or problems that require a response from one or more persons in the case. The decision must be one on which reasonable persons would disagree. The authors are thus challenged to "enter" the situation and present a balanced portrayal of conflicting viewpoints. Parties on both sides of an issue need to agree that their perspective is fairly represented. The case writers have sought to be faithful to this challenge.

In this approach to case writing, which is sometimes called the Harvard or HBS case method due to its development at the Harvard Business School, the central figure(s) authorizes the use of the case as faithfully representing his or her view of this event or series of events. The case thus becomes, in an appropriately disguised form, a "gift" from the participant(s) to the reader and learner. The authors understand this gift of experience to be a gift for ministry as an educational resource.

It is also important to comment on the limited use of disguises within the cases. The names of public figures identified in the cases, e.g., President Anastasio Somoza Debayle, General Idi Amin, Mrs. Yasuko Nakaya, The Rev. Fred Morris, Premier Bjilke-Peterson, or Bishop K. H. Ting, are, of course, actual. However, the names of those persons who personally shared in each case their dilemma with the authors are disguised to protect their privacy. In some cases, such as "The Eye of the Needle," the location of the case events is also disguised at the request of case participants. A footnote on each case distinguishes disguised from actual names.

In each of the twenty or more foundational cases initially researched through interviews with civil and religious representatives, we posed the following question: "What do you see as the most important issue of human rights in your part of the world?" In the eight cases selected, there was agreement between those interviewed on the issue or the events around which the case study was prepared. The criteria applied to all of the cases were that they:

(1) Address a central concern for the given nation or broader region of the world;

(2) Involve an issue of human rights that encourages international dialogue because it touches on similar concerns in other regions of the world;

(3) Focus on issues where theological reflection might be fresh and the case approach might be distinctive;

(4) Provide a balance in the group of cases, both as to issues and geographical distribution; and

(5) Be based on data accessible to the researchers.

There are obvious specific areas of the violation of human rights that many would expect to be represented here: racial discrimination in South Africa, or a homeland for Palestinians in the Middle East, or torture and summary execution in El Salvador. In each instance those interviewed thought these problems could be approached from a different perspective. The case study on Nicaragua is symbolic of struggles against oppression in other parts of the world. Some colleagues argued for a different approach to human rights on the African continent, so the case selected focuses on Uganda rather than South Africa.

At times individuals asked us not to publish material gathered for a case because it might jeopardize their work or even result in reprisals on individuals or groups. Such requests were honored; case studies begun on Egypt, Israel, and the Palestinians do not appear in this collection.

We make no claim of comprehensiveness or of strategic priority of one region or problem over another. Our concern was rather that the case studies be representative of and faithful to human situations that were accessible within the scope of the project. What is amazing is the "transfer potential" of the cases—something we have experienced whenever they are discussed. The Swiss case study on migrant workers refers to a condition that involves one-seventh of all Europeans, but also reflects the issue of workers shifted from one country to another on each of the six continents. Land rights become a universal issue, as pressing in Africa or South America or North America as in Australia.

The aim to break down national or theological "territorialism"—the notion that only Africans have the right to comment on African issues, Latin Americans on South or Central America, and so forth—was included in our intentions. Commentators were selected along the same guidelines as those that governed case selection. However, to provide not only depth but also contrast, some commentators were asked to write on one case from their homeland and on another case from a different part of the world. Most colleagues in this experiment, originally cautious if not skeptical, risked their judgments on controversial issues in another area of the world to initiate the cross-cultural dialogue we sought to encourage.

The authors are grateful to the contributors for adjusting packed schedules to meet deadlines and for graciously preparing second and even third drafts at our request to strengthen already good commentaries. However, we thank them most of all for their generosity of spirit, their insights on the case studies they reviewed, and their dedication to the cause of human rights reflected in their work and personal lives.

The project's original design required adjustment for special resources or unexpected circumstances. The pattern was modified when we discovered that Heinrich Ott would bring not only theological expertise but experiential involvement as the only theologian in the Swiss Parliament, and one who had worked directly on the complicated migrant-worker legislation. After teaching the Australian case on location, it seemed imperative to provide an Aboriginal commentary. Working in a communal setting after traveling thousands of miles, Terry Djiniyini and Don Carrington collaborated to produce a commentary that is a report of an Aboriginal council discussion of the case. This pays tribute to the cultural integrity of the Aboriginal people.

The list of contributors represents only a few of the individuals and institutions that have given of themselves for this project. A complete list of those who were dialogue partners and hosts, who became adversaries or friends, who shared a slice of their life in the hope of throwing light on a serious problem, would be even longer than the Introduction. It would especially include those whose stories did not and often could not appear in the final collection. Bishop Samuel of Egypt, with whom we met at length, died from an assassin's bullet. To all in this company go our thanks and our prayers.

This project was made posssible through the continuance of a ministry of peace and justice across the globe carried out most creatively and persistently by the Maryknoll Fathers, Brothers, and Sisters. Officially known as the Catholic Foreign Mission Society of America, with headquarters in Maryknoll, New York, the Fathers and Brothers made funds available through a fellowship that honors their cofounders Bishop James A. Walsh and Father Thomas F. Price. The Walsh–Price Fellowship and the financial support it provided, along with an earlier grant from the Cuesta Foundation of Tulsa, Oklahoma, were indispensable. But the crucial gift that we describe as an extension of their ministry was the guidance, care, mutual support, and accountability that we experienced with Maryknollers around the world. No project, no book, even one produced under the kindly tutelage of Philip Scharper and John Eagleson, editors of Orbis Books—who really know and care about their authors as well as the issues of liberation—could discharge our indebtedness for surprising encounters that changed our lives. Special appreciation is extended to all the members of the Maryknoll Mission Research and Planning Department who coordinated the Walsh–Price Fellowship program.

In the Introduction that follows, Bob will try to share what we learned from the field research that we conducted from 1978 to 1981. It is only a sample of what we experienced and, by Bob's own admission, may be distorted to a degree by the focus of his vision. However, he has sought not to intrude on the case studies or the commentaries or tell readers how they should understand or organize the rich material that follows, although he confessed that he intended to do just that at the beginning of the project. We hope you will profit from it, and be provoked by it, and celebrate it as much as we do. The research stands on its own, as do the commentaries and the case studies. Both the dialogical Introduction, which contextualizes the research, and the confessional Conclusion, which interprets the research, stand as personal, provisional and positive statements of Hope in the gracious God who alone can enable us to listen to, respond to, and love one another across all the barriers we erect.

A word of praise must go to our International Advisory Council. Orlando Costas, Kosuke Koyama, and John Mbiti provided suggestions, counsel, support, and often a great deal more work—because they wanted it done better. And they were correct. Mbiti suggested that the original cases we had assembled on the first round of research were too narrowly focused. So we started over. Koyama flew thousands of miles and recruited a commentator. Costas sat in our living room and tore the plan for the North American case to pieces—and then helped us put it together again. These are illustrations of the work of friends and partners.

The advisory council was almost as crucial as the support system provided by our children Mellinda, Judith, and Allen, who ran a hundred errands, and waited a hundred hours, and grew a hundred ways, while we researched and wrote and missed some precious moments. But they have forgiven us—we think. As has Pam Bartle, our typist, who heard us say so many times, "just one more page and I need it before I catch the plane tonight." Pam laughed and even said she loved what we wrote. What more could one ask?

Introduction

ROBERT A. EVANS

HUMAN RIGHTS IN A GLOBAL CONTEXT

God has showed you . . . what is good;
   and what does the Lord require of you
   but to do justice, and to love kindness,
   and to walk humbly with your God? [Micah 6:8 RSV]

"Is this where it happened?," I asked as we scrambled down the wet, muddy bank of a steep slope on the border between Thailand and Cambodia.

"Yes, over a thousand people died in less than an hour—most of them children," responded the exhausted, sunken-eyed young physician. He worked with one of the international aid agencies in Bangkok. "Soldiers under orders from the Royal Thai government, in June of 1979, conducted what is known as the forced repatriation of 40,000 Cambodian 'illegal immigrants' back to their own country. What that means is that thousands of civilians who had only recently crossed the border into Thailand seeking food were forced back down this very slope into a mine field. They had been brought in buses from another area on the Thai border. Children were forced into the buses first, so the parents would have to follow. Men, women, and children were marched at bayonet point down into the hell of those mine fields. Some were literally blown apart. When others tried to move back up the slope, they were shot by the Thai soldiers. There was no water over there, no food, only the Khmer Rouge waiting to take revenge on those who had fled their native country of Kampuchea. How many more starved to death or were murdered upon their return, we will never know. To talk to the survivors now in the new Thai refugee camps like Kao-I-Dung is heartbreaking."

1

"Was there anything you could do?," I asked, searching desperately for a way to be consoling as the doctor seemed to relive the horror of the experience.

"Only weep, as I stood by the road and tried to flag down the buses. Only weep when they refused to stop," he murmured to himself as much as to me.

Back in the agency office in Bangkok, the physician reflected on our trip to the border. "How can we debate about human rights in Geneva and New York when thousands of people, mostly innocent kids, starve to death and are killed every year? I know that people say that Cambodia is the exception—the holocaust of the seventies. Perhaps three million people out of seven million have been wiped out in Cambodia alone in what has been called the 'decade of destruction.'[1] Everyone has been involved. It began with the massive bombing by the United States during the Vietnam War, then there was the genocide of the Pol Pot regime supported by the People's Republic of China, followed by the invasion of the Vietnamese and the Heng Samrin regime supported by the Soviet Union. Finally, even the international agencies, through diplomatic dancing, bureaucracy, and inefficiency, allowed delays in the delivery and distribution of rice and medical supplies in Cambodia and Thailand. This resulted in more death.

"The ancient culture of Angkor, that used to have not only enough rice to feed its citizens but also enough to export to hungry Asia, has been all but obliterated as neighbor kills neighbor with encouragement and assistance from the rest of the world. Hardly a developed nation in the world is without complicity in this living tragedy known as Cambodia.

"Nor is the Thai government a special villain," declared the physician. "Thailand is a nation of the Third World that can hardly play willing host to three hundred thousand refugees. It has not even ratified the U.N. covenant on the care of refugees. Thai farmers who live in the area of the newly established refugee camps are bitter. They complain that while they themselves labor to ward off starvation, the refugees who have been fighting among themselves in Cambodia are being prepared for a new, fat life in the United States, Canada, or Western Europe. They ask, correctly, I believe, if this is the justice to which we refer. Secretly, some Thai officials admitted that forced repatriation was necessary to survive politically in Thailand and was the only way to draw world attention to the magnitude of the problem. Long-term interests are served, they argue, even at the cost of lives. Do you think the Cambodian children who perished appreciate that perspective?"

"Where do we go from here?," I posed as he shuffled through the papers on his desk to find a medical form requested by a gaunt Thai nurse who had entered the office. As he located the form, signed it, and handed it on with a slight bow of his head to the nurse, the doctor continued.

"We have got to cut out the causes, not merely alleviate the pain for the twelve million refugees around the world. The Cambodian Holocaust is no exception! It is only the symbol of a community of nations so preoccupied with their own interests that they refuse to stop or strenuously object to the destruction not only of human rights but of human beings. Adults cry for revenge; children cry for hope."

He rose as he ran his hand through his hair, sandy from our struggle back up the border ravine. "The journalists say we need a political solution to the problem of Cambodia. I say we need a human solution to a world problem of inequity and injustice mirrored in the pool of blood that is Cambodia today. But that takes risk, vulnerability, and sacrifice on the part of powerful states for the sake of weak children. You know who protested that border massacre? Not the U.N. High Commission on Refugees, not the Christian churches in Thailand, not the multitude of international organizations that were the 'guests' of the Thai government. Only one young doctor with the International Committee of the Red Cross."

"Did it make any difference?," I asked hesitantly.

"I don't really know, to be truthful," my host replied. "A few months later we got an 'open-door' policy on Cambodian refugees declared by the Thai government, and millions of dollars of aid flowed in. Through groups such as Oxfam, British children sold their toys to provide food for their friends in Cambodia—an event that may have been one of the more significant components of the aid program. However, it now appears that the announcement of the 'open-door' policy was a factor in the fall of that Thai government. Much of the food and medicine never reached its intended destination; it was stored, diverted, and even sold. The problem is off the front pages of the world's newspapers, and the globe has a short memory. So a temporary aid fix gets submerged in the litany of Biafra, Bangladesh, Lebanon, Ethiopia, El Salvador, Afghanistan, and the boat people of Vietnam. There must be a way to prioritize rights that we dare call human. Sick and starving children are on the top of my list! How about you?"

This encounter came within the first two weeks of an eighteen-month research project on human rights. It was to lead the two principal researchers to six different continents and to distinctive but parallel accounts of the personal dramas that emerge from the struggle for human rights. It is not surprising that the product of the research was a series of case studies that seek to capture the issues, persons, alternatives, and resources—especially resources of grace, both human and divine—in unique settings within our global village. Twelve colleagues from around the world then joined us in preparing commentaries on these case studies, thus initiating the dialogue we sought between various representatives of the world community.

Images of the Thai-Cambodian border continue to haunt me—the slope, the soldiers, the mine field, the rifles, the tears, the blood, and most of all—the children. The young physician and I were at the side of that road, in that bus, alongside that ravine, as surely as were the Thai soldiers. Our presence was by virtue of a series of sins of commission and omission on the part of the human community—but we were there. I will never forget it. It confirms the greatest personal learning from the study for me. The motivation of basic human rights can never again become a matter of statistics, or theory, or strategy, or legislation, or judicial decision. It will always be, for me, the violation of the dignity of other children of God. Justice has become defined as protecting and enhancing the condition of human dignity that is the foundation of human rights.

". . . what is it that the Lord requires of you? But to do justice, to love kindness, to walk humbly. . . ." In my judgment, this has become the primary mandate of the gospel for the last two decades of the twentieth century for the entire global village. This mandate requires that we define rights more broadly, more humanely, more positively than do the majority of present declarations and covenants. It means that the global community must establish priorities within the catalogue of rights that undergird the fullness of life. Finally, the weak, the innocent, the poor—the child in our midst and in our person—must be given preference for the sake of the humanity of us all.

The Need for Agreement

So Jesus spoke again: . . . I have come that [you] may have life, and may have it in all its fullness. I am the good shepherd; the good shepherd lays down his life for the sheep. . . . But there are other sheep of mine, not belonging to this fold, whom I must bring in; and they too will listen to my voice. There will then be one flock [John 10:7–16].

Is there any agreement on the meaning of human rights in an international context which would allow the establishment of priorities? This was a question the research sought to answer. Special attention was given to the role of the religious community, especially the churches, because their leaders have played a rather prominent and often controversial part in the disputes over human rights. Presidents and popes, congresses and councils of bishops, assemblies of the United Nations and of the World Council of Churches have all issued declarations about the importance of human rights and a commitment to their protection and enhancement. One test of an operative consensus on priorities was to be agreement on the selection of issues represented in cases that evidenced the violation of specific human rights.

Perhaps not surprisingly, our study revealed that no such agreement exists on the order of priorities among conflicting "human rights." However, there is profound interest in discovering a path to such an agreement. Interviews with government, religious, and civic leaders in twenty countries and territories were conducted: Australia, Japan, the Philippines, Hong Kong, People's Republic of China, Thailand, India, Nepal, Pakistan, Tanzania, Kenya, Uganda, Egypt, Switzerland, Germany, Great Britain, United States, Puerto Rico, Nicaragua, and Brazil. This process resulted in the selection of the case studies contained in this volume. The cases were not only researched and written on location but also reviewed and revised in dialogue with the principal parties in each account. The interviews frequently provided learnings that could not be revealed in the cases; many participants urged confidentiality and disguise. We have attempted to honor this in every instance. In other situations, the cases were discussed and taught in that country during a testing period. The discussions were lively, often heated, but always reflected the authenticity of the human drama. The authors trust each reader will experience similar excitement and illumination in an encounter with our global brothers and sisters and the decisions that face them daily.

There was an extraordinary range of suggestions around the world as to the central issues of "human rights." However, in the midst of this diversity there was particular agreement on one issue. It was often voiced by those involved in national and international commissions or committees on human rights. The one area of consensus and frustration was that there is more rhetoric about than embodiment of human rights. This was seen within particular societies and was even more obvious when applied to relationships between nations.

A legal scholar from Sri Lanka, C.G. Weeramantry, has articulated the views expressed about this discrepancy in the application of human rights:

> When, therefore, the world talks of the equality and freedom of all human beings, it must give its mind to the emptiness of this concept in the eyes of vast numbers of those for whose benefit it is meant. . . . All the declarations of equality ever made will have no effect unless some attempt is made to understand the problem of human inequality as it appears to Third World eyes.[2]

We talk—but we do not respond.

A similar view from a religious perspective is found in "An Open Letter to North American Christians" prepared by thirteen Central and South American Christian leaders, five of whom dared not sign their names for fear of reprisals in their own countries, declares:

> Friends and fellow Christians, it is time that you realize that our continent is becoming one gigantic prison, and in some regions, one vast cemetery; that human rights, the grand guidelines of the gospel, are becoming a dead letter, without force. And all this in order to maintain a system, a structure of dependency, that benefits the mighty privileged persons of a minority of your land and of our land, at the expense of the poor millions who are increasing throughout the width and breadth of the continent.[3]

We talk—but we do not respond.

In the privacy of offices and in strolls through parks, the confession emerged, often by those charged with guarding human rights, that every nation has substantial groups of persons whose rights are not honored. They are the weak and powerless, often minority groups for whom the enforcing agency cannot successfully stand as an advocate because of a narrow or technical interpretation of the rights in question, or because of another claim of a human right that takes precedence. The claims to land rights by Aborigines in Australia or Blacks and Hispanics seeking adequate housing in the U.S.A. are the subjects of cases in this volume that reflect this conflict.

Again and again, research revealed agreement that each case involved one or more instances of the violation of human rights present in a particular country or region of the world. These rights were seen as the right to employment, education, personal security, or freedom of expression. However, it was impossible to find concurrence on the degree of significance of the various infringements of human rights, i.e, does the right to housing take priority over freedom to own property? This is the consequence, I believe, of diverse interpretations of the priorities of human rights. Perhaps, before we can move from rhetoric to response, we need a clearer, broader, and more positive interpretation of human rights. Patterns of interpretation that emphasize particular human rights appear consistently in the interviews and supporting documents. The patterns seem linked to whether one primarily holds a First, Second, or Third World perspective.

First/Third World Terminology

Let me acknowledge immediately that the First/Third World terminology is inadequate and for some has arrogant and condescending implications which some members of the International Advisory Council of this research project, especially John Mbiti, find repugnant. Orlando Costas, another member of the Advisory Council, reminded me that historically the terms "First/Second/Third Worlds" were developed by those who identified themselves as Third World. This occurred at the 1955 Bandung, Java, Conference of twenty-nine Asian and African nonaligned nations. "Third World was employed to define the nonaligned nations over against the industrialized nations of the capitalist bloc linked to NATO and the socialist states linked in the Warsaw Pact. Additional designations such as "developed/developing" or "north/south" are also employed. The nations of the South Pacific island chains have sometimes spoken of themselves as the Fourth World. There are groups of "Third World Ecumenical Theologians" whose conference members in March 1982 in Bangkok described themselves as "evangelical mission theologians from the Two-Thirds World." The Two-Thirds World has been used to highlight the strength in population and territory in contrast to the First and Second Worlds.

Acknowledging the difficulties and insisting that our use of the terminology "First" and "Third" does not intend to be discriminatory, the terms do communicate. In the title of C.G. Weeramantry's book *Equality and Freedom: Some Third World Perspectives*, or in a title such as *Human Rights: A Dialogue between the First and Third Worlds*, the representation of the human community is symbolized in the partiality of the language. It is a reversal evocative of the biblical passage (Mark 12) that eschews the presumption of those who would argue about who is the greatest in favor of those who would be servants of all.

"The last shall be first" is not discordant with the thesis offered by Weeramantry concerning the moral leadership to be offered by representatives of the Third World. Here, he claims, we have a fundamentally simpler "sharing society." Both by its traditional values and as a consequence of its location in the less developed world, the Third World has "been able to preserve itself from the relentless pursuit of 'progress' and 'efficiency' purchased at the expense of individual values."[4]

Let us also note that Third World and First World designations are not merely geographical. The characteristics that tend to identify a nation with one camp or the other are also those that portray individuals and groups in any nation as sharing a First, Second, or Third World mentality. It is precisely the division between the traditional views of the rich and the poor, the powerful and the powerless, that makes what was once only a gap—the abyss so familiar to us all, no matter where we live on the globe.

The authors were tempted to replace "First" and "Third" with such terms cited above: "developed" and "developing," or "north" and "south." However, this change would have helped to disguise the political, economic, and social divisions that are the mark of our time. Moreover, such a terminological switch would not have saved us from a primarily self-protective and negative definition of human rights. The mood of the rights debate is not only persistently rhetorical, it is also often so negative as to be less than humane. Not only the substance but also the tone needs conversion.

Our goal is a positive perception of human rights that urges and enables change. However, unfortunately, the dominant tendency is to view human rights merely as a minimum definition of the human condition. Thus we are tempted to negotiate acceptable trade-offs between conflicting rights. A positive, productive vision, in which the promises of "fullness of life" can be celebrated by more and more of the world's inhabitants, needs to be found.

The term "Third World"—or, for that matter, "Second World" or "First World"—defies precise definition. However, if we are willing to live with tentative definitions and some ambiguity such descriptive guidelines can alert us to directions we might otherwise miss. Kosuke Koyama, the third member of the Advisory Council, argues that such ambiguity is a reality of religious faith and life in contemporary society.

The "Third World" refers to groups of nations and persons who are economically disadvantaged or poor, politically impotent, and excluded from decision-making processes that determine their own future. For individuals these factors include poverty, racial and ethnic discrimination, and political domination. For nations these factors may be the consequence of a less developed economy, dependence on agriculture and primary products, recent emergence from colonial occupation, or lack of access to advanced technology.

Several of these categories might be applied to the community of nations and yet it would not constitute a denial of the enormous diversity of values and cultures that exists among Third World peoples.[5] However, to deny that there are poor, dominated, or marginalized peoples is to avoid the mandate for change. To allow these facts to be construed pejoratively in terms of the contribution of Third World peoples to the world community is to endanger not only the integrity of their own human dignity but also, ultimately, that of those who have cooperated, whether intentionally or not, in impoverishing, dominating, and marginalizing more than two-thirds of our globe's inhabitants.

This characterization distinguishes the Third World from those nations and groups of persons that belong to or benefit from the world of industrialized capitalism or industrialized socialism. These are sometimes referred to as the capitalist and communist blocs, liberal democracy and Marxism, or the First and Second Worlds. The categories are broadly descriptive because the patterns of emphasis in human rights on which we are focusing are informed by these distinctions. China presents a special problem because, in terms of many of the categories noted above, it is a Third World nation. In other respects, China is a Second World nation in terms of its perspective on most issues of human rights. However, it is my conviction that China constitutes a new category that stands apart from the three-way schema employed here. This distinctive stance is reflected in the eighth case study and the commentaries on "China and the Church."

Three Perspectives on Rights

A division between the three worlds, drawn on the basis of which particular groups of human rights are stressed, has been developed by several scholars. These divisions were confirmed by our own research.

First World

The emphasis in the First or capitalist world is on the rights of the individual. Civil and political rights become the standards of liberty. The liberal democratic state promises to guarantee such rights as freedom of religion, speech, and assembly; the right to be secure in one's person and property; and the right to due process of law. The common foundation that binds these rights together, according to one student of human rights, David Hollenbach, is "the freedom of the individual person."[6]

The foundational right is to be free. This freedom allows persons to order their actions, dispose of their possessions, and conduct their lives without depending on the consent of any other person. The equal right of all to be free is rooted in the West European philosophy of Hobbes and Locke and enshrined in the Bill of Rights of the U.S. Constitution. Hollenbach notes that if all rights are

. . . the extrapolations of individual freedom . . . then, rights are negative. They are defenses of individual liberty. They are immunities from
interference by others. . . . Rights are the fences around the field where
the individual may act, speak, worship, associate or accumulate wealth
without restriction by the positive action of either other persons or the
state.[7]

According to this perspective, when individual human rights are denied in
any part of the world by what are described as "authoritarian regimes" of the
left or right, then the core of human dignity has been violated by the offend-
ing party or country. In the Soviet Union the religious liberty of some Jews
and Christians and the freedom of speech of dissident intellectuals is restricted. Imprisonment without due process, and even with torture, is employed against political opponents in Indonesia, Iran, Uganda, and El Salvador. The right of free assembly is denied to Africans in South Africa and to
Christians in Egypt. Capitalist morality is outraged. The First World places
its trust in a pluralistic understanding of society in which the defense of liberty is the key to the human condition. One may not know what the good is
for other persons, but they must be free to pursue it, controlled only by the
commitment not to infringe on another citizen's liberty. Obviously, restrictions on civil and political rights around the globe make this mission to protect individual human rights urgent and appropriate in the eyes of the First
World.

Second World

The Second World, a term employed less frequently, designates an alternative to the capitalist model of the liberal democratic state by posing a socialist
model shaped by a Marxist worldview. The socialist democratic republic focuses on the rights of social participation in the benefits of society. Economic
and social needs become the standards of real liberty. The guarantees stressed
are the right to work and to material security, including the right to health, to
education, and to housing. Civil and political rights of expression, assembly,
and the press are also promised, but in conformity with social needs. According to the Marxist interpretation, real freedom is always a social reality. Social solidarity sets the boundaries of personal freedom.

Leonid Brezhnev cites a section of the Communist Manifesto as the practical principle of the state: "An association in which the free development of
each is the condition for the free development of all."[8] Because personal
freedom is linked to solidarity, then genuine freedom demands the transformation of the entire economic and social structure of the given society. The
Marxist tradition declares the need for a socialist revolution because the
rights of individuals, especially the right to be free producers and proprietors, appear to safeguard only the rights of a privileged class. The protection
of the rights to unrestrained personal freedom to own land or the means of

production makes the rights of the underprivileged a vacuous abstraction. Socialism, therfore, stresses economic and social rights so that the rights of society take priority over the interests of individuals. The Second World would affirm that without the necessary economic and social conditions, it would be impossible for individuals to experience personal, political, and cultural rights.

Therefore, in the Soviet Union and other Marxist-influenced nations of the second or alternative worldview, civil and political rights are guaranteed to the extent that they do not conflict with the needs of socialism. The state determines what builds socialism, and thus the class analysis of human history determines which human rights are to be emphasized as the key to other rights. As Hollenbach reminds us, the human rights highlighted in the Second World also "possess a negative or defensive content. They are protections of the Soviet people against any who would act contrary to the interests of a developing socialist system."[9] In this perspective the state not only claims to know the needs of persons, but also has the responsibility and right to protect them from individual license that might exploit or oppress them.

Conflict arises when dissident voices within the socialist system charge that the state has confused social solidarity with state control. Social participation, which the state sought to protect, is often suppressed by the state itself when it limits political participation to one party and denies the right to dissent.

The important contribution of the socialist approach to human rights is the recognition of the significance of economic and social rights that must be protected by law if equality in personal freedom is to be obtained. The evidence of economic and social exploitation in various parts of the world makes the mission to protect society's human rights appropriate and urgent in the eyes of the Second World. This concern surfaces in cases such as "To Bear Arms," "I Was a Stranger," and "China and the Church," even though their settings are First and Third World.

Our project seeks to promote international and cross-cultural dialogue that can illuminate the conflict between these two differing perspectives on human rights. This struggle is embodied in a "value difference." It is not that there is an absence of value or integrity on one side or the other. Nor is it that one culture violates human dignity persistently or intentionally, whereas another enshrines it. At a distinctive point in human history, the pressure of certain human needs and requirements will result in a contrast in values. The American and the Chinese cases, when set side by side, reveal the conflict between civil and political rights versus economic and social rights, not only between nations but also within them. Ross Terrill has a simple but powerful vignette which captures this contrast:

> Red Guards smash the fingers of a pianist because he has been playing Beethoven's music, which they find decadent. To a Westerner who ex-

pects to be able to do his own thing, such action suggests a tyranny without equal in history. In New York City, two old folks die of cold because the gas company turned off the heat in the face of an unpaid bill of $20. To a Chinese, who honors the elderly, it seems callous beyond belief.[10]

The conflict is dramatized on a global scale by the United Nations' Universal Declaration of Human Rights adopted by the General Assembly in 1948. However, the interpretation of this declaration came in the two covenants adopted and opened for signature in 1966. The "International Covenant on Economic, Social, and Cultural Rights" is given priority by the socialist states, and the "International Covenant on Civil and Political Rights" is endorsed by capitalist nations. The Helsinki Agreement, Principle VII, on respect for human rights, sought to bridge the gap in understanding but did not meet with dramatic success.[11] The value difference is theoretical. In practice the battleground where the perspectives of the First World and Second World often engage in combat is within the Third World.

Third World

The nations and, I have argued, groups of persons who sometimes refer to themselves as being of the Third World have another view of human rights.[12] There is, obviously, no coordinated position on this question, but rather an expression of common priorities expressed in pleas for understanding. These reached a climax around the North-South economic summit at Cancun, Mexico, in October of 1981. The poorer nations, residing primarily in the southern hemisphere, demanded "global negotiations" on a new and more just world economic order under the auspices of the U.N. It was argued that the organizations that distribute foreign aid at present, such as the World Bank, are controlled by northern more developed nations and have been consistently insensitive to the needs of the less developed nations. The demand is not for charity but for justice, not for weapons but for willingness to share appropriate technology. Weeramantry cites this concern in another context:

> Indeed a basic reason for failure by the other worlds in their attempts at assistance to the Third World is a lack of understanding of the importance of this aspect. Assistance given with condescension is self-defeating in its objects.[13]

The Third World perspective focuses neither on individual political rights nor on collective rights to social participation. Rather, the focus is on the right to human survival and liberation. Both industrialized capitalism and industrialized socialism are experienced by Third World peoples as being similar in their manipulative building of First and Second World prosperity on the backs of Third World poor. The natural resources and the labor of the southern hemisphere are purchased at a low price and kept low to fuel an economy that produces manufactured goods, especially armaments to sell back to the Third World at ever higher prices. Finally, the less developed nations see themselves as the battlefield where the world powers wage wars of influence that destroy the population, the resources, and the culture of the war-zone nations but seldom touch the lives and lands of those who initiate and often escalate the conflict.

In the Third World, the basic human rights are survival and liberation. With famine, war, and cultural corruption the real enemies, the rights to food, shelter, health, and education at the survival level take priority. Any person or structure, whether domestic or international, that prohibits the exercise of those basic rights must be their concern. Following these rights comes the right to cultural integrity after years of colonial occupation. This entails: the right to hope for a better future as something that is not hopelessly out of reach and the right to freedom from racial or geographical discrimination that leads to exploitation at both national and international levels.

Human rights in the Third World also assume a negative focus. Survival and liberation rights are often seen by some as merely restricting some persons from removing conditions necessary for sustaining the lives and cultural integrity of other persons. These rights are not frequently seen as a positive force for enhancing the quality of life of all persons and cultures.

The Third World perspective would affirm both individual and social rights, but not at the expense of the two-thirds of the world's population who reside in the Third World. There must be some way, demand the peoples of the Third World, to prioritize human rights so as to distinguish rights of necessity from rights of preference. Giving priority to the rights to survival and liberation may be the first step toward resolving the enormous disparities among the three worlds.

Beginning the Journey

The following section on "Teaching and Learning with Cases" is intended to equip readers to enter the varied worlds of the case studies with more openness, sensitivity, and anticipation. The "slices of life" that follow call us temporarily to suspend our disbelief and experience the contrasting world-views presented by the cases. The cases seek to concretize issues of human rights and consequently enable readers to dialogue more realistically about alternatives.

The commentaries that follow each case may lead the individual reader or member of a discussion group to become more sensitive and critical. The promises and problems of protecting and enhancing the rights of our global sisters and brothers are complex and the strategies often compromising. The move from rhetoric to response in areas of human rights requires that priorities among conflicting rights be established. We invite you to enter into dialogue with the commentators and with other readers. We trust the experience will not only be stimulating but rewarding.

"From Reflection to Action" is the theme of the Conclusion in which the researchers share their findings, disclose their conclusions about priorities, and—for the sake of children and church—call for simple steps toward a theology of letting-go. But that is a later stage in the journey. Join us first on our pilgrimage to the First and Third Worlds.

NOTES

1. For more background see the excellent series by British journalist William Shawcross, "Cambodia: Decade of Destruction," which appeared in the *Washington Post,* March 1980, and for which he won the George Polk Award for investigative reporting on U.S. policy in Cambodia.

2. C. G. Weeramantry, *Equality and Freedom: Some Third World Perspectives* (Columbo: Lake House Publ., 1976), p.5.

3. G. H. Anderson and T. F. Stransky, eds., *Mission Trends No. 4* (New York: Paulist, 1979), p. 74.

4. Weeramantry, *Equality,* p. 187.

5. Ibid., p. 4.

6. David Hollenbach, *Claims in Conflict: Retrieving and Renewing the Catholic Human Rights Tradition* (New York: Paulist, 1979), p. 13.

7. Ibid., p. 14.

8. Ibid., p. 20.

9. Ibid., p. 24.

10. Ross Terrill, *The China Difference* (New York: Harper & Row, 1979), p. 12.

11. All four documents referred to here can be found in the Appendices of *Christian Declaration on Human Rights,* A. O. Miller, ed. (Grand Rapids: Eerdmans, 1977), p. 157.

12. Friends in the South Pacific, who feel they are far removed from participation in world decision-making, often consider themselves to be in the "Fourth World." In this book, however, they are represented in the category of Third World.

13. Weeramantry, *Equality,* p. 6.

ALICE F. EVANS

TEACHING AND LEARNING
WITH CASES

Tokyo, Japan. A lively debate on the case "Enshrinement" by a group of Japanese and American teachers and religious leaders had just concluded. As the group began to disperse, a Roman Catholic priest declared, "I had not seen the far-reaching implications of the Nakaya lawsuit before our discussion. Though I have lived in Japan for over twenty years, today I experienced from my colleagues feelings and ideas about Japanese culture in a new way. I have also gained some insight about how I perceive the world. Both of these learnings are invaluable to my ministry."

A woman teacher shared with the discussion leader as she left, "I was born in Japan. Reading in 'Enshrinement' about the possible revival of economic aggression against our Asian neighbors and a return to militarism distressed me. Here is a poem I wrote last night in response to the case. It is my own confession of responsibility."

•

Melbourne, Australia. Many in the group of eighty-five pastors and lay leaders gathered for an annual church conference shifted uneasily in their seats as the case discussion began on "Sacred Sites." A Council of Churches' critique of Australia's relationship to the Aborigine people had just been released; conference participants held widely divergent views on the issue of Aborigine land rights. In the course of the open discussion that followed, several clergy shared their frustration with Australia's "conservative congregations." A lay leader condemned "liberal" church pronouncements on race which were followed by little or no real action. Some present honestly shared their anxiety about speaking out on controversial issues for fear of the backlash. Still others shared educational models and personal experiences that they felt had helped expand their own and parishioners' understanding of the Aborigines and the role of the church in the social and political arenas.

In a two-hour discussion new levels of understanding about the diversity of Christian witness and even some new friendships across ideological boundaries had begun. One church leader announced his intention to teach the case in a community meeting in Queensland the next week.

•

Rio de Janeiro, Brazil. Members of the woman's association of a large urban congregation discussed the central issues of an American case study that had been read to them in English and simultaneously translated into Portuguese. As the enthusiastic level of participation increased one woman declared, "I feel for the first time the struggle of an American family making decisions about the change of lifestyle. I thought that was a Brazilian problem. We must build bridges of friendship across the barriers both our governments have erected." The discussion leader said later she thought about the passage from Ephesians 2:13–14, "But now in Jesus Christ you who once were far off have been brought near. . . [he] has made us both one, and has broken down the dividing wall of hostility. . . ."

•

Pasadena, California, U.S.A. Fifteen development supervisors from around the world, working for an international organization, were discussing the difficult decision facing James and Mary Kyonka in "Returning Home." Several in the group shared their personal reaction to the deep emotional struggle of the East African couple in the case. One supervisor, who had remained quiet through much of the discussion, raised her hand to speak. She told her colleagues that the decision involving the high personal cost to oneself and one's family in order to do development work in life-threatening situations, as in the case, was remarkably close to the dilemma she and her husband had faced. "I see our decision in a new light," she concluded. "And I praise God for the sensitivity and understanding of this group."

•

These "snapshots" offer momentary glimpses into four of the many instances in which the eight cases in this volume have been taught and discussed. One of the authors' visions for this project is heightened awareness of the gifts as well as the needs of our brothers and sisters within the global village. One step in this direction may be through the effective use of case studies as instruments of understanding, insight, and hope.

As noted in the Preface, the cases that follow are not simply "stories" gathered from around the world. Rather, the selection and ordering of factual data intentionally focuses on specific issues or problems that require a decision or response from one or more persons in the case. It is the authors' goal that controversial issues of human rights are presented with a sufficient degree of integrity and balance that thoughtful persons of good will will genuinely disagree about what ought to be done. The case itself does not supply an "answer" to the problem but invites the reader to enter the situation, analyze the issues, and propose justifiable alternatives. Thus, responsibility for a decision is placed not only on the case characters but also on the reader or participants in a case discussion. Serious study of a case allows readers the opportunity to test the application of their human concern and their religious faith in real-life situations to bring together reflection about a case, often from a theological perspective, and the proposed practice of ministry that recommends a specific alternative. The authors have found that this imaginative connection between faith and action facilitates fresh insights, greater understanding, and commitment to new strategies on behalf of human rights.

Setting

Cases can be extremely useful for inducing reflection by an individual reader. However, as evidenced by the four introductory "snapshots," they are especially effective as instruments for discussion. Any of the eight human rights cases might be used in congregational gatherings, retreat settings, community meetings, university, seminary, or high school classrooms, or with any group seeking to gain new perspectives on global issues and/or human rights. In non-English-speaking settings, the authors have found that the cases can be translated and even condensed and read aloud in a local dialect. We have found that groups numbering from five to fifty (or more) can engage in a fruitful case discussion. The most important factor is that the group be a supportive community open to new learnings.

Responses

Within a variety of settings the authors have found several distinctive responses from those who experience a case discussion.

Often the case functions as a catalyst, presenting concrete issues in such a way that participants turn to theological and biblical resources with renewed enthusiasm. Following a session in a Latin American setting using the case "I Was A Stranger," some participants requested biblical references. Others asked for additional resources on migrant workers throughout the world. Often the greatest learnings take place when participants are motivated to seek further information and explore new options. For this reason, the authors urge the study and discussion of a case *before* turning to the commentaries, each of which offers one theologian's unique insights and perspective.

Persons experiencing a case discussion confirm that cases provide a relatively non-threatening arena in which to discuss volatile issues. This was acknowledged, for example, following the Australian teaching of "Sacred

Sites." Several people present said that the high level of emotional involvement in issues concerning the Aborigines usually hindered or even prevented open dialogue with those of radically differing opinion. In their words, the case experience had been "a stimulating exception."

Participants in a case discussion are asked to creatively analyze situations, discern underlying assumptions, and propose creative and compassionate alternatives. The authors have found the value of this experience significantly increased by the interaction of a community of persons experiencing and learning to trust one another's insights. The honest dialogue that often results from a case discussion can reap the added benefit of building a genuine sense of community within the group. A number of businessmen who originally gathered for a discussion of "Prophet or Provocateur" decided to pursue additional case discussions. They subsequently formed a regular support group that meets monthly to discuss their own "cases."

Participants of a case discussion are often willing to risk decisions and take responsibility for the implications and/or consequences of those decisions within a community of faith. Persons who are encouraged to be critical of their own theological assumptions are also more open to hearing the positions of others. In this climate, participants can also enter into creative dialogue with the commentators.

Finally, the authors have found that by "living through" the case experience of a Ugandan refugee, a Swiss migrant worker, a Japanese secretary, a Nicaraguan pastor, or a Chinese farmer, participants often become more sensitive to their voices and responsive to our mutual need for dignity and self worth.

The authors must clearly acknowledge, however, that cases are not an educational panacea. There are clear limitations to the case approach that must be seen as only one of many educational instruments. Of particular note for many cultures is the difficulty of overcoming traditional understandings of the teacher/student roles. The case approach is student or participant oriented; the teacher assumes a non-traditional role. Second, though cases are an effective learning tool, they are not the most "efficient" way to communicate a body of new information. If a teacher is concerned primarily about data transfer, then a reading assignment or a lecture may be more time effective than a case discussion. Finally, as is indicated not only by the commentaries but also by bibliographies and additional readings listed with most commentaries and with each Teaching Note, an experience with a particular case should not be seen as a conclusion, but as the entry point for much deeper learnings about issues of human rights.

Preparation

It is possible to hand out copies of the shorter cases in this volume and ask participants to read them immediately prior to discussion (e.g., "Sacred Sites," "Returning Home," or "Prophet or Provocateur"). However, the quality of most case discussions is heightened by careful advance reading. A case leader could suggest that participants study a case by identifying the principal characters, developing a "time line" to indicate significant dates and events, analyzing the issues involved in the case, and thinking through a number of creative alternatives to the dilemma posed. Small groups meeting to prepare a case before a larger group discussion can also be extremely beneficial to the total learning experience. This type of case preparation is equally valuable for the individual reader. A structured process for "entering" each case provides a base that may be challenged, expanded, or affirmed by the commentaries.

Teaching Notes

Following each case is a list of suggestions for the individual reader or for a group discussion on that particular case. It is imperative to state that these are only guidelines for ways to "open up" the cases. The Teaching Notes are in no way definitive; many viable topics for discussion are not raised in these brief illustrative notes. The Teaching Notes are also not written primarily to focus on the commentaries. Rather the purpose of these notes is to help readers and discussion participants develop their own insights and personal commentaries.

Teaching the Case

As noted above, the role of a case leader does not follow a traditional model of the teacher as a dispenser of knowledge or information. The excitement and power of cases as learning tools is in assisting discussion participants to discover for themselves not only the most responsible decisions the case characters might make, but what decision the participants themselves might make in a similar situation and why. Thus the primary functions of a case leader are to facilitate meaningful dialogue among the participants, to highlight insights they mutually discover, and to assist in summarizing the learnings from the discussion. This does not mean, however, that the case teacher in any way relinquishes appropriate leadership. As a facilitator, the case leader is responsible for clear goals and objectives for each discussion session and for guiding the quality and rhythm of the discussion. While cultural patterns may vary, this would usually involve limiting the contributions of very vocal participants and encouraging more reticent members to enter the process.

Several suggestions for guiding a case discussion have been proposed by experienced case teachers throughout the world. Many suggest that the most crucial factor for a rewarding case experience is the case leader's style; openness, affirmation, and sensitivity to the group create the climate in which genuine dialogue can occur. Second in importance is that the case leader thoroughly master the case facts and develop a discussion plan or teaching note.

The case leader should prepare in advance the general direction of the discussion as well as clear, leading questions to move from one topic to the next. It is often most involving and least threatening to "enter" a case by identifying the case characters and raising questions about their feelings or attitudes. In the course of the discussion other general topics to be covered might be the issues, the alternatives, rationale for each alternative, and the possible resources for resolution available both to the case characters and to the participants. The Teaching Note following each case is intended as an aid to the teacher's own creative imagination.

The case leader should take care not to allow the group to speculate far beyond the case data or get caught up in arguing about minor issues. Some teachers find that simply asking "What evidence do you find in the case to support your suggestions?" keeps discussion centered on the case. Many case instructors report that recording the essence of participants' contributions on newsprint or a chalkboard gives order and direction to the discussion. A skilled instructor is able to organize participants' remarks and show the relation to other contributions. The teacher should be willing to probe respondents for additional clarification of points. However, the leader needs to be aware that this form of discussion can be unusually effective in drawing out personal responses. Care should be taken to be supportive of participants who become vulnerable through self-disclosure during or after the discussion of a case.

Honest conflict of opinion is usually characteristic and can be quite constructive in a case discussion. The case leader may need to assume the role of referee and urge participants to listen to one another and to interpret the reasoning behind their conclusions. It is often helpful to put debating participants in direct dialogue by asking, for example, "Anne, given your earlier position, how would you respond to Alberto's view?" The leader's role of mediator is also significant, especially as a discussion nears conclusion. It is helpful to encourage the group to build on one another's suggestions. One constructive process for "closing" a case is to ask participants to share their learnings from the discussion. A case teacher may also wish to summarize important insights. However, experienced case teachers find it is crucial for further dialogue for the leader to avoid the temptation of giving "the" definitive answer or otherwise imposing on a group a dogmatic interpretation of the case. Such a summary lecture may cause participants to feel they were cut down or "topped" by the leader's conclusion and thus their original contributions were not really valued. However, a confessional sharing which says, "This is one approach which may be useful to consider," is usually well received as one form of concluding a case.

Additional Teaching Techniques

Two techniques mentioned in the Teaching Note are often employed by case teachers.

1. Voting. The discussion may often be focused and intensified by calling for participants to vote on a controversial issue, e.g., in a discussion of "China and the Church" one might ask "How many of you believe that Chang should accept the offer of Bibles and money from Wong?" "How many of you believe he should refuse?" Most case teachers record the vote on the board. The dynamics of case teaching reveal that once persons have taken a stand, they assume greater "ownership" of the decision and are eager to defend or interpret their choice. Voting provides an impetus for participants to offer the implicit reasons and assumptions that stand behind a given decision. It can also be a test of the group's response, especially if one or two outspoken participants have taken a strong stand on one particular side of an issue.

2. Role Play. An exciting way to heighten existential involvement in a case is to ask participants imaginatively to assume roles of the persons in the case for a specified period of the discussion. In a group role play or simulation experience, the leader might ask the entire group, for example, to become Sue Edwards's study group responding to her questions of what specific lifestyle change or response to the urban problems might best reflect her growing concern for the urban poor ("Eye of the Needle"). When individuals are asked to assume roles before the group, e.g., Ricardo Campos speaking with one of his Pentecostal pastors ("To Bear Arms"), experienced case teachers have found that rather than making assignments or asking for volunteers, it is better to ask permission of participants who have given evidence in the discussion that they can identify with the characters and understand the issues. It is often most helpful for individuals in a role play to move into chairs visible to the entire group. The personal integrity of those who assume individual roles is then guarded following a five-minute role play by allowing them space to "de-role." This is done by asking them, for example, how they felt during the conversation and by asking them to return to their original seats. Then the group may be called on to share learnings from the experience.

A Final Note

Notwithstanding the preceding hints and principles for case teaching, the authors wish to acknowledge that a good case discussion is not ultimately dependent on a trained professional teacher or on a learned group of participants. A gifted leader is one who listens well, encourages participants to do the same, and genuinely trusts the wisdom, insights, and personal experiences of the group. The same is true of a reader willing to wrestle honestly with the issues in the cases and willing to evaluate with an open mind the insights of the commentators. As citizens of the global village, those of us with different worldviews have much to learn from one another. We need occasions when this can occur. The authors are also convinced that there can be grace-filled moments in open dialogue when the Holy Spirit speaks to us through one another, opening new channels of service and understanding. This is what "mutual ministry" is about.

ADDITIONAL RESOURCES

For further information on additional cases, a bibliography of case books, and more extensive guides for case teaching and writing, contact the Association for Case Teaching, P.O. Box 243, Simsbury, Connecticut 06070, or the Director of Case Development for the Association of Theological Schools, P.O. Box 396, Vandalia, Ohio 45377.

For those who would like to make further use of the case method, there are a number of resources that provide not only cases but interpretative aids from commentaries to teaching notes.

Case Books

Baird, Forest, and Rogers, Jack. *Introduction to Philosophy: A Case Method Approach.* San Francisco: Harper & Row, 1981.

Evans, Robert A. and Alice F. *Introduction to Christianity: A Case Study Approach.* Atlanta: John Knox Press, 1980.

Evans, Robert A.; Lewis, G. Douglass; and Davis, Marjorie Hall. *Explorations in Faith, Participants' Packet and Leaders' Guide.* Washington, D.C.: Alban Institute, Inc., 1981.

Evans, Robert A., and Parker, Thomas, eds. *Christian Theology: A Case Method Approach.* New York: Harper & Row, 1976.

Evans, Robert A., and Alice F., and Weeks, Louis and Carolyn. *Casebook for Christian Living: Value Formation for Families and Congregations.* Atlanta: John Knox Press, 1977.

Houck, John W., and Williams, Oliver F. *Full Value: Cases in Christian Business Ethics.* New York: Harper & Row, 1978.

Lewis, G. Douglass. *Resolving Church Conflicts: A Case Approach for Local Congregations.* San Francisco: Harper & Row, 1981.

Bibliography

Cases in Theological Education. 1981 Bibliography, Garth Rosell, ed. Published by the Association of Theological Schools and the Case Study Institute, 1981. Over 600 individual cases are listed in this bibliography. The cases and the bibliography are available through the Association of Theological Schools (ATS), P.O. Box 130, Vandalia, Ohio 45377.

Case Articles

Evans, Robert A. and Alice F. "Theological Education and the Case Method." *Ministerial Formation,* No. 3, July 1978. World Council of Churches, P.O. Box 66, Geneva, Switzerland.

Handspicker, M. B. "How to Study a Case." Available through 1981 Case Bibliography.

Meyers, Ann, and Weeks, Louis. "Writing and Teaching Cases." Available through 1981 Case Bibliography.

Theological Education (Spring 1974). Entire issue devoted to "Case Study in Theological Education." Order from ATS, P.O. Box 396, Vandalia, Ohio 45377.

Association for Case Teaching

The Association for Case Teaching (ACT) is a professional association composed of individuals (professors, pastors, lay leaders) and institutions (seminaries, colleges, churches, and service agencies) committed to improving the quality of teaching by use of the case method. Through the office of the Executive Director, the Association provides counsel on the use of cases, Case Method Institute Summer Workshops for two-week intensive training in case teaching and writing, and short-term workshops from one to four days for faculty, church staff, and lay leaders in locations in the U.S.A. and overseas. For further information write: Association for Case Teaching, c/o Robert and Alice Evans, Co-Executive Directors, P.O. Box 243, Simsbury, Connecticut 06070.

Case Study 1

NICARAGUA: TO BEAR ARMS

Ricardo Campos began to speak slowly, and then his voice grew stronger and became laden with emotion. "I must visit our churches and talk with their pastors. I know that those evangelical pastors under my supervision have counseled their people not to take up arms in the Sandinista insurrection to free Nicaragua from the Somoza regime. I have heard that they are threatening to discipline those who are fighting with the FSLN [Sandinista National Liberation Front]. They will not like to hear what I have to say now, for I must tell them what has happened to me in the last few days. The pastors know that I have taken a stand against violence and have refused to fight. But at this moment my decision is seriously challenged. After accompanying some of the young people from my parish to join the guerrillas on the outskirts of Managua, I faced a startling dilemma: to go back home as I had planned, or to stay and bear arms beside them!"

Ricardo paused, searching for words to describe his feelings. He met the eyes of his two friends who had agreed to meet with him in a modest building in downtown Managua. They had arranged to meet at the headquarters of CEPAD [Ecumenical Committee for Development Aid], an organization that coordinated the work of thirty-four Protestant denominations and groups in Nicaragua. Ricardo looked deeply into the face of Miguel Silva who, like Ricardo, was a Pentecostal pastor in the Church of God. There, too, was Ramón Ramírez, a CEPAD coordinator, medical doctor, and Baptist lay missionary.

In the moments of silence that followed, Ricardo reflected on the events that had culminated in the revolution, recalling that he had known about the activities of the FSLN for a long time. However, it was just in these last few months that so many Christians had joined in their support.

It was then the end of June 1979. The revolutionary forces, led by the FSLN, were showing signs of victory over the National Guard, which supported the Somoza regime, although the outcome was still unsure. There was devastation everywhere. Even in the midst of chaos, there were already estimates that more than fifty thousand were dead, one hundred thousand were wounded, forty thousand children were orphaned, and two hundred thousand persons were homeless.

The FSLN

The FSLN traced its origins to General Augusto Cesar Sandino's conflict with the U.S.-supported Conservative Party in 1928. U.S. Marines had been sent to Nicaragua in 1909 after Nicaragua's Liberal Party President José Zelaya had imposed restrictions on foreign investment and denied the United States the rights to build a canal that would have made use of Nicaragua's natural lake and river system. The United States supported the Conservative Party, which agreed to place the economy under the control of U.S. banks and to accept the presence of the Marines. Sandino was a general in the army of the Liberal Party, which opposed this foreign intervention and called for the right of self-determination for Nicaragua. By 1928 the long-standing conflict between the Liberal and Conservative Parties escalated to the point of open warfare. There was a U.S.-mediated settlement with the Liberal army, but General Sandino refused to lay down his arms until the Marines left. For nearly six years he fought a guerrilla war against the Marines. He also organized literacy classes for his *campesino* army, believing that ignorance was "the most powerful method of oppression."

In 1933 the U.S. Marines withdrew after training a newly formed National Guard to serve as both police and army. Anastasio Somoza García was appointed its head. When Sandino stopped fighting and went to Managua to sign a peace agreement with the new government, he was abducted by the National Guard, taken to the airport, and assassinated. Both Conservatives and Liberals agreed that Somoza had ordered the killing. It is also generally agreed that three years later, in 1936, it was Somoza who forced out the civilian president and secured his own election to the office. He held the presidency from 1937 to 1956. His son Luis was president from 1956 to 1963. Then in 1967 Luis's brother Anastasio Somoza Debayle became president.

During the forty-year period beginning in 1937, the Somoza family gained control of one-sixth of the total land (one-third of the arable land) and the twenty-six largest companies of Nicaragua. In this small country of 2.4 million persons, 5 percent of the adult population came to control 28 percent of the national income, while the lowest ranking 50 percent controlled 15 percent. Studies conducted by outside organizations concluded that 50 percent of the population—up to 90 percent in rural areas—were illiterate and lived in extreme poverty.

Although U.S. firms already controlled most of the production of Nicaragua's exports by as early as 1909, Ricardo believed that the United States had more interest in the strategic geographical location of the country than in its economic value. After the canal, crucial to U.S. interests, was built through Panama, it needed to be protected from hostile governments. Ricardo believed that Somoza García sought to strengthen his own position by serving U.S. strategies. President Roosevelt once said of him, "Somoza may be an S.O.B., but he's our S.O.B." Nicaragua was the staging base for the 1954 invasion of Guatemala, for the 1961 attack on Cuba's Bay of Pigs, and for the 1965 U.S. Marine invasion of the Dominican Republic. In return, the Somoza family directly controlled millions of dollars that came into the country designated for economic assistance. Ricardo was convinced that few of these funds ever reached the people.

During the years that followed Sandino's death and the Somoza family's rise to power, there was an occasional hit-and-run attack on the National Guard, but it was not until 1962, under the leadership of Carlos Fonseca Amador, that the Sandinista National Liberation Front officially came together by the fusion of several independent opposition groups. In 1974 the group, numbering less than a hundred, attracted national attention when, on December 27, an FSLN guerrilla band invaded a Christmas party in Managua and held hostage twelve of Nicaragua's top business and political leaders. In exchange for the hostages, the band was able to obtain the release of fourteen political prisoners, a ransom of one million dollars, and safe passage to Cuba.

In response Anastasio Somoza Debayle declared a state of siege with press censorship and martial law. Many *campesinos* (indigent landworkers) now refer to this time as the "reign of terror" as Somoza became determined to wipe out the FSLN. The *campesinos* reported that thousands of persons were tortured and killed by the National Guard and thousands more disappeared. This occurred primarily in the northern part of the country, in the towns of Zelaya, Matagalpa, and Segovia, where the FSLN had been active. To convert the rural areas into a fire-free zone, 80 percent of the mountain population were uprooted and moved into resettlement camps.

The opposition against Somoza increased with this new wave of oppression. Not all agreed, however, on the same strategy for working for Somoza's defeat.

In November 1976, after Carlos Fonseca Amador was killed in combat, the Sandinistas split into three factions, called "tendencies." One group, the GPP (Prolonged People's War Tendency) continued the strategy of rural-based guerrilla warfare. The TP (Proletarian Tendency) initiated political work in the cities, helping to organize labor unions, strikes, and protests against high prices and poor living conditions. The third group, the Terceristas (Insurrectional Tendency) believed that opposition to Somoza had become nearly universal, and they advocated a strong military organization to encourage popular insurrection. The three tendencies worked independently for several years, creating separate organizational structures and leadership.

The Christian Churches in Nicaragua

During the years of the Somoza family's dictatorship, Ricardo had seen critical changes taking place in the church and in the understanding of what it meant to be a Christian in Nicaragua. Beyond the political situation, a national disaster significantly affected the organization and the role of the church. The earthquake and subsequent fires in Managua in December 1972 devastated twenty-five city blocks and left seven thousand dead, fifteen thousand injured, and half the city's population of some four hundred thousand homeless. The landscape of downtown Managua was radically changed. There was devastation everywhere.

The Protestant Churches

Four days after the earthquake, CEPAD was formed to coordinate the efforts of the different Protestant denominations to meet the immediate and intense needs of the victims. CEPAD's statement of purpose was:

> the promotion of well-being of Nicaraguans in the following fields: integral development of individuals and communities; health in the physical, mental, and spiritual spheres; adult basic education; adequate housing.

Ricardo's congregation joined dozens of others that mobilized to help their neighbors in this time of emergency, using their buildings for shelter, preparing meals, and distributing clothing. Ricardo's denomination, the Church of God, worked with CEPAD from its beginning, as had 60 to 70 percent of the Pentecostal churches. Now the fastest growing churches in Nicaragua, the Pentecostal churches had their roots mainly in the United States. The majority of Pentecostal church members were working-class poor and *campesinos* in the rural mountain areas of the country.

Following the earthquake, the churches faced an immense challenge. Their response took many forms, which then began to address conditions much more far-reaching than the earthquake devastation. Ricardo recalled hearing Ramón describe the significant effect the earthquake had on the churches: "The earthquake made us all aware that we are brothers and sisters, and to be faithful meant to help others. So it made us get together and work together, and out of this work came our reflection."

CEPAD began to work with hundreds of communities, training local leaders in health care and agriculture in an attempt to reduce the malnutrition that affected more than 60 percent of the country's children, 40 percent of whom died before reaching their fifth birthday. The organization gave support to an adult basic education and literacy program, to the formation of cooperatives, and to low-cost housing programs. Ricardo learned of Pentecostal pastors and lay members, encouraged through the organization of CEPAD, who had helped to provide health care in remote rural areas. It took two days of walking to get to some of those rural areas where no doctors or nurses had previously been willing or able to go.

Ricardo believed that CEPAD, representing Nicaragua's two hundred fifty thousand Protestants—11 percent of the population—in all of its programs had aimed to help persons discover their human worth and potential. He was sure that CEPAD had helped to stimulate their self-confidence and initiative, and thus to find their way out of poverty. Both pastors and lay persons had been trained to reflect on the conditions surrounding them and to determine the Christian response to bring about changes in those conditions. However, Ricardo recalled, "the missionaries who originally came to us from the United States thought that it was sinful to be involved in politics. They taught us that and then they left."

The Roman Catholic Church

Although there were no regular programs between CEPAD and the Roman Catholic Church, which counted 85 percent of the Nicaraguan population, the two bodies shared materials and emergency services. Ricardo knew that what some called a "conversion" in the Catholic Church had played a significant part in the impact of Christians on the revolution. This was in contrast to the service orientation of the evangelical churches.

As early as 1963, individual priests and Catholic Christians were known to be involved in the FSLN. In 1968, a statement by Latin American bishops in Medellín, Colombia, had asserted:

To us, the Pastors of the Church, belongs the duty . . . to denounce everything which, opposing justice, destroys peace. [The bishops affirm the] duty of solidarity with the poor, to which charity leads us. This solidarity means that we make ours their problems and their struggles, that we know how to speak with them. This has to be concretized in criticism of injustice and oppression, in the struggle against the intolerable situation which a poor person has to tolerate.

In 1970 the Nicaraguan Catholic bishops publicly criticized the Somoza regime for violations of human rights. They accused the National Guard of "humiliating and inhuman treatment ranging from torture and rape to summary execution." It was accepted as fact that the National Guard subsequently responded by killing several priests and machine-gunning the home of the Bishop of León.

After Medellín, it was Ricardo's understanding that the values of justice, human rights, and social change began to be preached more openly in many of the Roman Catholic churches. Within some of the local parishes, small groups of twelve to fifteen persons, known as *comunidades ecclesiales de base* (Christian base communities) began forming to pray, to study the Bible, and to reflect on the meaning of the Bible for their own lives as Christians in Nicaragua. These groups grew out of a grass-roots movement and were not based on any particular political thought or strategy. Emerging from them, however, were new understandings with which Ricardo agreed. He had heard one Catholic layman declare that "poverty is not God's will and need not be the destiny of the people. There are concrete causes that create conditions of poverty, and they can be changed." However, Ricardo also knew that this movement in the churches was not without risk. One group of Catholic laity known as "Delegates of the Word," who traveled between the villages leading Bible study and teaching catechism, also taught *campesinos* to read and led discussions on the social consequences of their Christian life. Ricardo had learned that several Delegates were arrested by the National Guard, and some were tortured and killed.

An increasing number of Christian university students—both Catholic and Protestant—became involved in the movement to better the conditions of the poor in Nicaragua. Ricardo knew that some students went to live in poor parishes to work with the people, to try to understand their conditions, and to encourage community efforts to solve immediate needs for water, electricity, schools, health clinics, and paved streets.

After the 1972 earthquake, several Catholic religious orders moved to the slums to share the problems and hopes of the poor. One nun had told Ricardo of her growing conviction that "to do the work of Christ means to work with the poor." Ricardo heard priests express their realization that the church had been supporting the more affluent minority and had previously shown its interest in the poor only by works of charity. Some began to state that being a Christian meant getting involved in political work with the people. Others voiced their belief, as the bishops at Medellín had affirmed, that "justice, and therefore peace, conquer by means of a dynamic action of awakening (conscientization) and organization of the popular sectors that are capable of pressuring public officials who are often ineffective in their social projects without popular support." Capuchin priests working in Zelaya helped the people to elect representatives to be trained as teachers, midwives, agronomists, and religious leaders. They helped to establish rural schools, agricultural clubs, homemakers' associations, and health care units. The Maryknoll sisters found new ways to live out their constitution's affirmation that evangelization "not only is proclaiming the Good News with truth, clarity, and challenge, but witnessing it in life and service. We have an urgent call to announce the brotherhood of all men in Christ and to denounce that which deprives man of his legitimate claims for dignity, equality, sharing, and friendship."

Ricardo recalled a letter published by the Maryknoll nuns in four Nicaraguan cities. It said: "We cannot sit with our arms crossed in our convents, as some have said we should. Our role is to be with the people in their struggle to achieve a life of dignity and justice."

The social and economic devastation that followed the earthquake also prompted revolutionary Christian students to organize support for the FSLN within the universities. In 1976 Jesuit priest Fernando Cardenal, a teacher of philosophy at the National University of Nicaragua, was expelled, together with eighty students, for revolutionary activity. He had told a U.S. House Subcommittee on International Organizations that the Somoza government had been responsible for the killing of 224 *campesinos*. Religious poet and priest Ernesto Cardenal was threatened after he charged the government with misuse of AID (U.S. Agency for International Development) funds. Ernesto's reflections on the Bible with the *campesinos* of the Solentiname islands in Lake Nicaragua were suspect because of their conscientization effects. In 1977 two young men from the village joined the FSLN. Soon after this the community at Solentiname was bombed and virtually destroyed by the National Guard. Ernesto Cardenal himself subsequently joined the FSLN, saying: "Authentic revolutionaries prefer nonviolence to violence, but they are not always free to choose."

Students as well as priests and nuns supported a teachers' strike, which moved Somoza to retaliate by closing the schools for six months. Ricardo was convinced that the participation of youth in the revolutionary movement was significant; more than half of Nicaragua's population was under fifteen years of age.

An Explosive Recipe

Ricardo recalled that although some Christians, both Catholic and Protestant, had joined the FSLN, many were afraid of its ideology, believing that its leaders were communists who did not believe in God. Other Christians found it difficult to accept a revolutionary movement that had to use arms. Most did, however, believe in the goals of the FSLN: to build schools and hospitals and to do away with poverty. Ricardo also believed that Christians had great respect for those who were willing to do what the Bible said was the greatest thing: to lay down their lives for others. Thus through a very difficult and painful process, many Christians began to acknowledge that "legal means would not work with a dictatorship, and they would have to fight."

In turn, some FSLN leaders who were not Christian began to see that many Christians, rather than using their religion to escape from life, were becoming revolutionary from Christian motivation. In order to reach victory, the FSLN would have to include all the people.

Ricardo regarded the union between the churches and the emerging FSLN, based on a common concern for fellow human beings, to be an historic event. One youth had remarked, "Christianity and revolution, when integrated, form a recipe that is explosive." Christians began to join the FSLN and took up many different tasks, as fighters and collaborators, offering safe houses and transportation. Several base communities in Nicaragua evolved into Sandinista Defense Committees. Christian men and women were taken into positions of responsibility and eventually comprised about half of the FSLN membership. Almost a third of the guerrilla fighters were women.

A Managua priest had observed, "The Sandinistas were born in the mountains, as only a small light in the mountains, but they began to affect the people. Christian revolutionary students have made possible the transfer of the struggle in the mountains to the cities, and make victory a real possibility." Many members of one group, the Revolutionary Christian Students, which had organized after the 1972 earthquake, moved into FSLN leadership roles.

The sequence of events was clear in Ricardo's mind. In October 1977 the Sandinista offensive began with a series of small-scale attacks on National Guard garrisons in five cities. They were forced to withdraw.

In December 1977, forty thousand youths participated in sit-ins in churches, calling the people to awakened Christian consciousness and creating pressure for the release of an estimated three hundred fifty prisoners who had completed their terms. The National Guard attacked the students by throwing tear-gas bombs into the churches.

In January 1978, middle-class citizen Pedro Joaquín Chamorro was assassinated on a street corner in downtown Managua. Ricardo could picture that corner in an area still not rebuilt since the earthquake. It resembled a desolate countryside, despite $76.7 million from AID and other international funds designated for reconstruction. The growing realization that the funds were being appropriated by the Somoza family and the taking over of the construction industry by the same small group had sparked opposition to the regime from the middle class. A growing economic crisis caused dissatisfied members of the middle class to join the UDEL (Democratic Union of Liberation), an anti-Somoza organization that campaigned for an end to press censorship and the state of siege and repression. They demanded political and trade union freedoms and the release of political prisoners.

Chamorro had been a founder and leader of UDEL and the editor of *La Prensa,* a newspaper that opposed Somoza's policies. Chamorro's latest editorial campaign had been against a Somoza-owned blood export firm that bought blood from the poor and sold it abroad for high prices.

By the time Chamorro's body had reached the hospital, more than a thousand persons were following after. Although Chamorro was buried secretly early the next morning, more than five thousand persons marched in the memorial service conducted by his church. Such public participation was unheard of. Ricardo knew that "If you did that under Somoza, you were as good as dead." Following Chamorro's death, there was a spontaneous uprising, resulting in a two-week general strike by the business community to enforce its demand for Somoza's resignation. The FSLN added its endorsement to the strike and named Pedro Joaquín Chamorro a "National Hero of Public Letters."

In retaliation, Somoza ordered the National Guard to bomb and burn several cities and villages. Hundreds of *campesino* families were killed. The government's harsh repression of the January uprising prompted U.S. President Carter to make a public condemnation of the violation of human rights in Nicaragua and to reduce U.S. military and economic aid.

This was also the time when Ricardo Campos had become directly involved. As he began to recall vividly the events of the past few months, he began to share his thoughts with his friends.

The Growing Crisis

"Do you both recall when CEPAD was asked by Somoza to give him a letter stating that there were no violations of human rights in Nicaragua? I was on one of the CEPAD commissions to go out into the mountains in the north to investigate. In the beginning, people were afraid to tell us."

Miguel Silva, who had gone with Ricardo, added, "After the people began to trust us, I heard of a Pentecostal pastor who was denounced as opposing the government. He was taken prisoner, tied up, and thrown out of a helicopter."

Ricardo continued his account: "We found that both Evangelicals and non-Evangelicals were suffering brutalities from the National Guard. We must acknowledge that there were also atrocities committed by members of the FSLN, particularly the attacks on members of the National Guard. Neither side is blameless in a war. But the people suffered far more at the hands of the National Guard. Guerrillas would come to homes looking for food or clothing and the people would give them what they had. Then the Guard would come and kill those who were suspected of helping the guerrillas. Women were raped and children were murdered.

"We wanted to talk to Somoza directly about these problems and complaints, and when we had information we planned to meet with him. That was in the beginning of May in 1978. I remember that the rains then were particularly heavy. Once it starts raining, it gets too muddy to get to some areas.

"Somoza claimed to have no knowledge of any problems in the mountains and said that 'it wouldn't happen again.' Our committee of three Evangelical pastors emphasized that we were not speaking just for Evangelicals, but for all the people without distinction of religion or politics. Of course we were never able to give the kind of letter that Somoza wanted. And I was angry to learn that President Carter sent a letter to Somoza not long after that to congratulate him on his improved human rights record and to announce the resumption of U.S. aid. I ask each of you to stop now and remember which events of this time touched you most deeply."

In the silence that followed, Ricardo traced in his memory the events of the next several months. Somoza's oppressive policies finally caused many in the middle class to add their support to the struggle being carried out by the rural and urban poor. In mid-1978 many from the business and professional community joined with the more radical groups opposing Somoza to form the

FAO [Broad Opposition Front]. And in July 1978 a group of influential businessmen, clergymen, and intellectuals returned to Nicaragua from exile in Costa Rica. Known as "The Twelve," they endorsed armed insurrection as the only way to remove Somoza.

In August an FSLN guerrilla band attacked the National Palace while Congress was in session, taking fifteen hundred hostages whom they exchanged for fifty-nine political prisoners and a flight to Panama. A new general strike that paralyzed the economy followed the palace assault, and in September the FSLN sparked mass insurrections, leading the people in an attempt to seize five of the country's largest cities: Matagalpa, León, Estelí, Chinandega, and Granada. The insurrections were put down. Then the Guard went through the streets with tanks, throwing grenades and entering houses and killing anyone found inside. The Sandinistas withdrew after three weeks and the Guard "mopped up" with hundreds of executions. More than five thousand civilians were killed by U.S.-supplied arms. In addition, there were ten thousand missing, more than fifteen thousand wounded, and more than twenty-five thousand left homeless. Somoza denied the accusations of the Human Rights Commission of the OAS (Organization of American States) that the National Guard had committed widespread atrocities in the September fighting.

In November the Catholic bishops of Nicaragua issued a pastoral statement supporting the revolution. By the following March, in 1979, the three "tendencies" announced unity within the FSLN. Ricardo had heard a Baptist pastor express his belief that it was the Christians within the three groups who enabled them to unite. One could no longer live in Nicaragua without being affected by the conflict. Few lives had been untouched by anger and grief over the loss of family members and friends and the continual fear of more executions.

Miguel Silva looked up at Ricardo and broke the silence that had followed Ricardo's question. "I remember during this time that members of our congregation felt compelled by God to pray for all the problems Nicaragua was going through. The scriptures say to pray for the government leaders because they are put there by God. So we prayed for Somoza, that God would illuminate his mind. At the same time we prayed for those in the jails and in the mountains fighting for justice. For three months before the insurrection started, in May, we began the day with prayer services at 5:00 A.M. This has helped us to have the courage to make decisions and to help our church members and neighbors in the difficult times that have come."

Ramón Ramírez added, "I have been touched by the Evangelical pastors I know who are fighting with the guerrillas, along with members of their congregations. Some have been killed. Other pastors have counseled their congregations not to support the Sandinistas, saying that the church is apolitical and that our faith does not allow us to kill."

"But persons from the churches are participating in many ways," affirmed Miguel. "They are risking their lives to provide food, safe homes, medicine, and message services. In our church, we have protected women and children and helped the wounded. We give refuge to all who ask—including the Guard. The Guard hasn't always respected the places of refuge. Both the FSLN and the Guard signed an agreement with the Red Cross not to attack churches housing the wounded. But churches in two barrios have been bombarded by the Guard."

Ramón reached over to the shelf near his desk and took down a large mortar shell. "This was found in a Pentecostal churchyard. It says somewhere on here, 'Made in USA.' "

Ricardo joined the conversation. "I learned of a Church of God pastor who was conducting a worship service in a barrio in Managua. Guerrillas were in the neighborhood, and they wrote graffiti and threw some lighted gasoline bottles at a nearby bridge. Following the explosion, a National Guard jeep came. The guerrillas ran to save their lives, and one of them came into the church and sat down with the congregation. Someone gave him a hymn book and Bible and a different shirt, so he would not be recognized. The pastor stayed with the young man until the Guard was gone.

"Catholic churches are involved in the same way, and we have helped one another. There is a Catholic church about a block from us. It has an artesian well and was the only place we could get water after the recent bombings of Managua. Some women asked me to go with them to get water. They hoped that the Guard would not shoot so readily, because I am a pastor. After we arrived, there was an outbreak of shooting. The two priests who were there were very nervous and the women were afraid and wanted to run. I stopped them from running away because they would have been machine-gunned. I persuaded them all to lie flat on the floor and I prayed for them. Afterward the priests thanked me and gave us some food. During that time I learned that, when we share common needs, Roman Catholics and Protestants can work together."

"There was fighting near my house too," added Miguel. "My neighborhood was a zone of bombardment because there was a Sandinista post two blocks away. There was great devastation. Nearly a block and a half disappeared altogether. After the bombing, which they did with Israeli-made planes, the Guard set the rest of the houses on fire with the people inside. We later brought out the charred bodies."

Ricardo's voice grew strained as he shared with his friends an incident that happened just a few days before. "Some of the guerrillas came and asked me, 'Are you an Evangelical pastor?,' I answered, 'Yes.' They continued, 'We want to give you a gun so that you can fight to free your people.' I let them know my stand. I told them that I loved my people, that I saw the struggle as a good cause because I knew of the atrocities, but I also said that as a minister of God I was not able to take up a gun and kill other human beings. They asked me, 'What if a gun is given to you by the Guard? Would you fight then?' I said that I would not. 'Even if they would kill you?' they pressed me. I told them that I was ready to die. Then I asked them, 'Are you willing to break your commitment and agree not to fight?' They said that nothing could convince them not to fight. I explained that in the same way I, as a minister of God, could not change my stand.

"But I was deeply moved when the young people in my barrio made the decision that they would take up arms to fight. They knew that if they stayed home, the Guard would kill them. At first I didn't understand that. But when the guerrillas took over our barrio, we heard that the Guard was planning a 'clean-up operation.' We had come to know what that meant. At first I cried. But then I came to understand that there comes a moment when people have to make a decision, as those young persons made."

"In my barrio," Miguel broke in, "there was a time when the Guard came in pickup trucks. A guard would kick open closed doors, take the young people by the hair, and tie them up. They piled their bodies in the trucks on top of one another like sacks of potatoes. I saw a truck with about thirty young people piled up. That was a moment when I felt impotent with anger. It is a deep anger that burns like fire, when you see machine guns and are not able to do anything. We knew that hours later those young people would be dead. The Guard threw their bodies behind the National Theater near the lake. They threw them away like garbage, and smashed their faces so their relatives couldn't recognize them. There comes a moment when the fear of the Guard disappears and people fight with whatever they can find: hunting rifles, old machetes, cans full of powder, picks, shovels, and sticks. When I felt impotent with anger, I was tempted to fight. I knew how to use arms. My own son had become a guerrilla fighter. It is one thing to see other persons suffering, and another thing to see your own children suffering."

Ricardo took a deep breath and looked straight at Miguel. "You, then, will understand what has happened to me. When the young people from my barrio left to join the guerrilla forces, they had to get to the other side of Managua. I decided to go with them to protect them. Being with them during that time taught me that their struggle was necessary, because to stay at home was to die with their hands crossed and tied. They are fighting not only for their own lives, but for thousands of others. I saw why they feel that the only way to be free is to take up weapons.

"It has been only a week since I refused to accept a gun from the guerrillas and told them that I would not fight. It has been only two days since I left my young people behind the battle line. Those two days of my life have seemed like at least two months. I wasn't even sure for a time whether I would go back home. I asked the Lord to help me show that I was his servant. God says, 'Thou shalt not kill,' and his only son, our Savior, asks us to turn the other cheek and even to love our enemies. Yet my young people are prepared to take other lives as well as to give up their own for the sake of justice and freedom. If I truly love my people, is not my place beside them bearing arms? How can I explain this conflict to our fellow Christians in the mountains, some of whom have already threatened to discipline those who fight? Even my consideration of bearing arms may be seen by them as a betrayal of the gospel—and perhaps it is.

"I come to you now, friends, to ask for your guidance."

TEACHING NOTE ON "TO BEAR ARMS"

Ricardo Campos is asking his friends to share with him in a decision which many Christians face in areas of the world where there is long-standing, widespread and desperate poverty, and a clash of political factions of the right and left. The case raises numerous issues: pacifism vs. revolutionary activity; violence vs. nonviolence; structural violence vs. personal violence; ecumenism; church-state relationships; social action; solidarity with the poor; sacrifice; anger; grief; love of neighbor; love of enemy; forgiveness.

The case discussion could assume a variety of objectives:

A. To identify the kinds of violence that can be inherent in governmental and economic structures.
B. To explore the witnesses of the Christian pacifist and the Christian revolutionary.
C. To explore the relationship between Christianity and politics.
D. To explore the implications of "solidarity with the poor."
E. To understand the relationship of Christianity to Marxism in the Nicaraguan revolution.

CASE PLAN

Opening: What would you be willing to die for? Ask participants to identify one or more things—values, principles, persons, etc. Share briefly with the person next to them.

1. The case discussion could center on a series of questions. Responses could be listed on newsprint or a chalk board under "Issues."

—How is Ricardo's decision not to fight being challenged?
—What factors support/challenge his pacifist decision?
—What are the ways in which violence is present in Nicaragua?
—What basic human needs are not being met?
—What do you hold to be "basic human rights"?
—What is implied by "solidarity with the poor"?
—How would you interpret "God's will" to the poor?
—What goals might Christians and Socialists hold in common?
—How do they differ?
—What possibilities exist for the Church to remain neutral?
—How can a church best serve its people in time of revolution?
—What is the role of ecumenism?

2. At this point call participants to list possible "Alternatives" by asking how Ricardo can best express love of neighbor. Call the group to then vote on the alternatives each recommends. Urge participants to share the reasons for supporting a particular alternative.

3. A helpful way to close this case might be to ask participants to share whatever learnings they had from the case and the discussion. Where is forgiveness in this case? What other resources of God's grace are available to Ricardo, whatever he decides?

SUGGESTIONS FOR ADDITIONAL READING

Books

Gutierrez, Gustavo. *A Theology of Liberation*. Maryknoll, N.Y.: Orbis Books, 1973.

Lernoux, Penny. *The Cry of the People: United States Involvement in the Rise of Fascism, Torture, and Murder and the Persecution of the Church in Latin America*. New York: Doubleday & Co., Inc., 1980.

Articles

Berrigan, Daniel. "Open Letter Berrigan to Cardenal: 'Guns don't work.' " *National Catholic Reporter.* May 5, 1978.

Cardenal, Ernesto. "In my opinion," *National Catholic Reporter.* February 3, 1978.

Erlick, June Carolyn. Cardenal: "To Berrigan I say: 'Arms gave life.' " *National Catholic Reporter,* September 14, 1979.

Leo Grande, William M. "The Revolution in Nicaragua, Another Cuba?" *Foreign Affairs* 58:28–50, Fall, 1979.

For additional information on Nicaragua, write to:
National Network in Solidarity with the Nicaraguan People, 1322 18th Street, N.W., Washington, DC 20036

ORLANDO E. COSTAS

COMMENTARY ON "TO BEAR ARMS"

Seven days after the overthrow of General Anastasio Somoza Debayle, I found myself on a two-engine Cessna plane traveling to Managua, Nicaragua, from my home in San José, Costa Rica. I was one of a group of Protestant church leaders who were to consider how the Protestant world community could respond to the challenge of reconstructing war-torn Nicaragua.

From Costa Rica I had followed, step by step, the war of liberation spearheaded by the Sandinista National Liberation Front. Along with thousands of other Christians, I had prayed for the downfall of the Somoza regime. I had vigorously advocated the just cause of the liberating struggle of the Nicaraguan people. I had raised funds for and personally contributed to the cost of caring for the nearly one hundred thousand refugees in Costa Rica as well as for the provision of food, medicine, and clothing for the Sandinistas. As a servant of Jesus Christ, however, I could not see myself spilling blood no matter how justified the cause might seem.

Pastor Campos's dilemma was shared by many colleagues in the ministry throughout Central America. Although it must be acknowledged that for those of us who were outside Nicaragua the dilemma was not as profound as for Campos and other Nicaraguan colleagues of his, the way I tried to deal with the situation may well illustrate how Ricardo Campos could have solved the problem.

No Moral Judgment

First of all, I did not (and could not) make a moral judgment on those who decided to join the armed struggle. In spite of my commitment to nonviolence, I was too well aware that the issue in Nicaragua was not simply violence versus nonviolence. Regardless of my convictions, thousands of persons were being killed by one of the worst tyrants Latin America has ever known. He had no moral scruples. He had no respect for the civilian population or for human life in general. His troops invaded homes, killed babies, youth, and women, destroyed churches and flattened entire cities with air strikes and bombs. He refused to adhere to the pleas of the international community. He refused to settle the conflict politically and furthermore was known to be, like his father, a traitor (who ordered the assassination of Augusto Sandino). It was clear, therefore, that the only way more bloodshed could be avoided was by overthrowing the Somoza regime.

Moreover, it was not possible for me to put the children, women, and men who had joined the armed struggle in the same category as Somoza's National Guard. Not only did the Guard have highly sophisticated arms supplied by the U.S.A. and Israel to protect invested economic interests, but had been from its inception an instrument of violence and injustice. The violent and treacherous record of the Somoza National Guard has been amply documented.[1] In contrast, the masses had only .22 caliber guns and machetes. They were simply defending what they had. In many cases, it was either to be killed by the Guard or to survive by killing them. As Ricardo says, for the youth of his barrio "to stay at home was to die with their hands crossed and tied." This was both an uneven and qualitatively different struggle. The blood spilled by the Sandinistas and the people cannot be compared with the numerous assassinations executed every day by the Guard. The motivation as well as the end were radically different. As Ernesto Cardenal also stated in his response to Daniel Berrigan's criticism for defending the armed struggle, the arms of the Sandinistas and the Nicaraguan people "were used not to kill but to give life." It was a war that "was fought to end violence." Although it is true that "no principle—no matter how high—[is] worth [spilling the] blood of even just one child," Cardenal added that "for the same reason [he felt] no principle—no matter how noble, even the principle of staunch nonviolence— is worth more than the blood of this one child."

Hence I could not condemn, much less discipline—as the pastors in the churches under Ricardo Campos's supervision were threatening to do—those Evangelicals who had joined the armed struggle. On the contrary, I had to admire and demand respect for those who had given up everything to participate in such a struggle, even if I could not in good conscience bear arms myself.

Nonmilitary Assistance

But secondly, I did not (and could not) make or accept a moral judgment upon those such as Ricardo (and myself) who would not take up arms. Not everyone who refused to bear arms was against the revolution. There were many who served the cause by doing what Ricardo did: accompanying the struggle with their moral and spiritual support. Indeed, it took more courage for Ricardo Campos to refuse to bear arms and continue to be a pastor to his flock than it would have had he taken up arms, because in so doing he became more vulnerable to the National Guard. It is easier to kill an unarmed person than someone who has a gun, especially if the unarmed person happens to stand for justice and the person with the gun for injustice.

It is a fact that had it not been for those who did not bear arms but dedicated themselves to help the homeless and the wounded, the war of liberation would have had a far greater social cost than it did. Take, for example, those who transformed their homes into shelters for families left homeless. CEPAD dedicated itself to deliver food and medicine in areas where the line of supplies had been cut off. The Red Cross struggled fearlessly and tirelessly to treat the wounded, thereby saving lives that would have otherwise been lost. These actions reflect a decision to serve persons in need. Such actions may not have been as dramatic and heroic as the responses of those who directly resisted the tyrant through military action, but they were socially and politically significant. Indeed they not only kept alive persons who would be involved in the reconstruction of the nation, but indirectly frustrated Somoza's attempt to wipe out all opposition. Little wonder that the National Guard not infrequently went after those who were engaged in humanitarian aid.

Bearing arms is but one way to deal with tyrants. In the Nicaraguan struggle for liberation there were many who, though committed to the revolution, made their contribution in nonmilitary ways. How far would the armed resistance have gone had it not been for the nonviolent support it received from the religious community, especially the Catholic hierarchy, for the tactical support of such moderate nonmilitary coalitions as the Broad Opposition Front and the Democratic Union of Liberation, or the political leadership of the Committee of Twelve in exile? Not very far! As a matter of fact, the Nicaraguan struggle was not carried out simply on the military front; it had to be carried out in the political, economic, social, and ideological arenas as well.

Not to bear arms in a situation where all other peaceful means of resistance have been exhausted is thus not *necessarily* morally wrong. For the "conscientious objector" there is the possibility of contributing to the resistance by other than military means.

Ricardo did not need to doubt the consistency of his decision to bear arms. For him it was not a cop-out, but a question of conscience. Nor did he need to feel guilty about not taking up arms alongside the youth of his barrio. On the one hand, it was *their* decision of conscience; they believed that this was the only option left open for them as Nicaraguans. On the other hand, he did the work of a pastor, which is not to bear arms but to stand in solidarity with his flock. By accompanying them to the front lines, he showed them that he respected their decisions and cared for their well-being. His next *pastoral* task, therefore, was not to take up arms but to go to the mountains and talk to the pastors under his supervision and enable them to understand their pastoral responsibility in such an hour. Rather than discipline their church members because of their decision to join the armed struggle, they were to preach and teach God's gift of human life, the command to promote and defend it, and the right to resist any regime that threatens and works against it. Moreover, they were to provide alternatives by which their members could fulfill their Christian responsibilities. As Nicaraguan pastors, they had as much a responsibility to provide spiritual support for those members who had conscientiously opted for the armed defense of the nation as to provide nonmilitary options for those who could not see their way clear to participating in the armed struggle.

The Life-Criterion

Thirdly, the fundamental factor in the issue of bearing arms or not is *life*. Does the armed struggle promote life or death? Is nonviolence prolife or antilife?

Somoza and the National Guard did not promote life. They used their arms to exploit the poor, oppress the weak, and put an end to all opposition by recourse to torture, imprisonment, and murder.

The Sandinistas, and the people's militia that emerged throughout Nicaragua, sought to abolish such a regime of death by establishing a just social order. They were not simply seeking to stop the physical violence of the established regime. For them life was not simply biological; it was social, economic, political, cultural, and psychological. Thus they did not simply overcome the institutional violence of the Somoza dynasty, but once in power began to create the material conditions for a fuller life: the elimination of illiteracy, the redistribution of land, an economy geared to satisfy the real needs of the country, the establishment of a just legal system, a participatory political democracy, the provision of basic health services, education for all, employment for the healthy and social care for the disabled, and the guarantee of freedom of religion and expression. Whether or not they have been able to achieve all of these goals in the aftermath of the insurrection is still a matter of dispute. Well-informed observers have said that many of these goals have already been reached. Be that as it may, it was to that end that the Sandinista government committed itself, and in so doing it promoted life.

There were some during the insurrection who, out of fear or conviction, refused to get involved in the struggle. Some of them helped out with the wounded and homeless; others simply tried to stay out of the war zones; and yet others fled the country. All of them claimed to be neutral. Sadly, it must be said that among them were several Christian leaders. In fact, such seems to have been the position of the pastors under Ricardo Campos's supervision. Consciously or unconsciously their neutrality and nonviolent principles became an instrument for the maintenance of the status quo and the immolation of the people. In so doing, they did *not* promote life, but death.

It is in this context that we can appreciate the nonviolent action of Ricardo Campos. Although he refused to bear arms—in obedience to God's command, "you shall not kill"—he also felt that his country could not continue under the terrorist regime of Anastasio Somoza Debayle. He had learned to respect the youth of his barrio; for them fighting was a matter of survival. If there was to be life in Nicaragua, it would have to be won by the people through sweat, tears, and blood. As Augusto César Sandino had said, "Freedom is not won with flowers."

Yet God had not called Ricardo to bear arms but rather to bear the message of life and resurrection imbedded in the gospel. The one who had commanded "turn the other cheek" and even "love your enemies" was also the one who said, "The thief comes only to steal, to kill, to destroy; I have come that men may have life, and may have it in all its fullness. I am the good shepherd; the good shepherd lays down his life for the sheep" (John 10:10–11). In a world of injustice and death, robbers and murderers, Jesus, the Good Shepherd, came to give life by laying down his own life and refusing to take the life of others. Thus, he not only atoned for the sins of a fallen world but set the model for those whom he calls to shepherd his flock. It was to this task that Ricardo Campos was called.

His dilemma was, thus, not between violence and nonviolence, but rather between the call of his homeland to defend its right to freedom, justice, and well-being, and the call of Jesus Christ to lead his flock through the shadow of death by being willing to lay down his life for them so that they might have a sign of the most basic requirement of abundant life: selfless love. As a Nicaraguan, Ricardo understood and deeply sympathized with the decision of the youth from his barrio and thousands of other young persons elsewhere, to fight for the freedom of their homeland. But as a pastor, he had been called to another task. To adhere to this calling was not to deny his solidarity with the struggle for justice and the liberation of his homeland. It was rather to enrich his contribution to it: to be a sign of sacrificial love, along the model of the Good Shepherd, which was the only basis on which a new Nicaragua could guarantee true freedom, justice, and well-being to future generations.

NOTE

1. See, for example, Richard Millet, *Guardians of the Dynasty* (Maryknoll, N.Y.: Orbis, 1977); EPICA Task Force, *Nicaragua: A People's Revolution* (Washington, D.C.: EPICA, 1980).

JOHANN B. METZ

COMMENTARY ON "TO BEAR ARMS"

Nicaragua is getting increasingly bad press in Europe. The picture of this country and its revolution appears darker and darker. But why this negative attitude and propaganda? There are, to be sure, difficulties and a considerable number of contradictions in Nicaragua's revolutionary enterprise, which I will discuss, and only some of which are reflected in the case "To Bear Arms." In my opinion, one of the primary reasons for this negative criticism of the Nicaraguan revolution is the fact that the situation of the country is judged too much from the outside, according to our criteria and our alternatives. (Of course, Nicaragua produces enough evidence and voices to support this critique.)

The Relationship Between Religion and Revolution

The case attempts to present a view from the inside and also reveals the contradictions and conflicts concerning the revolution within some dimensions of Nicaraguan society itself, including the Christian community. Other commentators may address the question of violence and the Christian faith in a revolutionary situation. However, I am going to attempt to illuminate one particular aspect of the situation from the inside. This aspect presents a new problem for those like Ricardo, Carlos, and Ramón. I wish to portray the new Nicaragua as reflected in the present ecclesiastical situation of the country. This is a legitimate viewpoint; in fact, it almost forces itself upon us, since the recent revolutionary history of Nicaragua demonstrates a singular, and so far historically unique, relationship between religion and revolution, between political opposition and the church. It is a picture of a revolutionary battle of resistance in which, above all, devout Christians, the faithful *campesinos*, participated in the struggle and the uprising motivated by their

---

This commentary was translated from German by Eileen Fitzsimons.

faith—in contrast to the Cuban revolution, the revolutionary process in Chile, and the great revolutions of modern Europe.

In Nicaragua, the relationship between church and the revolution seemed relatively unproblematic for the Roman Catholic Church as long as it was a matter of participation in the revolutionary battle itself. The difficulties did not really arise until *after* the victory—when it was no longer a matter of participating directly in a revolutionary uprising, but rather a matter of participation in and support of the revolution as an "historic enterprise." The difficulty arose in seeking the reorganization of the country "in the spirit of the revolution"—the realization of the revolution as cultural, social, and economic, in brief, as a new political enterprise, but beyond that, as a pilot project for Central America as a whole, and ultimately for the development of all of Latin America.

Who Owns the Revolution?

At this point, the question of the inheritance and development of the revolution surfaces. To whom, in short, does the revolution belong? Who bears the responsibility? Does Ricardo (whether he bears arms or not), his young people or their parents, the Pentecostal pastors or the Catholic bishops? The current situation in Nicaragua, as mirrored in the country's ecclesiastical processes, can be characterized by the fundamental (and historically paradigmatic) question: How is a revolution inherited?

1. Difficulties in dealing with the revolutionary inheritance on the part of the Roman Catholic Bishops.

a. It appears to me that the majority of the Nicaraguan episcopacy tends to regard the revolution itself merely as an episode and wants to bypass it and revert to the established, paternalistic church. These bishops fail to realize that such a revolutionary experience has an impact on all dimensions of life, particularly the religious, and that it evokes a new subjective consciousness in people, especially in the poverty-stricken and the oppressed, a consciousness which neither can nor will stop at the door of the church. The revolutionary experience is, at the same time, an experience of new ecclesiastical identity. If the bishops do not take this into account, they will find themselves in a schismatic relationship to the people who fought decisively and who suffered most in this revolution.

b. Furthermore, there is the fact that the bishops obviously find it difficult to recognize that there are other leaders with moral authority besides themselves, namely those revolutionary leaders recognized by the people. During the Somoza era the bishops were more or less the only moral authority for the poor and the oppressed.

c. Finally, the bishops appear to have chosen a questionable concept of reconciliation ("the bishops are there for everyone"), which blocks the partisanship historically necessary for the poor and oppressed. The bishops, whether they will it or not, are again forced too far toward the side of the bourgeoisie, and they become accomplices in the "grief of the bourgeoisie" and the fight for their endangered privileges.

2. On the Sandinista side there are clearly emerging dangers and contradictions concerning the development of the revolution. I think it is important that the dangers be recognized, articulated, and thought through. Part of the historical dignity of this unique revolutionary enterprise is precisely this process, and, in my opinion, the long-range success of the revolution is dependent upon it.

Now, for the difficulties and the contradictions.

a. First of all, there is the question of the historical theme of the revolution. The Sandinistas emphasize again and again that this is a revolution of the poor people. But, in order for this to be not only a revolution *for* the poor (as happened in Europe), but also a revolution *by* the poor themselves, it must first of all listen to the poor and learn from them. Only then can this revolution be the voice of the poor and raise its voice in the name of those without a voice. In view of the difficulties—in the economy and in foreign policy—there is the danger that a substitution for the poor as subject of this revolution will be sought, that, for example, the Sandinistas, or the Sandinista military itself, will see themselves as subjects of this revolution and as responsible for the long revolutionary educational enterprise.

b. Secondly, this danger is intensified by the fact that the country is forced dramatically onto the defensive by the danger of counterrevolution from the inside and threatened invasion by former Somozistas from the outside. This increases the temptation to discontinue the revolutionary educational process and to misconstrue it as a process of militarization of the entire people. This militarization distracts the revolution from the social and cultural dream on which this historical undertaking is dependent.

c. Thirdly, if one considers the apparent catastrophic economic situation of the country, the pressure for action, the drive for success, and protection of the revolution from the enemy, then the danger of a political short circuit is obvious. There is a great danger that imported revolutionary theories will be superimposed on the Nicaraguan enterprise from the outside. No revolutionary theory familiar to us, not even the Marxist-Leninist approach, is applicable here. The *campesinos* are anything but a proletariat, or even a subproletariat, in our sense of the word.

3. Gaining time, setting up a protective "time screen," which would enable the authentic development of revolutionary enterprise, ought to be, in my opinion, the main slogan of Sandinista politics. This slogan contains, above all, a foreign policy challenge of corresponding alliances, which currently are almost nonexistent. Perhaps this involves rich European countries, which have democratic traditions, yet are simultaneously socialistic and critical of capitalism, or rich partners of the Third World. The historical and "spiritual" burdens of the United States are too great to enable one to envision a constructive political relationship to this world power in the foreseeable future, quite aside from the fact that one can hardly expect that American politics will support a socialistic option. And, as is the case with Russia, American politics constantly seem to succumb to a typical temptation of world powers, that is, to the loss of political sensitivity to foreign social and political cultures. This leads to the inability to recognize anything but themselves in other countries, and with this comes the danger that insight into foreign countries will be replaced by influence.

An Open Revolution and the Base Church

We start with the fact that Nicaragua's revolutionary enterprise is, in point of fact, an "open" enterprise. The struggle for the overall goal is not clearly delineated; there is no definition of the undertaking based on an end product. In the struggle for the inheritance of the "spirit of the revolution" there is, within the ecclesiastical scene, a process which at this point demands special attention. It is the germinating emergence of the so-called base church in Nicaragua, which sees itself unified as a religious-political church and therefore tries to understand the revolutionary impulse and the inspiration of the gospel as common stimuli for the realization of the new Nicaraguan social identity. To be sure (as is frequently the case with beginning base churches in Latin America), we are talking about a picture that is still unstable, but then real hopes are seldom pinned on the powerful! As these base Christians repeatedly assert, this is by no means the establishment of a "new" church or a sort of church of the opposition. These base Christians see themselves as members of the Nicaraguan church and strive now for shared political-religious responsibility.*

Lest there be any misunderstanding: When we address this church development as a hope for Nicaragua's revolutionary enterprise, it is not a matter of the revolution's being inherited, as it were, by the church alone. It is a part of the fundamental premises of the base church development that the church finally, even though it be a painful metamorphosis, is departing from its so-called legitimizing age, from that age in which the church lent legitimacy to social structures and relationships. The church today, however, is entering its so-called liberating and innovating age. The church itself is participating in a creative way in the attempt at liberating the poor and the oppressed. This is done, however, not "from above," but "from below," from its social basis. These base church initiatives in Nicaragua also seem to be led by a clear political alternative, which can be clarified briefly in two points:

1. The way of Nicaragua toward liberation from poverty and oppression, as well as that of all Central America and ultimately Latin America as a whole, is a non-capitalist, and in *this* sense, a socialist way.

2. The socialism proposed here, however, is not a copy of any existing (classical Marxist) socialism in Europe or anywhere else. And in this sense the revolutionary undertaking in Nicaragua comprises a revolution of socialism

---

*See the "Open letter of the Nicaraguan base communities from city and country to the bishops, priests, religious, and laity of the people of God" on the occasion of the First National Conference of the Nicaraguan Ecclesiastical Communities on June 27-28, 1981.

itself. These Christians see the innovative—and for the common culture of Latin America paradigmatic—fact that here, for the first time, Christian elements can become an intrinsic part of the socialist plan. They also have a large portion of base church beginnings and undertakings in other Latin American countries behind them, including a number of Latin American, especially Brazilian, episcopacies, who have intentionally spoken out in favor of the authentic development of the Nicaraguan revolution. And, finally, in their enterprises they can appeal to the church documents of Medellín and Puebla. The FSLN document on religion also encourages them, though at times the document creates the impression that the FSLN is the only authentic subject of the revolutionary enterprise in Nicaragua, and therefore qualified and authorized to define adequately this revolutionary process.

Critical Loyalty to the Revolution

The political option of the Nicaraguan basic church expresses itself in a fundamental and decisive loyalty to the "spirit of the revolution" and to the resulting directions for the country's new enterprise. To be sure, this loyalty gives them the authority to criticize in a spirit of loyalty the processes in the Nicaraguan society and church. This loyalty to the revolution does not mean that they unquestioningly allow themselves to be placed in the service of a predetermined revolutionary undertaking. Rather, it means they participate with solidarity on their part in the formation of this "open," albeit directed, enterprise.

1. In respect to the Sandinista, the base church will, with their critical loyalty, repeatedly raise the questions: To whom does the revolution belong? Is the revolution really the voice of the silently suffering poor? Furthermore, they will challenge the revolutionary virtues proclaimed to be the anthropological basis of the revolutionary enterprise by the Sandinistas, just as Ricardo challenges violence. They will protest institutionalized hatred as an identifying principle of revolution, as Miguel warns. They will insist on the possibility of guilt on the part of the revolution or the revolutionaries, as Ramón does, and work on revolutionizing all of the revolutionary understanding that has been practiced throughout history. They will remind the political leaders of the country that not only are Christians responsible for the revolution, but that political and military representatives of the revolution are responsible for the authenticity and identity of religion in an unprecedented way. At the same time they will repeatedly call attention to the identity-creating power of religion, which cannot simply be dissolved or transformed into the style of liberal or Marxist religious criticism.

2. Their loyalty to the revolution allows the base churches also to criticize the propertied middle class and the powerful foreign benefactors who support the middle class in the battle for its former privileges. They unmask the cynicism of the slogan "Return to Democracy," since, before the revolution, there was nothing in Nicaragua deserving of the name democracy. They rightly criticize the demand for unlimited play of market powers, because a

direct transfer of the marketing model on the Nicaraguan situation would mean nothing more than a reinforcement of the old dependencies and oppressions.

3. From the bishops, they demand a subjective basis for the church which works in shared responsibility under the leadership of these bishops. Base Christians fear that the episcopal church administration underestimates the revolutionary experience as well as the deep damage done to the Nicaraguan people by the so-called "inner Somozismo." Therefore, the bishops also fail to recognize the significance of and the necessity for new revolutionary identity symbols.

The Revolutionary Paradigm

Whether the inheritance of the revolution and the critical function of the base church can withstand the test in this revolutionary enterprise is a question which is important not only for Nicaragua itself, not only for the situation of the church in Central and Latin America, but for the situation of the entire church and for the situation of peace in our world.

1. Church renewal in the form of a "second Reformation" will come neither from Rome, nor from Central European churches, but from the poor churches of this earth. We in Europe do not in any way stand at the historical center of the church's development. The power of renewal, the revitalization and the metamorphosis of the legitimizing church into an innovating, liberating church, comes from the new lively impulses of the poor church of this earth. It is here that the situation of the revolutionary enterprise in Nicaragua has particular significance.

2. Whether Nicaragua's revolutionary enterprise succeeds for itself and ultimately for other poverty-stricken countries certainly does not depend only on the inner Nicaraguan process or on the ecclesiastical-political processes of Latin America. It ultimately depends on what happens in the so-called First World, on whether our anthropological revolution in the sense of our worldly needs becomes a possibility. Without this there can be neither liberation nor peace in the world.

The revolutionizing of our consumer society—the resistance to the capitalistic totality of "possessions"—which ultimately is also a condition for the long-range success of the revolutionary enterprise in Nicaragua, cannot begin with the weakest link. It cannot begin with the poor *campesinos* in Nicaragua. It must begin with us. Only when we here, in this First World, change, in the sense of such an anthropological revolution, only then does the Nicaraguan revolution have a chance, only then does this direction I have just described have a goal. Only then will there be a reliable foundation for world peace, a foundation which lies much deeper than the "balance of terror." The consequences of Ricardo's decision about how to interpret the revolution and the further question of how human beings, especially Christians, own an anthropological revolution is our concern as much as it is the concern of the Nicaraguan people.

JÜRGEN MOLTMANN

COMMENTARY ON
"TO BEAR ARMS"

The story of Ricardo Campos in Nicaragua is the story of a personal experience and a witness to a decision of conscience. I want to comment on this case study in terms of my own experience in this question of conscience and from there to engage in general considerations concerning the right to active resistance.

I was born in Germany in 1926. When Hitler came to power, in 1933, I was seven years old. When Hitler began the Second World War, I was thirteen. At age sixteen, in 1943, I was drafted into the German *Wehrmacht*. There was no right of conscientious objection then. Anyone who objected was sentenced to death and shot. In July of 1943 Hamburg, my home city, was destroyed by Allied air raids. As one of the few survivors, I was astonished at the annihilation of the antiaircraft batteries where I stood. In 1944 I was transferred to an infantry battalion and went as a machine gunner to the front in Holland where I was captured by English troops in February 1945. In April 1948, after five years in military barracks and prison camps, I returned home and began to study theology in order to become a pastor. My problem then was not "the right to bear arms" but rather "the right not to have to bear arms," or more exactly, "the right to renounce arms" and the right to live in peace without arms.

I had to sacrifice five years of my life in meaningless service to arms and a criminal war, without my consent—indeed, against my will. When I returned home after the war and could finally get out of uniform and throw it away, I swore two things to myself. First, war never again *(nie wieder Krieg),* never again to bear arms; better to be shot than to have to shoot again! And secondly, never to tolerate a dictator again, never again to allow a tyrant to come to power, and in extremity to be prepared to *murder a tyrant,* just as German officers on July 20, 1944, had attempted to kill Hitler, and as Dietrich

---

This commentary was translated by Wesley N. Campbell.

Bonhoeffer had also wanted. When we returned from POW camps and military hospitals and learned of Auschwitz and encountered the surviving Jews, many of my generation became prepared simultaneously to repudiate warfare and to engage in tyrannicide.

At the level of principle, that sounds paradoxical—even contradictory—because the first can be carried through only without violence, and the second is to be enacted only with violence. But for us at that time, at the level of our own concrete experience, there was no paradox. Instead, this two-edged response was the only real consequence that we could draw out of it. Those who, believing that they were fighting for their homeland, had carried weapons for a criminal dictator know against whom they will use weapons in the future if they want to live in peace and want to resist murderous warfare in any way. The consequences of war with modern weapons designed for mass annihilation are known to all those who have had a foretaste of such an inferno, and they know that war in the nuclear age can no longer be a political instrument.

Since 1948 I have participated in all democratic, nonviolent movements that have criticized and opposed the rearming of Germany and the stationing of atomic weapons in the Federal Republic of Germany. Even now the sight of someone in uniform startles me and brings back to me the most unpleasant memories of my life.

Preparations for a "limited nuclear war" in Europe, as is apparently being planned as a real possibility in the Kremlin and the Pentagon, is preparation for the annihilation of Europe. I believe that there can be no ethical justification for the preparation and triggering of a war with nuclear weapons. The guilt of mass annihilation would be unbearable. Therefore, we must unconditionally oppose every war that uses means of mass annihilation. Thus, I support the European peace movement and am prepared, even in the face of the so-called communist threat, to *live without arms (ohne Rüstung leben)*.

On the other hand, I admire and support the liberation movements in the Third World, which oppose racist and military dictators. Just because I recognized too late that my place was not in Hitler's army but in the resistance movement opposed to him, I must now support resistance offered to dictators and am prepared to be engaged in such resistance myself.

I have never understood how some of my contemporaries are able to take exactly the opposite course of action, supporting the rearming of Germany with nuclear weapons and opposing the liberation fronts in Africa and Latin America. Anyone who preaches nonviolence to oppressed peoples while seeking shelter under the nuclear protection of the armed forces of West Germany deserves not to be trusted. Anyone who maintains that nuclear rearmament is justified whereas a people's revolution against an oppressor is unjust speaks with a divided tongue.

There is a *right* to resist. There is also an *obligation* to resist. The right to resist is the foundation stone of every democracy. Democracy is based on a contract made between a people and a government. Democratic principles are enshrined for all time in a constitution. In every election this contract is concretely confirmed and concluded. When a government breaks this contract, the people and their chosen representatives have not only the right but also the obligation to resist and to overthrow it. In extremity this will be carried out with violence. "Resistance to tyrants is obedience to God."[1]

The medieval church, the Roman Catholic Church, and the major Protestant churches without exception have recognized and taught this right to resist a tyrant. According to Article 14 of the Scottish Confession of 1560, formulated by the Reformed Church, it belongs to the love of one's neighbor "to save the life of innocents, to repress tyranny, to defend the oppressed." In 1938 Protestant theologian Karl Barth commented on this Article:

> Faith in Jesus Christ active in love necessitates our active [political] resistance in just the same way as it necessitates our passive resistance or our positive co-operation when we are not faced with this choice.[2]

Norwegian Bishop Eivind Berggrav joined the Norwegian resistance against the German occupation forces. In 1952 he explained:

> When a government becomes lawless and acts with arbitrary despotism, the result is a demonic condition—that is to say, the government is godless. To obey such a Satanic government would be nothing short of sinful. . . . In circumstances of this kind, we have as a matter of principle the right to rebel in one form or another.

But how are we to identify and prove tyranny and oppression? And what sort of resistance is allowed or called for? Tyranny is verified where there is: (1) continual violation of law; (2) violation of the national constitution; and (3) violation of human rights even if legalized by laws and constitutions. Passive and active resistance in such cases is not "insurrection" or "terrorism" but legitimate use of justified political responsibility. For Christians, it is normal political participation in abnormal circumstances. For its part, resistance must be legitimized: (1) by restoration of legality; (2) by restoration of the constitution; or (3) by a new constitution in which human rights are recognized as the basic rights of all citizens.

Let us assume that in the case of tyranny in one form or another there is both justified and lawful resistance. Then we are faced with the problem of conscience in regard to the use of force because those attempting to substitute a lawful state of affairs for tyrannical injustice are obliged to use counterviolence in violation of the values that they want to embody in the new constitution. Yet we ought not to make resistance the only touchstone in this matter of conscience, and certainly not wait to do so until it is a question of active resistance. If resistance is legitimate, then it is a matter of the exercise of legitimate political power. Resistance is not the equivalent of a state of war, but is legitimate defense in a civil war that tyrants or a tyrannical class have begun against the rest of the population in order to make slaves of the citizens—for example, to make "second-class human beings" of Blacks.

The problem of conscience associated with active resistance is therefore basically none other than the problem of conscience associated with a government's normal exercise of power and the participation therein of Christians. Of course, active resistance does represent a totally different psychological burden. However, anyone who approves of the normal exercise of power by the state for the sake of love as unavoidable, cannot suddenly make resistance an extreme case of conscience. Anyone who holds up to those engaged in active resistance the principle of nonviolence as being consonant with the gospel, but who does not do so when the state exercises power, confuses the public conscience.

Nevertheless, it is difficult for a resistance movement opposed to a situation of legalized disorder, injustice, and terror to act lawfully and without resorting to terrorist methods. Understandably, the danger of letting the more powerful opponent dictate the battlefield and the weapons and of practicing only revenge instead of greater justice is always present. What form should lawful and legitimate resistance take in a country where the police lawlessly torture and liquidate persons and the courts are corrupt? Here it is not always possible or even wise for a people's countermovement to introduce legal proceedings, or the like. Instead, immediate active intervention by physical force is called for.

In situations of this kind, how can the legality of resistance activities be determined? In manuals of ethics this problem is often dealt with as a borderline case. For example, if the driver of a bus filled with passengers suddenly goes mad and heads for a precipice, the only thing to do for the protection of the passengers, if anyone can manage to do it, is to render the driver harmless and wrench the steering wheel out of his hand. Regardless of whether anything of this kind has ever happened, it is clear that killing is still killing, and as such cannot be justified. However, in such a situation it will probably be unavoidable, and in a theological sense the guilt of the one who does the killing can be forgiven. Guilt remains guilt, even if the one who stopped the driver was quite unable to act otherwise, because doing nothing would have meant being responsible for the death of many others. In itself then, such an act of violence cannot be approved, but it can be answered for. Responsible action in such cases demands a love that is ready to incur guilt in order to save. This is possible only in the awareness that all action in history is dependent on forgiveness.

Can the obligation to resist, and to resist actively, be justified in the situation out of which Ricardo Campos cries for guidance and help? A final decision cannot be expected from a European, who lives in a wholly different situation. The tyranny of the dictator Somoza, however, was publicly judged and condemned on all three levels of rights violation that I have named: the National Guard broke the laws and acted illegally; the dictator's laws contradicted the constitution and were illegitimate; and the dictator himself heinously violated human rights that are recognized by all civilized nations. Therefore, in my judgment, the right to resistance in this situation was verified.

To whom was this right given and who had the final decision in this question? The people of Nicaragua, I believe. A dictator set against the people is not to be tolerated. But there may also be resistance against a dictator that is not in harmony with the will of the majority of the people. Unfortunately, there are usurpers and revolutionaries who want power, not to free their own people but to terrorize them. Therefore, in this question, the will of the people is decisive.

Active resistance, when it is justified by the will of the people against that of a dictator, is directed not only against the dictator but also against all who are on the side of the dictator and who, by their participation in the dictatorship, have benefited from it.

In the case of Nicaragua that also means resistance against the National Guard. A distinction must also be drawn between the *unjust act* and the *human person* who performs the act. At no time does resistance direct itself against the human person, but is always only against the enactment of injustice. Resistance must therefore always keep open the possibility of the conversion of its misled opponents and may never threaten them with vengeance or liquidation. The generosity of the Sandinista Liberation Front toward captured members of the National Guard is a unique and impressive example of a *liberating resistance*. Because of this, the Christian character of the resistance and liberation in Nicaragua is clear to me.

NOTES

1. Cited from the Scottish Confession of 1560.
2. *The Knowledge of God and the Service of God* (London, 1938), p. 230.

Case Study 2

JAPAN:
ENSHRINEMENT

"As one of the women leaders of the church, Mrs. Kazuko Oshima, you must speak at the February 11 rally in Tokyo in support of Mrs. Yasuko Nakaya's fight not to have her husband enshrined as a war hero and Shinto god." These words were spoken by Rev. Yukio Deguchi, a member of the National Christian Council of Japan (NCCJ) Anti-Yasukuni Shrine Committee. He continued, "Your voice may influence others in Japan, especially women, to resist practices that encourage the return of the idolatrous emperor system, militarism, and restrictions on freedom of belief."

Mrs. Oshima replied, "It is difficult to speak at such nationwide rallies, but I will think and pray about it, and give you my final answer here at work tomorrow."

The Nakaya Case

Later at home, as she cleared the dishes from the evening meal she had prepared for her husband, her two teenage sons and one daughter, Mrs. Oshima had time for reflection. She felt that the pressure had been subtle but increasing during this January of 1980 for her to take a public stand on the Yasukuni Shrine issue and specifically on the court case of Mrs. Nakaya. As a secretary in the office of the NCCJ and an officer in the National Association of Kyodan (the United Church of Christ in Japan) Women, she agreed that

This case study was prepared by Robert A. Evans and Alice Frazer Evans as a basis for discussion rather than to illustrate either effective or ineffective handling of the situation. Copyright © by the Case Study Institute.

All personal names have been disguised with the exception of Mrs. Yasuko Nakaya, Takafumi Nakaya, Prime Ministers Ohira and Ikedo, and Japanese royalty.

53

she probably had some responsibility to make her views known. However, she was reluctant to speak not only because the crowds at the rallies made her nervous but also because she was less clear than many of her more vocal Christian brothers and sisters about what her Christian faith required of her on this controversial issue.

It was now February 8. The series of rallies scheduled throughout Japan was only three days away. The rallies were an annual event in which Japanese Christians joined with other persons from political and labor organizations to protest the reestablishment of National Foundation Day, a celebration of the founding of the nation by the first mythological emperor, Jinmu. Up to 1945, the date February 11 had been a powerful symbol for the ideology of "Japan the Divine Land."

Many Japanese who sponsored the rallies claimed that the designation of National Foundation Day and the nationalization of the Yasukuni Shrine were supported by those seeking the restoration of state Shinto, militarism, and emperor sovereignty. A majority of the sponsors claimed that these concepts violated the democratic basis of the postwar Japanese "Peace Constitution." Mrs. Oshima realized she had rather rashly promised an answer by tomorrow; she had best review the issues and attempt to settle the problem in her mind.

She recalled the debates and discussions at the NCCJ Triennial General Assembly held in Tokyo the previous March with the theme "Toward the Mission of the Church in the 1980s." At that time, Mrs. Yasuko Nakaya had asked the Assembly for continued support in her suit against the Japanese National Self-Defense Forces (SDF). This was the only official military organization in Japan; an offensive army was now illegal according to the constitution that came into effect in 1947 during the American occupation.[1] It had been subsequently debated whether the SDF were constitutional, and a number of postwar lawsuits had challenged but never definitely settled the issue.

An article in a weekly news magazine that Mrs. Oshima had read described Mrs. Nakaya as "a narrow-minded Christian whose radical stance against Japanese identity, culture, and the memory of the war dead was a disgrace." However, Mrs. Oshima had the impression that Yasuko Nakaya was a strong woman, rather gentle, even if persistent. She felt that Mrs. Nakaya seriously believed in the fight she had hesitantly assumed following the death of her husband, Takafumi Nakaya, on January 12, 1968. Mrs. Oshima felt Mrs. Nakaya believed her stand was not only a matter of justice but also of freedom of belief for the whole Christian church in Japan. Details of the Nakaya story had come to her around tea breaks at the assembly.

Lieutenant Takafumi Nakaya had been a soldier in the SDF. He was killed in an automobile accident while on duty during a recruiting mission. Mrs. Nakaya rushed to his unit but was denied permission to see his body, remain with him through the night, or bring the body to their home in Morioka for a civilian funeral. The funeral was conducted instead by the SDF unit. Mrs. Nakaya was a member of the Yamaguchi Shin'ai Christian Church. After her husband's death, she found a job in a home for the elderly in Yamaguchi, and she began a self-supporting life together with her son.

Four years later, in 1972, Mrs. Nakaya was visited by an SDF soldier who requested that she permit her late husband to be enshrined in the Gokoku ("Defense of the Motherland") Shinto Shrine in Yamaguchi. This would entail the erection in the shrine of a tablet bearing his name along with those of twenty-six other men who had died in military service. Mrs. Nakaya refused her husband's Shinto deification on the grounds that she was a Christian and attended an annual commemorative service for her husband at her own church where his ashes had been placed. She had added that although Mr. Nakaya was not a Christian himself, "he understood me and respected my faith."

Two months later a letter arrived informing Mrs. Nakaya that her husband had been enshrined and that a memorial service at the Shinto shrine would be held each January 12 to honor him as a military hero and god (*kami*). The required money for the annual service had been paid by the SDF Veterans' Association. Mrs. Nakaya said that when she received the letter and then read the public newspaper announcement of her husband's enshrinement, "I was filled with anger and sadness. Even my husband's death had to be used by the military."

Mrs. Nakaya questioned the SDF office about this action and expressed her surprise. The response she received was, "It is quite proper for us to enshrine Takafumi Nakaya, for he already belongs to the public after his death. Be thankful for what we did. The enshrining is also necessary in order to elevate the sense of pride among soldiers." Mrs. Nakaya responded that the SDF had exploited her husband after his death and had also completely ignored her own religious beliefs.

After attempting unsuccessfully to negotiate with the SDF, she brought suit against both the SDF and the Veterans' Association, demanding that the Shinto deification of her husband be rescinded because it was done without her consent. In the trial, which began in 1973, Mrs. Nakaya declared, "As a Christian I cannot accept deification of my husband by another religion." She contended that, inasmuch as the Veterans' Association was acting for the SDF and as an organ of the state, Article 20 of Japan's constitution had been violated; it forbids the state and its agencies from engaging in religious acts.[2] She charged that her basic human rights had been infringed upon by this action.

Broader Implications of the Suit

Mrs. Nakaya stated that she had taken her stand as a personal Christian witness against the violation of freedom of belief. However, in the months following, the divided public reaction revealed the broader issues at stake. Many persons who supported Mrs. Nakaya wanted to prevent the return of state funding and nationalization of the Yasukuni Shinto Shrine in Tokyo, which honored the war dead. National funding for the shrine had ceased following the Shinto directives issued on December 25, 1945, by the General Headquarters of the U.S. occupation. However, a bill reinstating government support was currently being considered by the government. Yamaguchi Gokoku was only one of a number of smaller shrines set up by the government in 1939. The prefecture shrines were viewed as virtual branches of the central Yasukuni Shrine in Tokyo.

Kazuko Oshima learned that Mrs. Nakaya received numerous derogatory letters and phone calls. Many who opposed her suit saw her attempt to end the enshrinement of her husband as a denial of her loyalty to Japan. Her action was thus perceived by them as bringing dishonor on all those who had given their lives in the service of their country. Even her father-in-law reacted against her action: "Why aren't you thankful? Selfish woman! How scandalous it is to defy the nation!"

The pastor of Mrs. Nakaya's church and many members of her congregation, including some women who had lost husbands and sons in the war, strongly supported her stance. They helped to organize a Support Yasuko Nakaya Society that listed over three thousand members nationwide. Prominent Christian intellectuals and labor leaders began to defend her struggle; five lawyers volunteered to work on her case and its constitutional issues. The court fight was long and difficult. Kazuko felt this must have been particularly difficult for a woman such as Mrs. Nakaya, who was unaccustomed to public exposure of any kind.

After seven years of litigation, on March 22, 1979, the Yamaguchi District Court ordered the SDF and the Veterans' Association to pay Mrs. Nakaya one million yen[3] for mental anguish. It also ruled that the enshrinement had been unconstitutional, based on Article 20 of the constitution, which forbade the state and its agencies to engage in religious acts. However, the ruling continued, because freedom of belief was also guaranteed to members of the Veterans' Association, and because Mrs. Nakaya was not required to pay homage to her husband's soul at the shrine, the association would not be ordered to remove his name.

Despite what some friends interpreted as a favorable ruling for Mrs. Nakaya, they agreed that the prospects for total success appeared dim. The SDF and the Veterans' Association were appealing the case to higher courts. At the 1979 NCCJ General Assembly, Mrs. Nakaya expressed her appreciation to the assembly and to those persons and committees that had given her support. She now sought wider support on a national scale for the appeal process.

Mrs. Oshima recalled the conflicting arguments she had encountered during the last ten months, when she had been urged to take a stand. Mrs. Nakaya's suit was seen as more than an issue of personal freedom of belief by persons such as Masahiro Ishikawa, the secretary general of the NCCJ, Kazuko's friend and employer. Masahiro, with others, linked the case to the subtle revival of the prewar emperor system and the potential reinstatement of state Shinto. The secretary general had reminded the General Assembly of the so-called modernization of Japan during the era of Emperor Meiji (1868–1912). Tenno (the emperor) was not only the political ruler but also the archpriest and the god of state Shinto. The term "Shinto" both then and now refers to the indigenous folk religion of Japan and is used to distinguish it from Buddhism, which was introduced to Japan from China and India, through Korea, in the sixth century A.D. Although there were amalgamations of Shinto and Buddhism in the following centuries, the Meiji restoration of Shinto reemphasized that Tenno was regarded as a "god incarnate" and ruler "in the line of emperors unbroken for ages eternal."

It was the argument of the secretary general that the Tenno system led to "an ethnocentric nationalism" and "a chauvinistic militarism" that "reduced persons to tools," in the drive for Japanese superiority and modernization. The system projected Tenno as a god who was the father of the Japanese people. The people, as his children, would then be interpreted as having a duty of wholehearted loyalty to Tenno extending to the destruction of his enemies and, if necessary, even to death. These beliefs were embodied in the famous "Imperial Rescript on Soldiers" (1882), which includes the statement, "Consider that righteousness is heavier than a mountain and dying is lighter than a feather. Do not be branded with infamy by failing to keep your fidelity." Through this mandate, the secretary general declared, "Citizens were instructed to find their national identity, mental stability, and moral values through Tenno, the center of the nation. Moreover, even when they died on the battlefield, Tenno showed mercy to them and delivered them from misery by presiding over the Shinto ceremony that honored them as military gods." In 1879 the Yasukuni Shrine was designated a national shrine for the war dead. The emperor presided over ceremonies held in this shrine and later in the regional Gokoku shrines. At the end of World War II there was a prohibition by the U.S. occupying forces against the Tenno's officially conducting such services. Furthermore, on January 7, 1946, the Tenno disowned his claim to divinity and from that point "his religious status was supposedly altered."

"The emperor system, seen as a religious system, helps one understand how the Japanese people can be mobilized as a unit and rushed off to war," explained the secretary general. "This approach, in which the powerful used the concept of 'righteousness' for their own interests and in which they treated human lives as lightly as a feather, brutalized the Japanese armed forces. In Nakaya's case, we discover that inhuman tendencies, to use people as mere tools, are still alive in postwar Japan. Mrs. Nakaya was not only denied the right to bury her husband's body; she was even forced to accept his enshrinement. All for the purpose of raising the morale of the armed forces."

The secretary general continued, "It is important for us to realize that Mrs. Nakaya's case is not an exception. This past April Yasukuni Shrine officials announced that the souls of fourteen Pacific war leaders had been enshrined a year ago. Seven of these had been executed as war criminals and seven others died in prison. The shrine staff said the enshrinement was done without any consultation with the families 'because some persons would not agree with the decision.' What is exceptional about the Nakaya case is that she has been courageous enough to protest."

This interpretation by her employer and friend appeared persuasive, but Kazuko Oshima recalled the strong opinion of another friend, a Catholic layman, Hiroshi Inoue, who had lived through World War II during his university education. "Japan lost everything in the war," Inoue declared, "yet in the beginning our professors appeared to support the philosophy of the old slogan, 'Revere the emperor, expel the barbarians,' which encouraged one to die for the honor of Japan and the emperor, as I was prepared to do. Neither the Kyodan nor my own church took a public stand against the war or the emperor." Inoue reflected, with his jaw set and his eyes flashing, "Then the professors changed overnight. When we were defeated in the war, some professors were supporting the new 'occupation' or 'U.S. constitution' with the same energy as they had supported the imperial philosophy. I gave up on the integrity of the university and the church on political issues. However, I have worked for the church because it does many good things.

"One must be practical. Japan needs an army," Inoue continued. "The U.S.A. will not defend us from communism any more than it was able to defend Vietnam. We must be prepared to defend our own interests and culture in Japan and not be dependent on America's changing attitudes toward Asia. Do you see the new friendship with our traditional enemy China? Some persons in the church are opposed to the proposed legislation in the Diet for the nationalization and funding of the Yasukuni Shrine. This has been proposed by the ruling Liberal Democratic Party (LDP), which seeks government funding for the shrine 'to accelerate respect for the war dead.' Some Christians say the legislation glorifies war, but they don't seem to object to American presidents' and foreign dignitaries' visiting the Arlington National Cemetery in Washington. Some Christians demonstrate against official visits to Yasukuni by the emperor or by Prime Minister Masayoshi Ohira. Ohira is a Christian and yet he recently made what he declared was a 'personal visit' to the shrine. Those anti-Yasukuni shrine protesters are concerned, I believe, with their own Christian minority rights in a nation where only about 1 percent of us are Christian. I wonder if the anti-Yasukuni protesters are equally concerned about our future as a nation and our culture. Thousands of Japanese, including Christians, go to the Shinto shrines on New Year's Day. It is a Japanese tradition. We Japanese must preserve our traditions against the university and the church, both of which are now too Western."

In contrast to Inoue's views, Kazuko Oshima remembered the report of the NCCJ Anti-Yasukuni Shrine Committee. This report stressed the danger posed to individual human rights and the transgression of the constitutional separation of church and state. Rev. Deguchi, a member of the committee who was urging Kazuko to speak at the rally, declared that to prevent the nationalization of the Yasukuni Shrine was a part of "our endless struggle for freedom. This struggle is a process to increase citizens' rights in order to limit the power of the state."

"Yasukuni Shrine in the past was the cornerstone of military aggression," a report from the committee stated. "The anti-Yasukuni struggle today is to oppose Japan's economic invasion of other Asian countries. We seek to resist Japan's economic control in Asia and to show solidarity with the people's struggle for democracy in other Asian countries. A primary concern for us is Korea, where many of our brothers and sisters in Christ have been imprisoned for speaking against their government in the name of freedom and faith."

Economic Implications

The *Asia and Pacific Annual Review* provided Kazuko Oshima with basic information about Japan's performing an "economic miracle." This involved going from the devastation of the postwar period to moving ahead of the rest of the rich world, in 1978, by having growth in real terms of more than 5 percent, compared with the average growth of all other industrialized countries of 3.4 percent. Unemployment in Japan remains at only 2 percent, compared with 6 or 7 percent in the U.S.A. Inflation is relatively low. Japan has a trade surplus of $25 billion, which evokes envy and anger in the U.S.A. and Europe. However, no other industrial nation faces Japan's shortages of raw materials: it must import 90 percent or more of all basic minerals and oil. Consequently, Japan is sometimes charged with exploiting the other Asian countries by purchasing materials and labor at a low cost and then selling to them high-cost manufactured products at an enormous profit. Economists predict that Japan will surpass the U.S.A. by the end of the 1980s as the richest country in the world in per capita terms.

The NCCJ Anti-Yasukuni Committee had stated that "obtaining this wealth at the cost of Asian poverty" was "a form of economic expansionism by Japanese monopoly capitalists." The report continued:

Under Prime Minister Ikeda's cabinet policy of high economic growth, Japanese have been required to cooperate in the government policy by earnestly dedicating themselves to business and industry without worrying about polluting the environment or the promotion of the economic invasions of other countries. Once again, the idea of the national religion of Yasukuni Shrine was revived, establishing the Emperor—described in the post-war period as a "symbol of integration of the people"—as the figurehead of the political ideology and the militarization of Japan. The Anti-Yasukuni Bill movement is a confession of our sin of disobeying Christ's teaching, "Love your Neighbor." For the sake of our Asian brothers and sisters the Church must resist this new Japanese aggression and exploitation of human and natural resources at home and overseas.

One member of the committee charged that the Yasukuni Shrine and in particular the honoring of the Self-Defense Forces by enshrinements such as that of Lieutenant Nakaya "gave support to Japanese industrialists who wanted to enter the arms production race using Japan's famous technology and dedication. Yet because of this we are described by some in the European Economic Community as 'a nation of workaholics living in what Westerners would regard as little more than rabbit hutches.'"

Kazuko Oshima remembered what Fred Robinson, an American missionary who was a consultant to NCCJ and a longtime resident of Japan, shared with her recently, "It is ironic that Japan should be criticized for doing efficiently in economic terms what the other industrial nations would like to do themselves in terms of growth and profit. America and Europe urge Japan to control exports and reduce tariffs so the West can reduce its trade deficit. The Constitution, which some Japanese describe as 'imposed' by U.S. occupation forces, prohibits Japan from establishing an army with offensive capabilities. Yet both the U.S.A. and China have urged Japan to increase its military strength by at least 30 percent. This is despite the fact that Japanese economic prosperity may be partially a result of low investment in armaments. A recent letter signed by thirty-eight U.S. senators expressed appreciation for the extension of the U.S.A.-Japan Mutual Defense Treaty while urging a stronger military stance as protection from the threat of the Soviet Union's expansion in Asia."

Fred shared with Kazuko, "I am impressed with the Christians who, though representing a tiny minority in the country, are attempting to prophetically critique economic and military positions taken by the industrialized countries of the world. This is courageous because some of the churches of these nations provide money and personnel to aid the Christian mission in Japan."

The Role of Women

Through her conversations with others about the Nakaya case, Mrs. Oshima had also begun to see the role of Japanese women in a new light. One of the women staff members of the Kyodan, Ichiko Kadokai, expressed her conviction that the industrial success of Japan was founded on the work of women who were poorly paid and did detailed but monotonous jobs under difficult circumstances. Ichiko noted, "Not only is there inequality of pay between men and women, but women are essentially cut out of any effective decision-making role in the economy. The number of women who reach senior positions is more limited than in any other industrialized economy. Women are meant to honor the family system, which is based on male supremacy and which places women in the home to look after the family or in farm or industrial communities as laborers. Although some unfair labor laws concerning women are being challenged, any consciousness of women's liberation in Japan is a recent development."

Ichiko continued, "I believe that Mrs. Nakaya had pressure applied to conform to the family system. As one supporter described Mrs. Nakaya's situation, 'Her father-in-law represents the social authority by which she is blamed for her disobedience to societal norms.' The idea that a woman is less valuable than a man and should obey him without claiming her own rights is prevalent in Japan. Perhaps the most popular and harsh way to criticize a woman is to call her a 'selfish woman.' It is assumed that a woman is expected to sacrifice all her rights, even to destroy her human emotions. Despite this pressure Mrs. Nakaya has continued to resist. It is above all a struggle to regain human dignity or humanness. We must continue to support her efforts."

After speaking with Ichiko, Kazuko Oshima realized that she had conflicting feelings about the role of Mrs. Nakaya and other Japanese women. Coming from a nonurban setting, she appreciated the support and security of the family system and the respect she received as a wife and mother. She had always believed that confrontations with men, such as that provoked by Mrs. Nakaya, often made men defensive and resentful. Kazuko reasoned that quiet competence in one's family and work brought both personal satisfaction and growing acceptance for women in a gradually changing world. Perhaps traditional cultures such as Japan's needed to change more slowly. Perhaps support for Mrs. Nakaya would not really benefit either those seeking to protect some traditional Japanese values or the need for change sought by some in her church.

Idolatry in Japan

In attempting to sort out the factors that should inform her decision, Kazuko Oshima acknowledged that her concern to be a faithful and responsible Japanese Christian was primary. She believed that one of the principal arguments of the NCCJ General Assembly for supporting Mrs. Nakaya and the anti-Yasukuni movement was based on the issue of idolatry. The committee report declared:

> Our fight of faith is a struggle of the self-evaluating process of the church's wartime responsibility. The glorification of the war dead seen in the Yasukuni Bill is only excusing the mistakes made during the war. The Japanese churches in wartime kept silent on Japan's invasions of other Asian countries, and the present churches carry some of the same attitudes as the churches in the past. The struggle for the anti-Yasukuni movement is a self-inquiry of the church's responsibility in society. It is a struggle against idolatry in Japan. Through the legislative bill to nationalize Yasukuni, the war dead, the emperor, the state, the war, and the Japanese are justified and absolutized by making them divine objects of worship. As it was difficult for the Israelites to accept the fact that the worship of Baal was a sin, so it is difficult to be aware of our own sin. The anti-Yasukuni movement is a struggle against our own sin.

Kazuko Oshima remembered that her own church, the Kyodan, in 1967 had issued its "Confession of War Responsibility" (Appendix 1), which sought forgiveness from the people of Japan and Asia for the fact that the church did not perform the role of watchman during World War II. The document affirmed the Kyodan's determination to struggle against the forces of aggression in the future. The confession was now realized to have been a major factor in splitting the Kyodan into a division between the so-called "church" and "society" factions.

The Federation of Evangelical Churches, representing the "church" faction, stressed that the church's mission must be concentrated on evangelism and the salvation of souls. A federation spokesman affirmed that neither the church nor its members should ever take up fixed positions when dealing with social problems of modern society. The "society" faction was represented by the so-called problem-posers, who were convinced that the church must address the pressing economic and political issues of modern Japan. A conflict developed between groups in each wing over sponsorship of a Christian Pavilion at the World Exposition held in Japan in 1970. The conflict became so bitter that a dispute over the role of the church in society and proper credentials for delegates had prevented the Kyodan for ten years from holding general assemblies with regular representation from all of its districts. Perhaps, Kazuko thought, such confrontations diverted the church from its primary mission and ministry. The anti-Yasukuni movement, which today included support for Mrs. Nakaya's case, was one of the issues of the so-called problem-posers. Does the present Japanese government, Kazuko wondered, really pose an idolatrous threat to the church through the Yasukuni bill? Are all Christians who fail to resist such societal movements idolatrous?

A Shinto View

Kazuko Oshima also recalled a report of a dialogue between the chief priest of a major Shinto shrine, the Rev. Tanji, and a professor of theology at the famous Kokugakuin Shinto University, in Tokyo, Professor Hori. This report, Kazuko felt, made her decision even more complex.

Professor Hori had said, "The Christian fears about the Yasukuni Nationalization Bill are misplaced. Some Christians have accused Shinto leaders of being reactionaries wanting to return to a religious basis for the state that will encourage militarism. It is important to distinguish between a rightist political stance and the recovery of the traditional values of Japanese society. Some politicians supporting the Yasukuni Nationalization Bill may be reactionary, but most Shinto leaders are not. Rather, they seek to preserve our traditional culture for the future. The Shinto religion seeks to contribute to the happiness of the Japanese people—not to support a particular political position.

"I see the issue as 'cultural identity.' Education after the war tried to make Japan Western and individualistic. We began to lose our sense of the community and our identity as Japanese when the traditional Shinto rituals were restricted."

The Rev. Tanji entered the conversation and declared, "The new Japanese intellectuals who are graduates of the modern university system are not really Japanese. As one of our Shinto laymen states, 'The modern Japanese is interested in work, money, food, and sex. Not in philosophy.' That is not the Japanese way. But I believe that even these persons, in the daily experience of the heart, still value the Japanese traditions. This is evidenced by the many who come to the shrine on New Year's Day or who visit the Imperial Palace to shout *Banzai* to the emperor and his family. No nation can deny its cultural identity and survive."

"The case of Mrs. Nakaya is an example of the Christian misunderstanding," Professor Hori stated. "Shinto is a national or group religion, often called a folk religion. If persons die for the sake of their country, they must be enshrined; this is the will of the community for whom they gave their lives. In the history of Japan there has always been a ritual to honor our ancestors. The Christians, although well-meaning, confuse the situation by talking about 'Shinto military gods.' The Japanese word is *kami*. This is a theological term referring to that which is above, superior, or divine. The world of *kami* gave birth to the land and people of Japan. Japan is called the land of the gods, and the mythical tradition of the first emperor, Jinmu, as the grandson of the sun goddess is acknowledged on Foundation Day, February 11. Every nation has its mythical history.

"One can translate the word *kami* as god or deity, but you need to remember that Shinto has no systematic theology or doctrine in the same sense that Christianity does. The essence of *kami* is the power of existence in the world. Everyone has *kami,* as does nature. We enshrine some *kami* that have benevolent powers and some that have harmful powers. In Shinto theology Jesus' *kami* could be enshrined. It is misleading to talk about worshiping Shinto gods as idolatry. Japanese culture includes acts to honor or to enshrine the contributions of some ancestors, as we do for the Emperor Meiji and Empress Shoken in the Meiji Shinto Shrine of Tokyo.

"Why would Mrs. Nakaya resist the enshrinement of her husband by the community? Shinto respects the church. A personal funeral in the Christian way is fine. The Self-Defense Forces want to raise Lieutenant Nakaya's efforts before the nation. As the judge in the recent Yamaguchi district court decision indicated, Mrs. Nakaya was not required to pay homage to the soul of her husband at the shrine. Just as the court recognized Mrs. Nakaya's freedom of belief and ordered compensation for spiritual anguish suffered, it also acknowledged the need to guarantee the freedom of belief of members of the Veterans' Association. Mrs. Nakaya's right to personal freedom of belief did not encompass the right of refusing to have her husband, who was not a Christian, commemorated in a national shrine.

"Christians are a tiny minority in this country. Perhaps they have an overly defensive minority consciousness that makes them anticipate discrimination when little or none exists. We must respect Christian rights, but not at the expense of the majority of Japanese and their traditional culture. Some Christians have joined with communists and socialists in opposing, in addition to the Yasukuni Nationalization Bill, the designation of National Foundation Day, and the bill to provide a legal foundation for dates based on the imperial era name *(Gengo)* system, and the designation of the *Kimigayo* ("Emperor's Reign") as the national anthem. These minority groups tend to resist all moves they think return to traditional culture.

"It is claimed by some Christians that all this legislation is intended to prepare for the acceptance of *Daijosai,* a ceremony that some minority persons interpret as a Shinto rite of deification of the emperor. This ceremony would be performed when the crown prince ascends to Emperor Hirohito's imperial throne. I believe Christians fear that if the emperor is recognized, they will be forced—as they were before the war—to bow before shrines such as Yasukuni. However, I don't believe that will ever happen again. We need not go the way of secularized modernization *or* the route of reactionary politics. There is a middle way advocated by the Shinto tradition that honors the best values of our culture and the best of Western culture. Presently, there is a cultural vacuum, especially for our youth.

"There is no special Shinto doctrine in the memorial events for the war dead. One is only invited to attend and to pay respects to the dead with a sincere heart and a free will. However, it would not be possible to move this event to an athletic stadium and strip the service of all the prayers. It would lose its religious significance and thus its meaning. This kind of nonreligious site and service has been proposed by minority groups as an alternative solution. One wonders whether these groups have become so influenced by foreign values of other religions or governments that they would be willing to destroy Japanese culture and pride in order to protect a minority privilege. Mrs. Nakaya and other Christians are being used, without intending it, by radical leftist groups in the Japanese and Christian community."

The Choice

It was getting late and Kazuko Oshima had still not made a final decision. Participating in the life of the church plus working at the NCCJ led her to believe that her answer should be shaped by her Christian faith *and* that it should be authentically Japanese. Though she did not always agree with the view of NCCJ Secretary General Masahiro Ishikawa, she respected his judgment. Kazuko reread notes she had made the last time she heard Dr. Suzuki address the Yasukuni issue. He affirmed his belief that the Tenno system led to the distortion of faith into idolatry. As he said, "The emperor—Tenno—is a pseudogod or idol that threatens to draw us away from worship of the true God. Tenno is quite similar to Christ in the claims for his function—in giving grace to believers. Many Japanese think of God in terms of the folk religion, whether official Shinto theology would agree or not. They believe Tenno to be God incarnate, dispensing mercy as a savior. What else is this but an idol, an object of human worship that deprives us of the ability to stand on our own two feet as free and autonomous human beings?

"What do the life and death of Jesus tell us about the nature of the Tenno system? Jesus was the one who, although 'the divine nature was his from the first; yet he did not think to snatch at equality with God, but made himself nothing, assuming the nature of a slave. Bearing the human likeness, revealed in human shape, he humbled himself, and in obedience accepted even death—death on a cross' (Phil. 2:6-8).

"Christ experienced and tasted the misery of his own people. In so doing he became the servant of the people. Japanese churches have acquired a special way of understanding the suffering of Jesus, of which K. Kitamori's *Theology of the Pain of God* is an example. However, this idea of suffering must be extended to the social realities that brought misery to millions in Japan and other nations in Asia. The emperor system nourished an exclusivist nationalism that stressed Japanese self-assertion.

"As Christians, we must seek a solidarity in mission that frees us from Japanese self-assertion. Behind the struggling Asians exploited by Japan we see our Lord Jesus who suffered for the oppressed and was resurrected. We are called to worship the crucified Messiah in our own mission."

Kazuko Oshima wondered, as a woman in Japan, one who loved her culture and her country, what she should say tomorrow about participation in the February 11 rally. If she addressed the assembly, what message would listeners hear? Would God's love be enshrined in her witness? Perhaps she would not go. Kazuko began to pray for the third time that evening, "Holy Spirit, guide me. . . ."

NOTES

1. Article 9 of the postwar constitution reads: "Aspiring sincerely to an international peace based on justice and order, the Japanese people forever renounce war as a sovereign right of the nation, and the threat or use of [military] forces as means of settling international disputes.

"In order to accomplish the aim of the preceding paragraph, land, sea, and air force, as well as other war potential, will never be maintained. The right of belligerency of the state will not be recognized."

2. Article 20: "Freedom of religion is guaranteed to all. No religious organization shall receive any privileges from the State, or exercise any political authority."

3. Approximately U.S. $5,000.

Appendix

CONFESSION OF RESPONSIBILITY DURING WORLD WAR II

The twenty-fifth anniversary of the establishment of the United Church of Christ in Japan (Kyodan) was celebrated during the fourteenth General Assembly of the Kyodan held in October 1966, at Osaka, Japan. Now we are faced with the serious task of building up the Kyodan. In order to express the sense of responsibility which the Kyodan has toward Japan and the world, we prayerfully take as our theme "Our Church—Tomorrow."

At this time we are reminded of the mistakes committed in the name of the Kyodan during World War II. Therefore, we seek the mercy of our Lord and the forgiveness of our fellow men.

At the time of the founding of the Kyodan the Japanese Government then under pressure asked that all religious bodies be brought together and that they cooperate with the national policy to bring the war to a victorious end.

Since the time that the Gospel was first presented in the early part of the Meiji era, Japanese Christians had desired to establish one evangelical Church in Japan, by the merging of denominations. Therefore, they entered into the Union and the Kyodan was established, taking advantage of an order of the government.

Concerning this founding and the continued existence of the Kyodan we recognize, with deep fear and gratitude, that, even in our failures and errors, the Providence of God, the Lord of History, was at work.

The Church, as "the light of the world" and as "the salt of the earth," should not have aligned itself with the militaristic purpose of the government. Rather, on the basis of our love for it, and by the standard of our Christian conscience, we should have more correctly criticized the policies of our motherland. However, we made a statement at home and abroad in the name of the Kyodan that we approved of and supported the war, and we prayed for victory.

Indeed, as our nation committed errors we, as a Church, sinned with it. We neglected to perform our mission as a "watchman." Now, with deep pain in our heart we confess this sin, seeking the forgiveness of our Lord, and from the churches, and our brothers and sisters of the world, in particular of Asian countries, and from the people of our own country.

More than twenty years have passed since the war, and we are filled with anxiety, for our motherland seems unable to decide the course that we should follow. We are concerned lest she move in an undesirable direction due to the many pressures of today's turbulent problems. At this moment so that the Kyodan can correctly accomplish its mission in Japan and the world we seek God's help and guidance. In this way we look forward to tomorrow with humble determination.

Masahisa Suzuki, Moderator

Approved by the Executive Committee, Feb. 20, 1967
Issued Easter Sunday, March 26, 1967

TEACHING NOTE ON "ENSHRINEMENT"

In deciding whether or not to support Mrs. Yasuko Nakaya's legal battle, Mrs. Kazuko Oshima faces a dilemma which has broad implications for freedom of belief, civil religion, economic aggression, and militarism.

A discussion of this case could focus on:

A. Right to religious freedom for both Shinto and Christian followers.
B. Cultural identity of the majority versus minority rights.
C. Right to national economic growth versus the right of poorer countries to be free from economic aggression.
D. Right to self-defense versus the right to peace.
E. Right to human dignity of Mrs. Nakaya and others who take a stand which may challenge societal expectations.

CASE PLAN

1. As this is a highly complex case, it can be helpful to begin by cataloguing, perhaps in parallel columns, the persons who are in favor of Mrs. Nakaya's case and those in opposition. Develop the positions of key characters such as Rev. Deguchi, Secretary General Masahiro Ishikawa, Hiroshi Inoue, Ichiko Kadokai, Rev. Tanjii, and Professor Hori. Consider staging a debate between Secretary General Ishikawa and Professor Hori focusing on national cultural identity versus individual religious freedom.

2. Briefly describe the current economic climate in Japan. What is the basis of the NCCJ Anti-Yasukuni Committee position? Discuss how claims of Japanese economic aggression are linked to the Yasukuni Shrine debate. What other positions in the case support the work of this committee? How does the issue of idolatry enter in?

3. What is the theological basis for the "Confession of Responsibility"? How did this Confession split the Kyodan? In what ways does this division affect Mrs. Oshima's decision? Why has the Confession, written in 1967, come to the forefront in the present Yasukuni Shrine debate? What are the implications of the Confession in light of the present Japanese movement toward rebuilding a military defense system?

4. Trace the history of Mrs. Nakaya's court case. What is the traditional role of Japanese women? Probe her personal feelings during these past few years of national publicity. What issues of human dignity are at stake? How

68

do Mrs. Oshima and Ichiko Kodokai differ on their understanding of the role of women?

5. Ask participants what factors are the most important for Mrs. Oshima to consider in reaching her decision. Asking participants to place themselves in her position, what would be their responses? Urge respondents to justify positions taken.

SUGGESTIONS FOR ADDITIONAL READING

Anderson, Gerald H., ed. *Asian Voices in Christian Theology.* Maryknoll, N.Y.: Orbis Books, 1976.

"Decade of Dispute in the United Church," entire edition of the *Japan Christian Quarterly,* 45:3, Summer 1979.

Osamu, Tsukada. "Christianity and the Emperor System," *The Japan Interpreter,* 10, Winter 1976.

Shoji, Tsutomu. "The Church's Struggle for Freedom of Belief—An Aspect of Mission." In *Witnessing to the Kingdom,* February 1979 (Christian Conference of Asia, Singapore).

RUBEM ALVES

COMMENTARY ON "ENSHRINEMENT"

I must confess that I do not know what to say. I listen, over and over again, to those who have made their voices heard. But my conscience is unable to find a resting place. I cannot, in honesty, say: "This is what I would do, if I were a Japanese." My feeling is that there are too many idols involved in this conflict and that we are not, by any means, absolved from sin. Many of the idols have their abodes right within our very eyes and minds.

This perplexity invokes, from the past, words once written by Dietrich Bonhoeffer. I go to one of my shelves and take down his *Letters and Papers from Prison*; the volume has been resting silent there for a long time. "Who stands his ground?," he asks. "The great masquerade of evil has wrought havoc with all our ethical preconceptions. This appearance of evil in the guise of light. . . ." (And I feel tempted to add: "And this appearance of light in the guise of evil. . . .") "The rationalist imagines that a small dose of reason will be enough to put the world right. . . . The fanatic imagines that his moral purity will prove a match for the power of evil, but like a bull he goes for the red rag. . . ." The man of conscience? "There are so many conflicts going on, all of which demand some vital choice, that he is torn to pieces. . . . The path of duty seems to offer a sure way out. They grasp at the imperative as the one certainty. But when men are confined to the limits of duty, they never risk a daring deed on their own responsibility. . . . Some seek refuge from the rough and tumble of public life in the sanctuary of their own private virtue. Such men, however, are compelled to seal their lips and shut their eyes to the injustice around them. . . ." What to do? "Every conceivable alternative seems equally intolerable. . . ."

It is not difficult to identify the military devil, because he does not wear masks. Wherever he goes one hears the drums and sees the dreams of power and eternity with which he wraps up the images of death that follow him. Is it not disturbing that one should be attracted by death liturgies? Yet, is it not precisely in this that lies the bewitching power of the military? Are they not a religious order? Do they not, as magicians and priests, transubstantiate death into immortality? How could we explain, otherwise, the hypnotic attraction of their processions and parades, their requiems and marches? No, the military devil does not live in the barracks only. His native land is right within us. He is there, asleep, maybe, as a longing, a desire. . . .

This is a lesson that we learn from anthropology and from psychoanalysis. Anything that is strongly forbidden is so because it is strongly desired. There are no laws against eating stones. Nobody desires that. But incest and murder are crimes. The stronger the prohibition, the stronger the desire. A devil is a strong desire that should never exist. If it were not desired, it would not be tempting. If it were not forbidden, it would not pose any danger.

If persons tremble when they hear the martial liturgies of power and death, it is because those symbols invoke, from their depths, longings that are there, dormant. And as Martin Buber reminded us over and over again, evil impulses cannot be destroyed. They cannot be wished away. Impulses are as real as are physical objects. They are not redeemed by their destruction but by their conversion: the energy that is flowing in a certain direction must flow in the opposite direction. I understand that the easiest way for the church is simply to say no to that which appears to be nothing less than pride and idolatry. It is more difficult for the church to take the risk of playing the role of interpreter of dreams. All religions, regardless of the idols, demons, and superstitions that they worship, have collective dreams, revelations of our most hidden love secrets (Feuerbach). The evil is not in the urge, in itself, but in the wrong object that it chooses to fulfill its longing.

In military mythologies and liturgies, one is no longer a solitary individual, standing before death: one marches with millions of others; one is seen with love and gratitude by all those for whom one will die. In sacrificial death, the drop of water returns to the ocean. . . . It seems that there is more dignity in this madness than in the mediocre virtues of work, money, food, sex.

If the church does not understand the beauty, the force, and the attraction of evil, it will be unable to preach conversion. If one is not tempted by the devil, in the desert, one is prevented from seeing the fascination of the vision of the kingdom. Buber again: "One must also love evil . . . even as evil wishes to be loved."[1]

If one does not love evil it is because one has not been tempted by it. And if one has not yet been tempted by it, one does not know its strength as evil. It is useless to say no to the evil urge. The question is whether we have a vision strong enough to tempt evil, even as it tempts us. Whatever this vision will be, one thing is for sure: it must provide a transfiguration of life and death, it must bring meaning to life and death, it must point to possibilities of solidarity in life and death.

In my country—Brazil—we lack a military tradition, not because of virtue but because of accident. I am afraid, therefore, that my thoughts could be meaningless in the Japanese context. I do not have the experiential analogies that would allow me to span the ocean.

But there are voices that sound familiar. There are complaints that Japanese Christians are alienated from Japanese culture. And I have the impression that I am hearing voices coming from my own backyard. Yes, this is what has been said of Protestants in this part of the world. Protestantism is an alien religion, strange to our native cultural soil. It was transplanted to Latin America, and to the rest of the world, by Europeans and North Americans, together with their postcolonial expansion. It is the religion of the rich, of the white, of the strong, of the masters. From the beginning of their influence, our many cultures were considered to be expressions of Roman Catholic superstition and idolatry. If one was converted from Catholicism to Protestantism, one was expected also to be converted from Brazilian ways to the more civilized, Christian lifestyle of the countries whence the missionaries had come. This is how the good news of salvation was spread, and also the good manners of the postcolonial masters. Faith against cultural solidarity? Faith as cultural invasion?

Do we have the right to try to convert the Indians? This is a question that is being asked by many missionaries. They have learned, perhaps too late, that the world of human beings is not a pure-nature setting; that identity and integrity are interwoven with a network of cultural values and attitudes; that every act against a culture is an act of torture, because the human body is a cultural body; that it is impossible to love the neighbor without loving the things that are dear to that person. Do we have the right to disrupt these cultural universes, even by our mere presence? Every presence implies the nearness of strange, threatening, unknown worlds.

By what right? Yes, we preach *our* truth. But every illusion from within the magic sphere of the cultural bubble is also a truth! Why *ours?* Do we try to understand *theirs?* Have we felt their temptation? How, then, do we dare? Again, I am not speaking to the Japanese. I am a Brazilian, speaking about my own context, provoked by these words that come from afar. From within, all idols are gods. Only viewers who are outside have the distance to see. Distance is like a mirror. It allows us to look at our own faces, and we see the devils that live within our eyes.

Is it not true that every country has its own mode of enshrining? Every society? Are we not related to our fellow human beings by ties of reverence, love for common horizons? In every act of love there is a god, however little, hidden.

Flags within sanctuaries. . . . "In God we trust"—so all those dollar bills affirm.

Ceremonial places and curses. . . . "Rather dead than red." Is exorcism called for? And there are the monuments . . . because the past is glorious. And bodies tremble with emotion.

Even societies that claim to be atheistic, do they not have their shrines? Lenin's tomb, for example. I recall the sardonic remark by Leszek Kolakowski about the situation in communist countries: "A rain of gods is falling from the sky. . . . The atheists have their saints, and the blasphemers are erecting chapels."[2]

Idols are found both in the past and in the future. If one turns back, to the reaffirmation of tradition, one says yes to a hierarchical world, dominated by an authoritarian ethos, which will then cover, as a sacred canopy, the whole Japanese world. And the value of individuality will be lost.

But the way to the future seems no less repulsive. Westernization, secularization, no gods and no devils, only the mediocrity and boredom of the capitalist way of life: hard work, money, food, and sex.

In a world dominated by the business ethos there is plenty of room for the freedom of the individual. I recall Alvin Toffler:

> So long as the shoe salesman performs his rather limited service for us, thereby fulfilling our rather limited expectations, we do not insist that he believe in God, or that he be tidy at home, or share our political views, or enjoy the same kind of food or music that we do. We leave him free in all other matters—as he leaves us free to be atheist or Jew, heterosexual or homosexual, John Bircher or Communist. To a certain point, fragmentation and freedom go together.[3]

Yes, there is freedom in this kind of world, dominated by business. Because our freedom does not make any difference. Respect for our human rights is the companion piece of our impotence.

A return to the past is resorted to by some in the attempt to preserve their lives. Resistance. Rejection of the capitalist invasion. True, there are idols in our memories. But there are idols, maybe more cruel, in capitalism—and communism. The destruction of seas, of forests, of the land, of bodies and souls: is not all this related to industrial expansion and progress? The longing for a return to the past, is it not a protest against progress? Do Christians have the love and compassion that could help them in this search for a lost time, a lost home, a lost soul?

I must make a final confession. I do not believe that the crucial thing is to be found in *what* is said. I would rather look at the bodies of those who say it.

The nostalgia of a slum-dweller, uprooted from the land, for the traditional world of childhood is something totally different from the nostalgia in the dreams of an ambitious general. And it is likely that modern executives, responsible for the ecological rape of the land, will find themselves more comfortable in a Western Protestant culture than in the old culture of their grandparents.

Less attention to what is said. More attention to those who say it. This is the key for the interpretation of dreams. And, if the gospel is right, truth comes from those who are suffering, who are poor, who are weak.

NOTES

1. Quoted by Maurice Friedmann, in *Martin Buber: The Life of Dialogue* (Chicago: University of Chicago Press, 1956), p. 15.

2. "The Priest and the Jester," in Maria Kuncewicz, ed., *The Modern Polish Mind* (New York: Grosset & Dunlap, 1963), pp. 325–26.

3. *Future Shock* (New York: Random House, 1970), p. 89.

KOSUKE KOYAMA

COMMENTARY ON "ENSHRINEMENT"

My comments will be focused on one point: What was a theological and constitutional problem for Mrs. Nakaya was simply a matter of cultural identity for the general Japanese public. Here lies the difficulty that faces Mrs. Nakaya and Mrs. Oshima.

H. Richard Niebuhr speaks about five types of relationship between Christ and culture: Christ against culture, the Christ of culture, Christ above culture, Christ and culture in paradox, and Christ the transformer of culture. The problem facing these two Japanese Christian women does not fall easily into one of these relationships, but rather cuts through all of them. The conflict is between the eschatological perception of salvation ("help comes only from the Lord, maker of heaven and earth"—Ps. 121:2) and the cosmological culture of salvation ("help comes from heaven and earth"). This conflict expresses itself in many cultural contexts. What we have here is an exemplary case; it is the conflict between Japanese indigenous cosmological culture and the biblical eschatological insight into history. In the former, enshrinement presents no problem, but it is indeed problematic in the latter. How hard it is to speak the language of Mount Sinai in the land of Mount Fuji!

Permit me to be personal for a moment. I was eleven years old when Japan rushed headlong into a reckless war. On December 8, 1941, the emperor issued the Imperial Rescript Declaring War against the United States, Great Britain, and the Netherlands. I still remember the impressive lines from the rescript:

We, by the grace of Heaven, Emperor of Japan seated on the throne of a line unbroken for ages eternal, enjoin upon you, our loyal and brave subjects; . . . the situation being as it is, our Empire for its existence and self-defense has no other recourse but to appeal to arms and to crush every obstacle in its path. Hallowed spirits of our imperial ancestors guarding us from above. . . .

74

It took me several years to understand better that Japan went to war with "three marvelous truths" about itself: (1) the divine emperor possesses the grace of heaven; (2) the nation was engaging in a war of self-defense; and (3) the country was under the protection of the hallowed spirits of the imperial ancestors. The self-defense doctrine was neatly tucked in between two inspiring religious ideas.

In August 1945 two nuclear bombs were dropped on Japanese cities. On August 8 the Soviet Union declared war against Japan. Japan, now a wilderness as a result of incessant air raids, accepted the Potsdam Declaration of unconditional surrender to the Allied Powers. The "marvelous three truths" of Japan had failed!

The new constitution of Japan, put into effect on May 3, 1947, is "autobiographical" and "confessional." It reviews the recent past of Japan, in particular its record of violence against its neighbors and itself, and it expresses the nation's resolve not to go to war again. I find this thirty-four-year-old constitution very important and in agreement with the message of the Christian faith. I quote from its Preamble:

> We, the Japanese people, acting through our duly elected representatives in the National Diet, determined that we shall secure for ourselves and our posterity the fruits of peaceful cooperation with all nations and the blessings of liberty throughout this land, and resolved that never again shall we be visited with the horrors of war through the action of government, . . . We, the Japanese people, desire peace for all time and are deeply conscious of the high ideals controlling human relationships, and we have determined to preserve our security and existence, trusting in the justice and faith of the peace-loving peoples of the world. We desire to occupy an honoured place in an international society striving for the preservation of peace, and the banishment of tyranny and slavery, oppression and intolerance for all time from the earth.

When I read this, remembering the devastation of the war, I am deeply moved. This Preamble is very similar in tone and contents to the Preamble to the Charter of the United Nations:

> We, the peoples of the United Nations, determined to save succeeding generations from the scourge of war, which twice in our lifetime has brought untold sorrow to mankind, . . .

If these two preambles share the same outlook, we may say that our Japanese constitution has been endorsed by the peoples of this planet. It has the quality of universality. We destroyed others and ourselves by the parochialism of "hallowed spirits of the imperial ancestors guarding us from above." Now we must discard that self-glorious parochialism and build our nation upon the principles of peace-loving humanity. This is also in keeping with the first of the ultimate objectives of the U.S. Initial Postsurrender Policy for Japan (September 6, 1945) which states that it is "to insure that Japan will not again become a menace to the United States and to the peace and security of the world." What can be done to uphold this principle of peace-loving humanity?

I have started with the impressive quotations from the Imperial Rescript, the Japanese Constitution, and the United Nations Charter. The challenge Mrs. Nakaya and Mrs. Oshima face must be understood in this greater historical context. It has to do with the dream of humankind. Christians must understand this perspective and must stand against the possibility of repeating the Tenno system, which "led to an ethnocentric nationalism and a chauvinistic militarism that reduced persons to tools in the drive for Japanese superiority and modernization."

Mrs. Nakaya's litigation has legal and moral implications in the disputes on the nationalization of the Yasukuni Shrine, National Foundation Day as a national holiday, *Gengo,* and related issues. "For our fight is not against human foes, but against cosmic powers, against the authorities and potentates of this dark world, against the superhuman forces of evil in the heavens (Eph. 6:12).

For Mrs. Oshima a nationwide rally in support of Mrs. Nakaya's fight not to have her husband enshrined as a war hero and Shinto god is approaching. I think the most difficult part of Mrs. Oshima's problem is to clarify the difference between the traditional way of Japanese thinking and the Christian viewpoint on the subject of the enshrinement of Lieutenant Takafumi Nakaya. The great missionary Francis Xavier, who came to Japan in 1549, was aware of this problem. Fundamental to the Japanese way of thinking is its optimism over the continuity of history. There may be critical disruptions, such as the unconditional surrender to the Allied Powers in 1945, but somehow the nation will continue. All will be put in the right place eventually by the power of nature. "My help comes from heaven and earth!" Humankind and gods *(kami)* share the energy of nature. They are continuous to each other. The eighteenth-century Japanese scholar Motoori Norinaga wrote about *kami:*

> Speaking in general, however, it may be said that *kami* signifies, in the first place, the deities of heaven and earth that appear in the ancient records and also the spirits of the shrines where they are worshiped. It is hardly necessary to say that it includes human beings. It also includes such objects as birds, beasts, trees, plants, seas, mountains, and so forth.

Lieutenant Nakaya, then, would not become divine in the Christian sense. He would become a *kami* in the traditional theology of Shintoism. Shinto theology is basically animistic and in this tradition we cannot speak about "idolatry" as we do in Christianity. It is in the monotheistic religions that the discussion of idolatry becomes centrally important. As R. R. Niebuhr writes:

Radical monotheism dethrones all absolutes short of the principle of being itself. At the same time it reverences every relative existent. Its two great mottoes are: "I am the Lord the God; thou shalt have no other gods before me" and "Whatever is, is good" [*Radical Monotheism and Western Culture*, p. 37].

If God is King, then earthly kings are kings only as long as they do the will of the invisible King. If they presume an ultimate kingship, they must be dethroned. This is a very strong principle. The Chinese view of imperial authority comes close to it. In that political philosophy an emperor can rule over the people only as long as he has the Heavenly Mandate. If that is lost, he must be dethroned. I think in 1945 the Japanese emperor lost the Heavenly Mandate. In monotheism, the one who claims to be absolute is dethroned because of the sin of idolatry; in our oriental culture the emperor is dethroned when he loses the Heavenly Mandate. Traditionally Asians do not speak about idolatry. Idolatry is not a concept in our culture. However, Christians in Japan are sensitive to idolatry. They have learned the eschatological theology of salvation: "help comes from the Lord, maker of heaven and earth." Destruction came upon Japan because of its corporate idolatry! Because this viewpoint is unfamiliar to our people, they will not understand the objection of Mrs. Nakaya and Mrs. Oshima to the enshrinement of Lieutenant Nakaya.

The idea of the Heavenly Mandate is not indigenous to Japan. It is too sophisticated an idea to be native to Japan. But the idea of taking care of departed spirits is indigenous to the Japanese mind. The pacification of the departed souls—"hallowed spirits of the imperial ancestors guarding us from above"—has given us the philosophy of continuity. When history is disrupted, as in the defeat in 1945, this discontinuity must be healed by some stronger cultural element indigenous to the Japanese mind. That element is the cult of pacification of departed spirits.

In postwar Japan almost everything was in a state of disarray. In that unsettled time the strong ideology of the enshrinement of departed souls was renewed as a symbol of national continuity. When the authorities took steps to enshrine Mr. Nakaya as a *kami,* they were expressing the deep psychological and cultural yearning of the Japanese people. Mrs. Nakaya and Mrs. Oshima are confronting this special Japanese "spirituality." Therefore I find their task very difficult. The issue involves the most sensitive core of Japanese culture.

Professor Hori views all litigation in terms of "cultural identity." The focal point of the dispute is that what Mrs. Nakaya takes to be a *theological* issue is, for the Japanese public, merely a *cultural* issue. Why do Christians get so disturbed about the conventional Japanese way of thinking and doing things?

Since the time of the Meiji restoration, the Japanese government has often insisted that Shinto is not a religion but a national custom. The National Diet Committee on the Study of the Constitution, meeting on March 9, 1960, recorded a highly revealing discussion between the Shinto representatives and the committee members. They questioned whether, if the Japanese emperor were to become Christian, the Shinto people would welcome the event. The consensus was that the people would be shocked. They were then faced with the problem of why this should be so if Shinto were only a national custom and not a religion.

The "Confession of Responsibility During World War II" of Kyodan was not well prepared. To whom was it addressed? To Christians only? To the general public? If it were addressed to Christians only, what do we mean by this confession?

> Concerning this founding and the continued existence of the Kyodan, we recognize, with deep fear and gratitude that, even in our failures and errors, the Providence of God, the Lord of history, was at work.

Were we making this confession to ourselves only? On the other hand, it is a substantial theological statement, but it is not intelligible to the Japanese public. Are we not then required to rewrite it?

It is this kind of challenge, at the more fundamental level of Japanese culture and psychology, that is the problem facing Mrs. Oshima.

Here I also would return to the theme of the conflict between cosmological culture (the concept of the healing of the world in terms of the interrelatedness of nature) and eschatological theology (the concept of the healing of the world by the power of "the finger of God that . . . drive(s) out the devils"— Luke 11:20). The latter way of looking at culture is not indigenous to the Japanese mentality. It is here that the problem surfaces.

What can Mrs. Oshima do in this situation? First, she could make of it an effective educational opportunity to prepare younger generations for a similar eventuality in the future. She could visit schools—particularly those that base their educational programs on Christian principles—and speak on the importance of a Christian understanding of the dignity of the human person. The story of Mrs. Nakaya can be presented as a cogent example of how an apparently innocent cultural custom can erode the principle of religious freedom.

In the face of the current upsurge of chauvinistic militarism in Japan, Mrs. Oshima could work with those persons who still take the "lesson of Hiroshima" seriously. Hiroshima blasted the destructive tribal god of Japan and began our search for a universal God who cares for the universal welfare of humanity. The tribal god cares only for the prosperity of its own people. It encourages its own people to sing a parochial doxology to its own country. The foreign policy of the tribal god places its own people at the center and all others on the periphery. Tragically, our world is full of tribal gods, and is governed by their foreign policies. In the tribal-god culture we do not experience the creative moment of singing a doxology to the universal God who is concerned about the universal peace of humanity. "My help comes from heaven and earth" is an inspiring philosophy of salvation. It gives, however, little protection from the domination of the tribal god. The Japanese people suffered greatly from this tyranny during the last war and in the postwar years the possibility of domination continues. Therefore those who remember Hiroshima must keep alive the awareness of this danger not only for themselves but for the inner life of all Japanese today. Mrs. Oshima is not alone.

SELECT BIBLIOGRAPHY

Elwood, Douglas J., ed. *Asian Christian Theology. Emerging Themes.* Philadelphia: Westminster, 1980, pp. 56–59, 213–19.
Fabella, Virginia, ed. *Asia's Struggle for Full Humanity.* Maryknoll, N.Y.: Orbis, 1980.
Koyama, Kosuke. *Waterbuffalo Theology.* Maryknoll, N.Y.: Orbis, 1974, pp. 95–105, 133–60.
———. "Ritual of Limping Dance, A Botanical Observation." *Union Seminary Quarterly Review,* Vol. 36, Supplementary Issue, 1981, pp. 91–104.

Case Study 3

UGANDA:
RETURNING HOME

James and Mary Kyonka sat quietly on the small porch of their Nairobi, Kenya, apartment in the cool of the evening. Their two children were watching television and the noise of the city traffic had begun to subside. The silence between them had also deepened since James had once again raised the issue of returning to Uganda. His last words hung in the air: "I've got to give the bishop a decision by the first of next week."

James had felt Mary's tension as she glanced down at the headline of the Nairobi *Daily Nation* that lay on the floor between them. Yesterday fourteen Ugandans had been shot dead in the streets of Kampala. They had been celebrating reports that ousted President Yusufu Lule was returning home in preparation for recently announced democratic elections. James remembered with a stab of pain his first reaction: "What are fourteen more added to the slaughter of fifty thousand during the past eight years of terror?" Then came a flood of memories of their secretive departure from their homeland five years earlier.

Uganda Under Amin

James had been appointed a lecturer in ethics in the Department of Philosophy and Religious Studies at the renowned Makerere University not long after Idi Amin seized power in 1971 by overthrowing the government of

80

Milton Obote. The initial rejoicing of the Ugandan people, fed by Amin's freeing of hundreds of political prisoners and promises of democratic elections, soon soured as General Amin began to build an elite personal bodyguard. He plowed the country's meager resources into a massive military program and later maneuvered the Parliament to vote him President for Life.

In mid-1972 in an attempt, James believed, to appease the people, Amin decreed the forced expulsion from the country of more than thirty-five thousand persons of Asian descent, many of them born in Uganda. Propaganda accompanying the expulsion order implied that Ugandan Africans would acquire thousands of middle-class homes and businesses owned by Asian Indians and Pakistanis. Amin declared that the Asians controlled the economy of Uganda (which, James acknowledged, was in many respects true) and that what was needed was economic independence to match political independence. In the ensuing "economic war" against the Asians, most of their property was expropriated and some were even murdered as they tried to flee with personal possessions. James grimaced as he recalled the socioeconomic chaos that followed the expulsion: Asians had held a majority of the professional appointments in education and medicine and had controlled a massive portion of the export-import business.

The university was one of the few institutions to withhold public praise for Amin's policies. As the ranks of military and secret police swelled with the disenfranchised and often illiterate, attacks on the university increased. The vice-chancellor of the university disappeared; there were rumors that he had been killed by Amin's secret police. Then came raids on the university dormitories, as well as the seizure of leaders of the Student Association and students from those tribal groups associated with the former Obote regime.

As James and a fellow professor whispered to one another in the faculty common room, they agreed that teaching conditions were almost intolerable and that the university was "gradually becoming a prison." It was increasingly difficult for faculty members to leave the country. Special individual permission by the minister of education was required. No research was possible, because anyone asking questions was immediately suspect. And James felt bound even in his lectures to refrain from any comment that could be construed as critical of the government; too many students were now paid informers. James and several other faculty members felt that the only way left to express their disgust and protest was to leave the university and the country.

Flight to Kenya

In October of 1976 James obtained permission to attend an academic conference in Nairobi. He then stealthily moved his wife Mary, their two children, Samuel (age eight) and Flora (age six), and a few possessions over the border into neighboring Kenya. After several difficult months, schools in Nairobi were found for the children. Mary found a stable job with a large

Nairobi research firm, and James accepted an administrative position with an international Christian organization. He then began using his free time for raising money abroad for the thousands of Ugandan refugees now in Kenya, as well as for support of the Christian churches in Uganda. Individual members were being persecuted in growing numbers, though Christianity was the majority religion of Ugandans.

In the winter of 1977 the persecution reached a climax after the homes of the archbishop of the Anglican Church of Uganda, Janani Luwum, and of the bishop of Bukedi were searched by secret police. Twelve bishops of the Church of Uganda, including Luwum, drafted a petition to Amin urging him to respond to the critical state of the country. In part the statement read:

The security of the ordinary Christian has been in jeopardy for quite a long time. It may be that what has happened to the Archbishop and the Bishop of Bukedi is a climax of what is consistently happening to our Christians. We have buried many who have died as a result of being shot, and there are many more whose bodies have not been found, yet their disappearance is connected with the activities of some members of the security forces. . . . When they begin to use the gun in their hands to destroy instead of protecting the civilian, then the relationship of mutual trust and respect is destroyed. Instead of that relationship, you have suspicion, fear, and hidden hatred. There is also a war against the educated, which is forcing many of our people to run away from this country in spite of what the country has paid to educate them. . . . Too much power has been given to members of State Research [secret police] who arrest and kill at will innocent individuals. Therefore, that which was meant to provide the Ugandan citizen with security is increasingly becoming the means of his insecurity.

Two days after release of the petition, the archbishop was arrested and then found dead in what the government declared was "an automobile accident." Six bishops fled from the country and thousands of other Christians were harassed and seized.

In the two years that followed Luwum's death, James and Mary housed and helped provide for many fellow Ugandans who fled to Kenya for safety and who were unable to find work of any kind. By the initiative of Archbishop Luwum, prior to his death, an emergency relief fund for Ugandans had been established through the Anglican Church of the Province of Kenya. Still, many Ugandans were eking out an existence on less than five Kenyan shillings a day (less than U.S. $1).

In late 1978 James and Mary's hopes were elevated when an army of exiled Ugandans and troops from neighboring Tanzania flooded across the border. They defeated Amin's army and "liberated" Uganda. Yusufu Lule, a former vice-chancellor of Makerere University, was installed as president following Amin's flight. But peace did not return. Another change of government followed less than three months later. Thousands of Ugandans were starving in the north due both to drought and theft of cattle by fleeing soldiers. Law and order in the cities were almost nonexistent. The victorious soldiers had emptied the jails indiscriminately, freeing criminals as well as political prisoners. Poorly paid Ugandan and Tanzanian soldiers began to loot and kill. In self-defense some Ugandan citizens armed themselves with hand guns and rifles abandoned by Amin's troops.

It had been in the midst of this turbulence that James's Ugandan bishop, Silas Majobe, had come to him and said, "I have a job for you." James responded that he was not prepared to take a new job right away. A few months later, on another trip to Kenya, the bishop came again, joking that his Church of Uganda diocese "extended to Kenya." He repeated the offer, James clearly recalled his own personal turmoil as he began seriously to consider the invitation of Bishop Majobe to return to Uganda and accept the top administrative post with the Diocesan Rural Development Project.

Committee for Moral Rehabilitation

James was certain that eventually he would return to Uganda, but how and—perhaps equally important—when were the nagging issues. At almost the same time his bishop approached him for the second time, James was exploring a job with the church-sponsored Committee for Moral Rehabilitation. His first acquaintance with the committee's goals had emerged during a week he spent in Uganda following the "war of liberation." He visited several dioceses and prepared a report on physical damage to churches for the Church World Service in Geneva.

James recalled telling Mary that he had been overwhelmed by the change he found in the people, and that he was anxious to understand the mentality of those who had lived through the ordeal of the past eight years. He reasoned that the people's struggle for mere survival, in light of rampant inflation, insecure employment, and scarcity of essential goods, had given them an insensitivity to the feelings of others. An increasing number of youth who had seen power and money seized by illiterate soldiers now scoffed at education as a way of advancement. James saw this as particularly ironic in a country that had formerly prided itself on having one of the most distinguished universities in Africa.

The primary work of this committee, for which James was interviewed, was to work directly on the decayed ethical fabric of the country, to encourage "love of neighbor" in a land rampant with hatred, fear, and suspicion. Its goal, in a country where residents had grown a "thick skin," was to increase sensitivity and to help once again develop a "thin skin."

James decided to submit an application to the central committee in Nairobi, although he had not made a final decision on the matter. His application was stalled for several months in the committee. Friends quietly shared with James that there were "several drawbacks" to his being offered the posi-

tion: he "was not an ordained pastor," and with a Ph.D. he was "overquali-
fied" for parish renewal work. His role "should be in the university, for
which he was trained." James then recalled several incidents in the interview
that might have led to this conclusion. One priest had asked, "Why do we
need a Ph.D. for this work? We are doing moral education in the church
every Sunday." When James posed the question, "If we are doing a good job,
then why is the country in the present state?," there was a series of defensive
objections. And James's suggestion of using educational drama and films to
attract and interest the people was greeted with skepticism by the committee.

Rural Development Project

Though his application had not yet been officially rejected, the delays
moved James to consider again his bishop's offer. In conversation with Mary
he shared his deep desire to contribute to the rebuilding of their country.
Mary had reminded James how much they had enjoyed the years in the university and that he had again been offered an appointment at Makerere.
James had responded that he "owed more to the church than to secular institutions."

James continued. "The university serves the elite, not the ordinary people.
I am critical of its failure to be integrated with the general development of life
in our country. After giving most of my life to study and learning, it is strange
to hear myself saying these things. They seem in opposition to what has been,
to this point, my life's work. But I also feel responsible to the source of that
training. All those years away at schools in the U.S.A. and England were
largely through church support. Now I need to respond to where the church
needs me most. Our grass-roots people are like a football, kicked around by
everyone who can gain power and manipulate them. The intent of the job the
bishop offers is to help alleviate the deplorable conditions under which the
people are now living."

James had described to Mary the bishop's Rural Development Project for
the diocese, which contained over one million persons, of whom 80 percent
were Christians and 40 percent members of his church. The project was
divided into five general areas: health; agriculture; women; youth; education
and training.

In the health sector the primary focus would be on small parish aid posts
and on preventive medicine. Following the "war of liberation" there were
neither doctors, medicines, soap, nor bedding available in rural areas. Drugs
and other supplies coming in from abroad were being sent to the government
and to the Church of Uganda. Yet, as James explained to Mary, "dispersal to
local aid posts is in chaos and in need of strong, coordinated administration.
Health conditions are deplorable and health is the key to development."

In the realm of agriculture, even if the rains came, James said, "there will
be no crops because the people have no seeds and no tools to prepare the
ground. There are ten thousand hoes waiting in Jinja, sent from Europe, yet

no organized system to distribute them has been set up." James stressed that education was also needed on basic farming methods, on the economical use of land, and on the need to grow food rather than cash crops, which had been the practice of Ugandan farmers for many years.

Work with women, the third area, would involve training in family nutrition to overcome severe malnutrition in children and to develop a strong healthy people. This sector also involved the encouragement of craft skills. James also saw deep trouble for the young. The educational system had been seriously threatened by an expensive pyramid system that left thousands of school dropouts headed for the city to find disappointment and often crime. Two of James's primary concerns were the development of vocational schools and the reintroduction of athletics in the schools to raise morale and overcome the growing apathy.

The education and training sector touched every part of the development program, but James saw a particular need for a program of Christian conscientization. One route to this would be model farms that would reflect basic human values of commitment and hard work. Again James voiced his strong feelings: "The people, not the men in cassocks, are the church. We must find a way to serve the real church, the lowly people."

James indicated that this project would be a new way to use his education for the sake of the people. However, he told Mary he would have to be present on the job before he could locate the most critical areas for immediate attention and establish directions and priorities. After eight years of political and economic destruction, each of the areas needed massive redevelopment.

The project had been promised funding for at least three years by a grant from the German Evangelical Church. James's bishop had already named a seven-member executive committee and was trying to oversee the project himself, along with all his other responsibilities, until an administrative coordinator was named. The bishop urged James to come immediately. As he told James the last time they were together, "The crucial work cannot really begin effectively without dedicated full-time leadership."

Family Concerns

As James and Mary discussed the decision before them, Mary verbalized many of the questions that had been troubling James. She expressed confidence in James's administrative ability; he had done a fine job with his current post and had been urged to renew his contract when it expired in two years. Yet, she asked, back in Uganda would he meet resistance from those under him—just as the church council had not been immediately receptive to his job application because he was not an ordained priest and because his education set him apart? James was also worried that the resistance he had experienced before from clergymen who wanted control and seemed threatened by lay persons, even those without graduate degrees, might block the very program he believed was crucial for his diocese. Given the present conditions in the country and in the church—where the clergy represented some of the few persons who still held authority in the eyes of the people—perhaps only an ordained person could succeed in this post. Was his proper role really in the university using the investment in his education to help equip future clerics to work constructively with the people?

Beyond these personal questions, family responsibilities seemed to loom even larger. Apart from the two children with them in Nairobi, James's and Mary's families were in Uganda. Since James's father had died, two years earlier, James, as eldest, had assumed responsibility for his mother, brothers, and sisters. Return to Uganda would allow James to give his family the support and guidance he knew was his responsibility. Yet, over the past few years of economic strain, the family had become increasingly dependent on the money he and Mary sent in from their combined income in Kenya. Returning to Uganda now, where it would be virtually impossible for Mary to get a job and where James would be taking a sizable cut in income, would seriously reduce the primary source of financial support for the family group. In addition, Mary had been promoted to supervisor in the research laboratory where she worked. She would have to sacrifice her own professional career for the move. James felt Mary shared his commitment to their people; she had expressed a desire to work with young girls on their return. But was he being a loving husband to opt for a return at this particular time in Mary's life?

Personal insecurity loomed as another drawback. Mary acknowledged her growing feelings of "maternal protectiveness" for the children. The new job would place the family in Kusaka, an industrial town over sixty miles from the capital city, Kampala. Decent housing was almost impossible to obtain.

Following the Asian expulsion, hundreds of rural families, unaccustomed to urban living, rushed to the cities. Families of ten or fifteen members took possession of Asian homes designed for five or six persons. Later, still more rural families came to the cities in search of work. As law and order eroded, trash collection and sewage treatment ceased. During Amin's rule, as outside trade was severed, building materials became scarce, then unavailable. The population of Kusaka—twenty thousand, before the "invasion"—had meanwhile doubled, yet there had been no new construction of homes and virtually no maintenance for eight years.

The reports by friends living in Kusaka and in numerous other towns were no less discouraging. James and Mary had been told repeatedly that each evening one went to bed uncertain of what that night would bring. There was no police force, food was scarce, and household robberies were frequent. Even driving an automobile was precarious, as there was no way of knowing when you would be stopped and the vehicle taken at gun point. James and Mary were told quite frankly that they would feel more insecure if they arrived with noticeable possessions—furniture, clothing, utensils—or even if it was thought they *might* have them. The educated were at a distinct disadvantage because it was assumed they had possessions. The value of human life was low, possession of guns unchecked, and many persons had been killed for their belongings.

Items James and Mary could take for granted in Nairobi—soap, tooth-paste, blankets, toilet paper, sugar, wheat flour—were often unavailable in Uganda. They had begun to gather a year's supply of many items in anticipa-tion of their return. They were seriously considering trading their fairly new automobile for an older, "less desirable" one. And though they had bought a new stove and freezer to take back, they were now concerned that these pos-sessions would endanger their safety. Yet these supplies would be necessary for the friends and relatives who they knew would be frequent and long-term visitors.

Mary had then raised with James one of the deepest concerns, that of education for their children. Ten-year-old Flora would be able to attend a mission school still in operation near Kusaka. But education for their thirteen-year-old son Samuel was more uncertain. He was now in a good school in Nairobi, but was a year behind his age group, because he had been placed back when they moved from Uganda. In another year he would take the all-important seventh-form national exams, which would determine his eligibility for future education. Should the family move now, Samuel would lose at least two more years. Preparation for the Kenyan and Ugandan exams differed considerably. Being three years older than his classmates could be a serious disadvantage to university entrance. Mary had said to James, "The wrong decision on our part could ruin Samuel's future. He might never forgive us if we sacrifice his education for a precarious project."

Alternatives

Mary had considered several alternatives. There were no relatives in Kenya with whom Samuel could stay and finish his last year of school, and on the new salary they would not be able to afford the expensive boarding schools. If Mary remained and James went alone to Uganda for the first year, she and Samuel would have to face the difficult task of finding housing, because Mary's salary alone could not support them and pay the rent on their present apartment. Mary also suggested that James could negotiate a contract with Bishop Majoba to arrange for a transitional period of one year; he would work twenty days a month in Kenya in his present job, and ten days in Uganda. This would allow time to see if things would really change.

James did not believe this would be feasible. The bishop wanted and needed him full-time—now. Total commitment to the new task by someone on the site was essential. Even if a transitional contract could be arranged, James feared this would involve too much travel back and forth by unreliable and unsafe public transport. Mary would need the car in Nairobi. Also, James argued, "We have always worked things through together. We may need one another now more than we ever did before."

James asked himself if he was being selfish by wanting to make a tangible contribution to his people at the risk of jeopardizing his family. Did his desire to make a difference in the lives of ordinary persons simply reflect his impa-tience with the slower, long-range goals of higher education? Some friends had suggested that he might not only be throwing away his training and God-given gifts, but also his life. He or the family could well be killed by thieves or even by someone jealous of his work. Reports of such things came in every day. However, as James recalled when writing to his bishop, "Since your last visit, I have persistently pleaded with our Lord to make it clear to me what he wants me to do and where I am to work. Increasingly, I have felt that our diocese is crying out, 'Come over to Macedonia and help us.' " James believed his decision was rooted in reflection on Matthew 25:35 and Luke 10:27–28. Yet, was such a risk to his family and such a new vocational direction the Lord's will or his own?

James reached out and touched his wife's hands as he asked, "Are our fears and uncertainties responsible considerations, or are they excuses for both of us to delay returning to the bitter conditions of our homeland? What are the values, Mary? How do we decide what our faith is calling us to do?"

TEACHING NOTE ON "RETURNING HOME"

Within the context of James and Mary Kyonka's decision about returning to Uganda, this case provides basic information about some dimensions of the political, economic, and religious conditions in Uganda. There are clear parallels with conditions in other parts of the world, wherever persons are experiencing the aftermath of war or internal revolution. The case offers a variety of possible responses by individual Christians and churches. A discussion of this case could focus on several topics:

A. Many Christians find that their sense of "call" conflicts with family responsibility. James appears to face a choice between Bishop Majobe's "call to Macedonia" (see Acts 16:9–10) and responsible care for his immediate and extended families. What are basic criteria upon which Christians can make decisions such as this?

B. James is also faced with the question of the role of laity. Are there roles that only ordained clergy should fill? Why or why not? The clergy as well as James question his move into a field which may not utilize the technical teaching skills he acquired at a high cost to the church. By what criteria do we evaluate how gifts are used?

C. How does an individual or an organization begin to restore the dignity of human life following the devastation of war? In rebuilding a victimized society, which human rights take priority? This leads to the examination of mission strategy and the underlying presupposition of development projects.

CASE PLAN

1. Open the case by testing and discussing the reasons to go and the reasons to remain in Nairobi as stated by James and Mary. Are there unstated reasons revealed in the case? What is at the feeling level for this couple?

Ask the group to vote for one decision or the other; record the vote, then ask participants to discuss the implications of the decision each made and the rationale behind that decision. Draw in the issue of James's lay status. Compile a set of criteria which could guide James and Mary in their decision.

Are there any alternatives open to them not considered in the case? Urge participants to be creative and to justify their responses. What resources of the Christian faith will undergird James and Mary whatever decision they make? (Consider prayer, confession, forgiveness.)

2. Discuss the economic and political situation in Uganda. What is the situation in Kusaka? Draw out specific illustrations. Ask participants if they lived in Uganda at this time what they would feel. What would be their greatest needs?

Outline the Rural Development Project organized by Bishop Silas Majobe and the work of the Committee for Moral Rehabilitation. What are the presuppositions of each approach? How do these programs respond to the needs of the people? Are there any other approaches which would be more effective? Why or why not?

3. Conclude the discussion by raising the biblical and theological criteria by which the church responds to dire human needs. Is the church also responsible for addressing the causes of war?

SUGGESTIONS FOR ADDITIONAL READING

Kivengere, Festo. *I Love Idi Amin*. Old Tappan, N.J.: Fleming H. Revell, 1977.

Kyemba, Henry. *A State of Blood: The Inside Story of Idi Amin*. New York: Ace Books, 1977.

Mbiti, John. *African Religions and Philosophy*. Garden City, N.Y.: Doubleday & Co., 1969.

Taylor, John V. *The Primal Vision*. London: SCM, 1973.

Tuma, Tom, and Mutibwa, Phares, eds. *A Century of Christianity in Uganda, 1877–1977*. Nairobi, Kenya: Afropress, 1978. A collection of articles written to mark the Centenary Celebration of the Church of Uganda in June 1977. Available from either Afropress Limited, Lusaka Close, P.O. Box 30502, Nairobi, or Uzima Press Limited, P.O. Box 48127, Nairobi, Kenya.

Wood, Jayne Miller. *Focusing on Global Poverty and Development. A Resource Book for Education*. Order from Overseas Development Council, 1717 Massachusetts Ave., Washington, D.C. 20036.

JOHN MBITI

COMMENTARY ON "RETURNING HOME"

This case study focuses on personal rights around the person of James Kyonka and his family. Ultimately, James, and his conscience, must determine which line to take. However, some observations can be made in the light of the specific information given and the dilemma posed for him.

James is right in keeping up his interest in the events in Uganda, his home country, from which he, his wife, and two children had been forced to flee in 1976. In fleeing, it is obvious that they could not take with them all their property, much less their relatives, their friends, and cultural roots. It is quite understandable—even to be expected—that his heart would also still be there.

In addition to the normal attachment to one's home, there is the question of serving one's country—the people, the church, the nation. The third area of consideration has to do with the family—a working wife and two school children, who have now settled down in Nairobi, Kenya, after some initial difficulties. But also there is the wider family, which embraces more than husband, wife, and children, according to African ideas of the family. Both James and Mary have many other relatives in Uganda, who are also members of the family. So, in effect, James's family is divided—a small part is with him in Kenya, and the greater part is still in Uganda.

To complicate matters, there is also the question of security. James is fully aware that Uganda has become extremely insecure for everyone. It was this insecurity that initially led him to flee with part of his family to Kenya. Although the military regime of Idi Amin had been overthrown three years later, arrests and killings, as well as robberies and other forms of violence, have continued. There is, therefore, no guarantee that by returning home James would be more secure than when he first fled. If, upon returning home, he would be killed, what then?

For me this is the crux of the matter in this particular case. James is not a free man as long as insecurity is so pervasive in his country. He cannot decide freely without reference to the question of security for himself, his wife, and

91

children, all of whom are safe as long as they are living in Nairobi. Is it fair to return to the same (if not worse) danger from which they had fled only a few years before? What does his conscience say to him?

Let us look at the issues more closely. James is fortunate to be living in a neighboring country from where he can maintain close contact with his country. Love and attachment to one's country can be stronger in someone who is living away from home than in those who are there all the time. James should have no fears that his commitment to Uganda would diminish because he is living next door in Kenya. After all, he had also studied for several years in the United States and Britain, and this did not weaken his attachment to Uganda. Furthermore, there are millions of persons in the world who, or whose ancestors, left their countries of birth, whether willingly or unwillingly, and settled in other countries. There is nothing sacrilegious about going to live in a country other than where one was born. Economic and sociological patterns of today make such changes common, normal.

It is to be appreciated that James wants to return and serve the church and nation at a very needy moment. Both the church and the country can certainly profit from the learning, the experience, and the vision of a man such as James. But we have to recognize that there are many other Jameses in Uganda. A post that he would occupy could also be occupied by another James. After all, the church and the country would not grind to a halt if James Kyonka were not around. They have functioned without him since he fled, and surely they can continue to function without him.

One wonders, too, whether the church and the country actually need James as much as he imagines that they do. Even his application for a job with the church's Committee for Moral Rehabilitation has "been stalled for several months in the committee," we are told. We hear also that "friends quietly shared with James that there were 'several drawbacks' to his being offered the position." Although James might embrace the new post because it provides opportunity for him to return home and serve the church and people of Uganda, do those whom he wants to serve really want to have him back? There are hints that give cause for doubt, and these could eventually surface in the form of serious opposition to him and deep disappointment or disillusionment on his part.

A further consideration is the fact that in Nairobi James is also serving the church in his present post with "an international Christian organization." One's people in Jesus Christ is the church everywhere and not just in one's home country or denomination. This organization provides great opportunities for serving different denominations of the church in different countries of Africa (including Uganda). It is a serious responsibility that needs the services and knowledge of someone like James. There is no pressing reason for him to abandon this post when he has been offered a continuation of his contract, which can also be seen as fulfilling a calling.

Equally important is the fact that Mary is doing her work in Nairobi. She is using her talents and answering a calling. If she returns to Uganda, she would not have a job and that would deny her the right of pursuing her career.

The family issue is extremely serious. One man's move to Uganda would put into great uncertainty the future of the whole family. Mary "would have to sacrifice her own professional career," the education of the children would be put into jeopardy, if not ruined, and the insecurity of the country would put the lives of everyone in danger. If James were to be killed, his whole family would be deprived of physical and psychological support, and his wife and children would presumably be unable to return to Kenya. We are told that "some friends had suggested that he might not only be throwing away his training and God-given gifts, but also his life. He or the family could well be killed by thieves or even by someone jealous of his work." James should pay attention to this voice.

There are difficult and agonizing elements to this case. But the most decisive are the considerations pertaining to security and the family. By returning home, James would be terminating the fulfillment of his wife's career and their children's secured education in Kenya. By returning home, James would put everyone into a situation of anxiety, if not outright exposure to danger of life. The threat to the family's future and the exposure to insecurity outweigh feelings of attachment and the call to return home and help in national reconstruction.

James should remain in Nairobi. I feel happier with this option. Here he is serving the Lord in the post he holds with the international church organization. From here he can still nourish his attachment to Uganda and explore and use other opportunities of responding to the present needs of his country and church. In the years ahead, the situation might alter considerably. James would still be able to review it and act afresh accordingly. He has a right to personal security; his wife has a right to fulfill her own calling; and the children have a right to a good education. These three personal rights seem clearly to be well protected in Kenya. But they would almost certainly be violated by returning home to Uganda.

J. DEOTIS ROBERTS

COMMENTARY ON "RETURNING HOME"

This assignment is both a joy and a challenge. It is joy because my own instincts are caught up in the dialogue between the First and Third Worlds; it is a challenge because of inadequate knowledge or experience on my part to fulfill the task. Those who invited me to write this commentary, as well as the one on "Eye of the Needle," were obviously convinced that my insights would be useful. Encouraged by their confidence, I take up the challenge.

The case is centered around Uganda in East Africa. The location of the principal characters is Nairobi, Kenya. Those who have traveled in those parts know that it is a brief flight over Lake Victoria from Kampala, Uganda, to Nairobi, Kenya. But the distance for James and Mary Kyonka is both near and far. They are asked to make a decision to return to Uganda. But because of the many issues involved, they have reasons to ponder seriously whether they should return.

The turmoil in Uganda, resulting from the rule of Amin, is well known. A graphic account of this human tragedy and its aftermath is set forth in the case study. Details do not need to be repeated here. The central focus will be on the right to civil security in light of the decision that James and Mary Kyonka are asked to make.

The Kyonka family fled Uganda for Kenya. James was a lecturer in ethics, philosophy, and religious studies at Makerere University. For the sake of academic freedom and the safety of himself and his family, a self-imposed exile became necessary. But now in the post-Amin period, when conditions are still unsettled and danger still lurks throughout his native country, he is being urged to return by Bishop Silas Majobe to administer the diocesan Rural Development Project.

Earlier he had been approached to work on the Committee for Moral Rehabilitation following the "war of liberation." His advanced degree (Ph.D.) and his proposed educative methods (drama and films) seemed to be unacceptable. These and other reasons kept him from this role. But the committee's goals were worthy. Its purpose was to restore ethics to public life and

94

encourage love of neighbor in a land rampant with hatred, fear, and suspicion.

The new offer in the bishop's Rural Development Project was no less important. It was a firm offer that required a serious decision. The location was to be Kusaka, over sixty miles from the capital, Kampala. Decent housing was unobtainable. Education for their children would be hard to come by. Living conditions were primitive. Furthermore, poverty was widespread, the value of life had cheapened, and the aftermath of war made living conditions unsafe.

The Kyonkas looked at several alternatives. None of them seemed feasible. Finally, the issue was related to the call of God and a question of values. James put it thus: "Are our fears and uncertainties responsible considerations, or are they excuses for both of us to delay returning to the bitter conditions of our homeland?" James, who was not an ordained minister, wanted to know whether such a risk to his family and a new vocational direction were the Lord's will or his own creation?

This points to certain issues that belong to the province of theological ethics. First, are the "powers that be" ordained of God? This question is presently being answered in America affirmatively by the Moral Majority. If the answer is yes, expediency and enlightened self-interest are usually nearby. But where human rights for the oppressed masses are taken seriously, there is a reluctance to answer in such a hurried and self-assured manner.

When questions of social justice and the humane treatment of other human beings are carefully considered, we must reckon with the fact of the demonic in all human orders. Human beings are fallen beings and their sins multiply into collective evils in the social order. We have, therefore, to analyze each political order carefully to determine whether it measures up to goals appropriate for human life, personal and social. In any social order, we are charged with the responsibility of working for the highest and best values we know. All social orders are to be measured by standards of rightness and justice that transcend the givenness of any social order. The kingdom of God, a kingdom not of this world, is the proper frame of reference. Christians, who claim membership in the redeemed community, are to become fellow laborers with God in making life more human.

The decision James is to make regarding his return home properly belongs in the context of this discussion. Where is the place of greater service to the masses of the Ugandan people? Is it at a safe and comfortable distance in Kenya, or is it in the heart of the struggle, in solidarity with the oppressed?

Secondly, what is the relationship between law and morality? Human rights are often violated because laws are unjust. This is true in well-established governments where discrimination based on race, sex, or class is manifest. This state of affairs is also present in countries emerging from colonialism and underdevelopment. The issue of law in the body politic in conflict with justice was raised early in Christian history by St. Augustine in his *City of God*. It has been repeated forcefully in recent theological history by

Dr. Martin Luther King, Jr., in his "Letter from a Birmingham Jail."

Any society in turmoil raises the issue of law and morality in conflict. Uganda, during and after Amin, had to deal decisively with this matter. The restoration of ethical and personal values among the citizens of Uganda necessarily has to be related to the reign of law in relation to justice. A lawless government cannot provide the context for the functioning of just laws among its citizens. Love of neighbor and the writing of justice into law are two sides of the same coin. Theologically, God can be said to be lovingly just. It follows that those who seek to do the will of God among fellow humans must seek to establish laws that are just.

What makes the decision to return to Uganda exceedingly difficult is that ministry to the needs of the masses will include involvement in the transformation of the political economy. When one gets involved in that way, those in charge of the unjust established order try to limit the activities of churches to private religious matters. There is, however, in the Ugandan situation no real escape from a ministry of liberation. Anything less would be a denial of the gospel itself.

Thirdly, what is the relationship between means and ends? In recent ethical reflection the question of violent or nonviolent means has been raised. The Ugandan situation seems to be a prime example of the failure of violence to provide a more humane order. In the wake of Amin's violence, the war of liberation and its aftermath, one sees little evidence that violence can produce a more viable social order. Even the Tanzanian soldiers turned to robbery and plunder, according to the case study. Illiterate soldiers were obsessed with the power of the gun. Youths lost the desire to be educated or acquire useful skills. Although the war of liberation appears to have been the lesser of two evils, its consequences were bitter.

Human beings in the quest for justice in an unjust world often face hard choices. On the plane of reality, too often our only choice is between bad and worse. Violence as a means has spent itself in Uganda. Bishop Majobe rightly calls James Kyonka to a ministry of healing. But it is also clear that the quest for liberation must continue. Liberation must be related to healing. It must be by nonviolent means. There must be due recognition of the dignity of human life and the fulfillment of God's purpose in the social order.

In conclusion, I find this to be a most rewarding case. It illustrates the demands of the gospel in the human social order wherever there is the absence of justice and equality. It places human rights at the center of faith considerations and it illustrates the unity of the human family everywhere in the quest for the values and resources that make life human. Here the right to civil security is central, but there is such an interdependence of human rights that the denial of one basic right is the denial of all. An understanding of the Christian faith based upon a proper reading of the Bible moves us to compassion and action against sinful social structures at the same time that we are called as individuals and families to the obedience demanded by that same faith.

Case Study 4

AUSTRALIA: SACRED SITES

Gary Wells was troubled as he stepped on the commuter train that would take him from the prosperous suburb of Glen Lea to the city center and a meeting of his church's National Board of Social Responsibility. The meeting of the board had been called hurriedly to consider a request from the secretary for permission to go to Noonkanbah in Western Australia. With other Australian church leaders and concerned citizens, he wished to join with the Aborigines of Noonkanbah to protest, and if possible bring an end to, the transnational Amax Exploration Company's drilling for oil on Aboriginal sacred sites in the area. Gary knew that many members of his congregation were strongly opposed to the church's involvement in such actions. What is more, he was uncertain in his own mind about what policy the church should adopt in this particular conflict. Yet in a short while he would have to vote on a specific proposal that could inevitably link the church with a demonstration that, he believed, would be construed by many as antigovernment, as well as antagonistic to the lawful activities of a large mining company.

Now in his mid-forties, Gary had been minister at Glen Lea for five years—two years in the Methodist congregation before church union, and three years since the Uniting Church of Australia (a union of Congregational, Methodist, and Presbyterian congregations) came into being in 1977. Because of the desire for continuity in schooling for his children, Gary and his wife hoped that they might be able to stay in Glen Lea the maximum ten years permitted by the Uniting Church regulations for pastoral appointments.

This case study was prepared by Gordon S. Dicker and Alice Frazer Evans as a basis for discussion rather than to illustrate either effective or ineffective handling of the situation. Copyright © by the Case Study Institute.

The names of Gary Wells, Bob Croft, Ron Avery, and Glen Lea are disguised to protect the privacy of the individuals involved. The names of all other places and public figures are factual.

When Gary entered theological college twenty years earlier, he had been very conservative theologically. During his three years of college, he fought against what he considered to be the excessive liberalism of the theological faculty. Yet over the years he recognized that his outlook had changed a lot. He could not be called a fundamentalist, but he believed he had retained what was important in his conservatism: a concern for evangelism and for the preservation of historical evangelical doctrine. What is more, he had developed a strong social concern. In part this was born of his admiration for John Wesley's social concern, and in part it was the result of five years of ministry in an inner-city parish.

Gary knew that it was his reputation as an evangelical that had gained him the invitation to the Glen Lea Methodist Circuit, as it was then called. He had been pleased with the invitation. His previous pastorates had all been in struggling congregations. Here at last was an opportunity to work with a growing congregation made up largely of families. He had found, however, that most of the really active members of the congregation were more conservative than he was theologically and did not share many of his social concerns. Union had not made much difference to the congregation. There had been no Congregational church in the suburb to unite with, and the Presbyterian church there had voted not to enter the union. Only a few Presbyterian families strongly committed to union walked out of their church and joined with the previously Methodist congregation.

Aurukun and Mornington Island

As he gazed out the window of the speeding train, Gary recalled the last time he had been caught up in the Aboriginal issue. It had been during the protracted struggle of the Aborigines of Aurukun and Mornington Island with the Queensland state government in 1978, and the part that the Uniting Church played. Many of these black-skinned persons—the original inhabitants of the Australian continent, who had occupied the land for at least thirty thousand years before the white settlers came—had been resettled and moved onto state-controlled land over the past hundred years. However, the communities in Aurukun and on Mornington Island had remained on their ancestral lands. For most of the century these two Aboriginal communities had been administered by the Presbyterian, and then the Uniting Church, as an agency of the Queensland government. But in mid-March 1978 the state government suddenly notified the church and the communities that it would assume direct control as of April 1, by which time all church personnel with the exception of a chaplain should leave. Both communities protested the decision and the Uniting Church supported their protests.

In local gatherings, there were some members of the Aboriginal communities who voiced approval of the change. They stated that they could receive more financial support and more community services if the state administered the communities directly. But the majority opposed the change, many stating they would have less independence and less control over their own affairs under direct state control. Over the previous decade the church had followed a policy of transferring to the community elders responsibility for decision-making and control in all areas of community life. Church-recruited workers regarded themselves as employees of the tribal council rather than officials of church or state. State government policy appeared to be just the opposite. On those occasions when it made decisions about the two Aboriginal communities in question, it did so with little or no consultation with the Aborigines, as in this instance.

The Aurukun residents said they were suspicious about the government's intentions for another reason. The twenty-five thousand square miles of their land included a rich bauxite deposit that the government was apparently eager to have mined. A majority of the Aurukun Aborigines declared that they did not want any mining on their land. Open cut mining operations would destroy their ceremonial sites, scar the land with which they had deep emotional and spiritual ties, spoil their hunting, cut them off from their natural resources of fruits, roots, and seeds, and disrupt community life. The position of the Queensland government was that the Aborigines would not directly receive any royalties. However, the state government would pay for additional services in their community out of royalties received from the mining. The size of these benefits was uncertain. Most Aborigines stated that this would never compensate for the destruction of their tribal life.

They were aware of the problems that mining had brought to other similar communities—for example, at Weipa, only a short distance away, where bauxite mining had resulted in the destruction of tribal life and the decimation of the community by disease and alcoholism. They did not wish to have this result repeated in Aurukun. During the dispute they tried to explain to white Australians through newspaper and television interviews the fundamental importance of land for the well-being of Aboriginal people. "It is the source of our tribal identity and cohesion," one of them explained. "It provides not only for our physical needs, but for our spiritual needs also. Just looking at our land keeps up our spiritual life the same way reading the Bible keeps up the spiritual life of Christians."

At one time mining nearly did commence. In the 1960s one of the aluminum transnationals had prospected for bauxite on Aurukun land with government permission. Some discussions had been held with Aurukun leaders, but the only point of agreement was that there would be further discussions before any mining proposal was developed. In November 1975, however, without any further consultation, the Queensland state government announced, in a news release to the media, plans for a massive open cut mining operation. The Aurukun people immediately took legal action to stop the operation—with success. Three years later, they were suspicious that the state government's decision to take direct control of the community was a new and devious attempt to force the mining of bauxite without further problems.

The struggle between the Aboriginal communities and the Uniting Church on the one side and the state government on the other continued for a month with daily press and radio coverage of moves and countermoves. The federal government entered the dispute in support of the Aborigines. It threatened to respond to a request from the two Aboriginal communities to assume owner- ship of the lands and give direct control to the Aborigines. At the time the land was considered "crown land" belonging to the state of Queensland, having been previously designated by the state as Aboriginal reserve land. Only minutes prior to the passage of federal legislation to acquire the land, the Queensland premier announced the abolition of the Aboriginal reserves. This in effect nullified the federal legislation, removed all state financial sup- port from the two communities, and could lead to eviction of the Aborigines as trespassers on state land. Rather than enter into a divisive and lengthy court battle on untested issues of state and federal constitutional rights, the two governments, which were controlled by the same political coalition, ef- fected a compromise. The Aborigines would be left temporarily in control of the land, but as lessees for a fifty-year period rather than owners. The two communities, which had not been consulted in the decision, accepted the compromise: it was the only thing they could do. The role of the church was undercut; a powerful joint state and federal advisory board was established to counsel the two new "shires."

Throughout the dispute ministers of the state government continually al- leged that the church persons in the communities were "do-gooders," "radi- cal stirrers," "outsiders manipulating the Aborigines," and even "com- munists." Gary had wondered at times whether this might be true. Neither he nor the board of which he was a member played any part in the dispute. He did not know the individuals in question, and he did know persons in the Uniting Church whom he himself would have called "social activists" and "stirrers." But members of the state government made similar allegations about church leaders at synod and assembly level who were officially in- volved in the dispute. Some of these Gary knew personally and he knew that the allegations were false, and if these were false, it seemed to him likely that the other allegations could also be false.

Gary was pleased to note that newspaper editorials, radio commentators, and television current-affairs programs were heavily in favor of the Aborig- inal cause and very supportive of the church's action. It was gratifying to see this because it seemed to him that the attitude of the media to the church in Australia in the past had been mostly critical.

Yet there had been unfavorable reaction to the Uniting Church's involve- ment by the congregation at Glen Lea. Gary recalled the brief conversation he had with Bob Croft during the dispute. About Gary's own age, Bob was company secretary of a large Australian manufacturing firm. He was also one of the most active members of the congregation. He taught Sunday school, was one of the adult advisors to the youth group, and was convener of the Mission and Evangelism Committee of the Parish Council. He had opened up the conversation in the vestry just before morning worship with what seemed like a humorous question:

"Can't you talk some sense into some of these ministerial colleagues of yours?"

"What do you mean, Bob?" Gary asked.

"I mean the way they are going on over this Aurukun affair. Why don't they keep their noses out of this business and let the Queensland government settle the matter?"

"Don't you think the church has a right to be involved? After all, it has administered the Aboriginal reserves for seventy years," Gary countered.

"They should never have been involved in that sort of thing. The church's business is to preach the gospel to people, not run their affairs and turn them against the government," Bob replied.

"What makes you think the mission staff has been turning the people against the government?" Gary questioned.

"It's quite clear what they have been doing. Mr. Bjelke-Peterson [the Queensland state premier] said just this week that they are a group of social activists manipulating the people," Bob continued.

"Well, even the premier might be wrong, you know," Gary argued.

"No, I think he is absolutely right. He is a Christian man—teaches Sunday school. He knows what is best for the Aborigines and is trying to achieve it. The church is trying to keep them back in the Dark Ages—keep them separate from the rest of the nation—it's a kind of apartheid. The church leaders are always decrying apartheid in South Africa, but that is just what they are trying to create here in Australia." Bob was becoming quite agitated.

"Don't you think there is a difference between forcing black persons to live in separate areas from whites, and allowing them, if they choose, to have their own protected reserves?" Gary asked.

"It amounts to the same thing, doesn't it?—separate development for two races within the same nation. I tell you, Gary, I am very uneasy about this Uniting Church. It is led by a group of radicals who want to stir up trouble wherever they can. You never hear them talking about evangelism and the saving of souls. If things keep on like this, we'll have to think seriously about transferring to another denomination."

"I hope you won't do that," Gary replied. "Let's talk some more about it sometime."

They never did take up the subject again. The dispute subsided, and Bob seemed to be carrying on his church activities as usual. Then, early in 1980, a conflict between the Western Australian government and the Aboriginal community at Noonkanbah began to seize the headlines. The church was not directly involved in this dispute, but now, as the situation was nearing a climax, Gary believed some church leaders wanted to get involved.

Noonkanbah Station

Gary tried to recall the background to the dispute from what he had read in the papers. Noonkanbah Station was part of the tribal lands of the

Yungngora people. For many years the remaining Yungngora worked as stockmen for the white pastoralists who held a long-term lease of the land from the state. At one time they walked off the station to protest the way they were treated, and for about five years they lived as fringe-dwellers around the town of Fitzroy Crossing, though they continued to visit their sacred sites at Noonkanbah. In 1976 a federal government commission, set up to settle Aborigines on their own land, purchased the Noonkanbah Pastoral Lease for the Yungngora people. They returned to the station and made good progress in establishing a profitable cattle industry on the land. Shortly after they took over the station, a number of mining companies began prospecting for minerals, diamonds, and oil on the leased land. Inasmuch as the land was "crown land"—that is, it belonged to the state—and the Yungngora people only held a lease on it, prospecting could be carried on without their permission. The state legally controlled mining rights on all leased land and had historically accepted mining contracts on grazing acreage managed by white settlers.

In 1978 one company, Amax Exploration, decided to proceed and drill for oil. The Aborigines claimed that during their initial preparation, Amax employees damaged their sacred sites. A bulldozer was brought in to cut long straight lines in the earth in a grid pattern. Apparently some of these lines were cut through burial and ceremonial grounds and a tree that they believed was the home of the spirit of Friday Muller, a former elder of the tribe, was damaged. The community took action in the courts to prevent further exploration by Amax, but the action was unsuccessful. They also sent a petition to the West Australian Parliament, written on bark in their own language, asking the parliament to prevent mining or drilling on their lands. The parliament gave no public response to the petition, and in the following month the state government announced that it had given Amax permission to proceed with the drilling. The Yungngora people then voted to obstruct Amax personnel physically from coming onto the station. As a result, Amax decided to postpone operations.

In March 1980 the company proceeded with exploration. Claiming that the proposed drill hole would be within a sacred site complex, the Noonkanbah community sought protection through the court under the Aboriginal Heritage Act, a bill enacted by a previous West Australian government to provide protection for Aboriginal culture, including sacred sites. This legal action failed, and it became clear from the numerous press statements, as well as provision of police escort for Amax workers entering the Noonkanbah site, that the state government saw the dispute as an important test case. Government spokesmen said that as much as a third of Australia could be closed to exploration if the Aborigines won this dispute. The state minister for cultural affairs claimed that sacred sites was not the issue, and that if the Aborigines held the mineral rights to the land, they would readily negotiate with mining companies for the huge financial gain they would receive. He claimed also that the Noonkanbah people were being manipulated "for political reasons."

The minister argued further that the state government could not give overriding land rights to the Aborigines. This, he said, would be contrary to the government's policy of one Australian family with equal rights and equal opportunities for all. He said that the government was anxious to protect Aboriginal rights and all places of significance to them, but these must be consistent with the needs of the entire Australian community, which is composed of more than a hundred different ethnic groups. All are members of the Australian family. None should have rights or privileges not available to others. Aboriginal reserves in Western Australia amounted to tens of thousands of square miles. If the Aborigines had the right to prevent mining on all these reserves, the Australian community as a whole would be deprived of needed reserves of minerals and oil, and the development of the state would be seriously impeded.

Having lost the legal battles and having failed in all direct negotiations, it appeared to Gary that the Noonkanbah community might now take action outside the law—or a group of white activists would. Gary was not sure in his own mind that the Aborigines really were initiators of the proposed action or that theirs was a cause he could support.

As he stepped off the train, Gary was trying to compare this dispute with the Aurukun and Mornington Island dispute. He believed he saw a difference. In that case the church was directly involved. Here there was no necessary involvement, but as he saw it, some church persons seemed to be trying to involve themselves—to get into the act, as it were—and he was not sure what their motives were. In the previous dispute the church's actions were through legal channels, but here it seemed that disputants were preparing to take action outside the law, not just against Amax, but against the duly elected government. In view of the strong support of Scripture in Romans 13 and 1 Peter 2:13–17 for submission to the government, how could Christians justify such action? What is more, the dispute was over protection of sites associated with a heathen religion. How could Christians be involved in protecting such sites? Would this not be like protecting idols? Surely the church's task was rather to convert these peoples so that they would give up their superstitions and practices. If a member of his own congregation, Bob Croft, had reacted so negatively to the church's role in the Queensland dispute, how could he, and others like him, react positively to this one?

Board of Social Responsibility

These questions were uppermost in his thoughts as Gary entered the meeting room. He said "hello" to a few of his friends, but his mind was too preoccupied for small talk. The chairman called the meeting to order and opened with prayer. "You know why this meeting has been called," he said. "The motion before us is that the Board of Social Responsibility give its secretary leave to go to Noonkanbah, to demonstrate the church's support of the Aboriginal struggle, and that his air fare be paid by the board."

Ron Avery, the full-time secretary of the board, was in his fifties, an ordained minister who had served in several parishes, and a man whose ministry had always been strong on social issues. He rehearsed the events that led up to what he called "the present crisis in Western Australia" and put his case for going to Noonkanbah. Gary was familiar with many of the details, but Ron had a different interpretation of some aspects of the dispute.

Ron argued that the government had itself acted unethically in the dispute, and by doing so had deprived the Aborigines of justice. The Aboriginal Heritage Act of Western Australia provided for the trustees of the Western Australian Museum to establish the location and genuineness of sacred sites. The museum had done this and had accepted the genuineness of the site in question, though its report had not been published. The act gave the minister the power to direct the museum trustees to permit mining on a particular site. The minister used this power, and it was on the basis of the approval that the trustees were thus forced to give that the Noonkanbah people lost its final legal appeal. Ron argued that the outcome may have been legal but was not fair and just.

"It is clear," Ron continued, "that the West Australian government is determined to have drilling proceed on the site and is prepared to stop at nothing to see that it happens. The Aborigines are clearly the poor, oppressed, and the powerless in this dispute. It was with such that the prophets and Jesus took their stand, and the church of Jesus today must do the same. There is plenty of land in Western Australia where mining can be carried out. If ever there were a modern parallel to the story of Naboth's vineyard (1 Kings 21), this is it. It may be that if the churches and other persons of goodwill support the Noonkanbah people, this desecration of their sacred site can be prevented. But even if we can't prevent it, we must demonstrate our solidarity with the Aboriginal people in their struggle. It is clear that the next few days will be decisive. I ask you to make it possible for me to demonstrate by my presence the fact that the Uniting Church cares about justice and cares about Aborigines."

Following Ron's statement, there were speeches of support for the motion, but also a number of questions were asked.

"How do we know they are really opposed to oil drilling? The government has said they are just playing for a share of the royalties from any oil found. And how do we know this is not just a lot of trouble manufactured by social activists and stirrers?"

In reply Ron read from the statement of Aboriginal elder, Ivan McPhee:

The old people of Noonkanbah are very upset about this mining coming onto sacred site. This sacred site important to Aboriginal people. We got *goanna*[1] inside sacred site. That *goanna* been there from Dreamtime.[2] Long time before European came to Australia. That story come from grandfather to grandfather and now they still telling that story. Noonkanbah people don't want mining on sacred site. Already we got old man, Bob Muluby, sick by this company setting up camp on sacred site.

Ron also read from the statement issued to the press by the Noonkanbah community:

> If Aboriginals give up their sites and special places there will be no more law, no more story telling, no more initiation ceremonies. It will be like it has all gone out into space.

He referred to a statement in the press by another Aborigine, Ribnga Green. In rejecting the charge that white "stirrers" are responsible for Aboriginal opposition to mining at Noonkanbah, he said: "It's a real insult to the intelligence of the Aboriginal people. They know what they want and are capable of making their own decisions."

Another board member asked if the board was not intruding in matters where it had no right to be. "I believe," he went on, "that white people should get out of the way and let the Aboriginal people make their own protest. Support them certainly; write letters to the state premier, write to the newspapers, but it is not our job to go and organize their resistance."

This time it was the chairman who replied. "Our church has had a pastoral relationship with these people and we have been asked to come and help them. Ron certainly would not be going to organize resistance. They are perfectly capable of organizing themselves. He would be going to stand with them and demonstrate by his presence our support for their struggle."

Gary asked if it was not very strange that Christians were wanting to protect sites associated with a heathen religion. "Should we not be more concerned about evangelizing these peoples than about protecting sites associated with their pagan rituals?" he asked.

Ron replied that the churches would have no right to evangelize these people, and would not be heard by them, if Christians stood by and permitted them to suffer what, in their eyes, was a gross injustice. "If we are ever to speak to these people about the gospel, we must stand by them now," he asserted.

Discussion continued for some time. At last the chairman intervened: "I believe we have discussed this motion sufficiently to enable each person to vote responsibly and intelligently. I will put the motion to the meeting. Those in favor will raise the right hand."

NOTES

1. A large lizardlike reptile, hunted for food by the Aborigines, but also featuring prominently in Aboriginal myths and legends.

2. "Dreamtime" is the term used by Aborigines to refer to the time, long ago, when, according to their mythological stories or "dreaming," their spirit ancestors created the world and their society.

TEACHING NOTE ON "SACRED SITES"

Gary Wells finds himself confronted by the complexity of the Australian Aborigine struggle for land rights. The universal issue of relationship to the land and the religious significance of that relationship give the case world-wide implications. Surrounding the central issue of land rights, especially for minority groups that have a special understanding of the land, are several additional issues:

A. The responsibility of individual Christians to wrestle with and respond to the mandates of the Gospel.

B. The responsibility of the institutional church in problems with broad political and economic implications. This raises the issue of the mission of the church.

C. The responsibility of national governments to protect often conflicting rights of its citizens.

D. The responsibility of the global community in terms of the impact of national governments and multinational corporations on individual lives.

CASE PLAN

1. Identify Gary Wells, Bob Croft, and Ron Avery. How does each perceive the role of the Uniting Church in the land controversies of the Aborigine? (What differences does Gary see between the controversy in Queensland and that in Western Australia?) Broaden the discussion to include how each perceives the mission of the church. What common understandings, if any, do they have? What are the significant differences? What resources inform these positions? Consider the images of the church as prophet and as evangelist. Are there different understandings for these men in the meaning of Christian witness?

2. Ask participants to state additional issues raised by the case. Focus on one or two. Particularly helpful can be a discussion of individual minority rights versus rights of the wider community. What issues are involved in deciding the priority of one over the other? Discuss the statement by the Western Australian Minister of Cultural Affairs: "All are members of the Australian family. None should have rights or privileges not available to others." What kind of rights does he mean? What do Ivan McPhee and the Noonkanbah community understand to be their rights? Based on statements made by Aborigine communities, discuss their understanding of the land.

3. Move the discussion to alternatives. Ask participants to "counsel" Gary Wells in making his decision, giving biblical and theological interpretations which would support their choices. What specific strategies could Gary adopt in his home parish to deal with the continuing national conflict over Aborigine rights? Consider the responsible personal, local, national, and international strategies for any congregation (e.g., education and conscientization, community building, work with media, addressing state legislation, etc.). How can those of a majority community become sensitized to the perspective and needs of a minority? Try to be specific.

4. What does Ron Avery mean by the need to "demonstrate our solidarity with the Aborigine people" whom he has identified as "the poor, oppressed, and the powerless"? What are the biblical and theological resources of the Christian faith which undergird an individual or a church that moves toward identification with the poor? (Consider scriptures such as Matthew 25:31–46 and 1 Kings 21. Consider as well an understanding of confession, forgiveness, Christ's life and sacrifice, empowerment, freedom to risk.)

SUGGESTIONS FOR FILMS AND ADDITIONAL READING

"The Aborigines and the Churches." *St. Mark's Review,* No. 96, December, 1978.

Blainey, G. *Triumph of the Nomads.* Melbourne: Sun Books, 1976.

Carne, Derek. *Land Rights, A Christian Perspective.* Sydney: APCOL, 1980.

Engel, Frank. *The Position of the Australian Aborigine.* ACC, 1978.

"Justice for Aboriginal Australians." Sydney: Australian Council of Churches, August 1981. (Report of the Human Rights Team for the World Council of Churches.)

Stanner, W. E. H. *After the Dreaming.* Sydney: A.B.C., 1968.

Tatz, C., ed. *Black Viewpoints.* Sydney: Australian and New Zealand Book Company, 1975.

Woodward, A. E. *Aboriginal Land Rights Commission: First Report.* Canberra: Australian Government Publishing Service, 1973.

Three films available from the Australian Council of Churches:
— "On Sacred Ground", 16mm, 58 minutes.
— "Words and Deeds", 16mm, 30 minutes.
— "A Matter of Identity, 16mm, 20 minutes.

GORDON DICKER

COMMENTARY ON "SACRED SITES"

This is a familiar story of oppression. It has parallels in many parts of the world. An immigrant group, in this case white Anglo-Saxons, with tighter social organization and superior physical force, has taken possession of a land originally inhabited by a different race. The original inhabitants, the Aborigines, have been largely dispossessed of their land without treaty or compensation. Only a few tribal groups, living in fringe areas long regarded by the newcomers as worthless and unfit for habitation by white persons, have been permitted to remain on their tribal lands. Genocide has wiped out most of the other tribes. Small numbers of landless, largely deculturated and demoralized Aborigines live in the cities and on the edges of country towns.

Now it has been discovered that the "worthless" lands on which the tribal Blacks were allowed to remain are rich in the minerals and oil the white population needs to feed its industries and increase its prosperity. So now these Aborigines also are threatened with the destruction of all that is most sacred about the land and even ejection from their territory. The trans-national corporations are involved, but it is state governments that are doing their dirty work, supported by individuals who value their own luxurious and wasteful lifestyle so highly that it must take priority over all other human values.

The case focuses on the issue of the relationship of oppressors to the oppressed and looks especially at the reactions of Christians who belong to the oppressor group. A number of possible responses are suggested by the participants in the case.

A typical reaction is denial: there is no oppression. This may take various forms. Many Australians would say that any disparity between Blacks and Whites is due to the laziness, drunkenness, and foolishness of the Aborigines. It may well be that Bob Croft would be of this opinion, but he would not express such views openly for fear of being branded a racist. He expresses his position with greater sophistication.

The West Australian government denies oppression by talking about equality. The minister for cultural affairs argues that the government cannot give overriding land rights to the Aborigines, because this would be contrary to its policy of equal rights and equal opportunities to all. The minister fails to recognize that the Aborigines have been dispossessed of their land in the first place. The request to get it back and have total control over it is then regarded as claiming a right and privilege not available to other ethnic groups! The minister also fails to take account of the ruthless destruction of the Aborigines' way of life and sense of identity—a destruction that has continued for over a century. In view of all the suffering inflicted by the colonists, Aborigines need concessions and opportunities not available to others just to regain equality, not to attain some position of privilege.

Bob Croft is also denying the existence of oppression. Though he does not say so openly in his reported conversation, one may infer from what he says that he believes the Aborigines are receiving favored treatment just by being permitted to retain their own land. He believes they should be forced off their lands and compelled to integrate into the predominant white society. There is no acknowledgment of the fact that wherever a policy of assimilation has been forced upon them, white attitudes have mostly prevented any real integration and forced the Blacks to be fringe-dwellers on the edge of white society.

Behind the attitude of persons such as Croft is a corporation mind-set that accepts the axiom that profits are sacred and "development," whatever its form, is a great good. Croft would never acknowledge this. Indeed, inasmuch as it involves the most blatant idolatry, a religious person such as Croft cannot acknowledge it. Rather religion itself is invoked to provide some kind of justification for oppression. The church's struggle with the Aborigines for their rights is condemned on the ground that the church's job is to save souls. High-handed and oppressive action by governments is sanctioned because government is accorded some divine right that goes beyond anything suggested in the scriptural passages invoked in its support.

Nevertheless we should not be too hard on Bob Croft. He has not made himself what he is. He is the product of many forces operating upon him, from which he cannot easily break free. His conversation with his pastor should be construed as a call for help rather than a threat. It is regrettable that Gary Wells has not seen it in that light and followed it up.

At the other extreme from denial is the activist response. Oppressors who become convinced of their sins sometimes try to make atonement by means of involvement of any kind. This may take the form of organizing or attending protest demonstrations, presuming to speak to governments and communities on behalf of the oppressed, organizing the activities of the oppressed, or trying to participate in their organizations. The result is frequently meddlesome interference and paternalism. The board member who says "It is not our job to go and organize their resistance" is correct.

Repentant oppressors need to set themselves to learn first of all how to be sensitive to the wishes of the oppressed. That means learning to listen. They must learn also that they cannot save themselves by their "many good works." In many situations they may serve best by getting out of the way, both physically and figuratively. This means giving the oppressed people the space and freedom to decide for itself what it wants to do and how it will do it, and not standing in the way of the implementation of its decisions.

No one in this case represents this response, but this may be a temptation that Ron Avery needs to guard against. It is of the utmost importance in the consideration of this case that we are given the assurance that Ron Avery has been invited to come by the Aboriginal people. We must hope that it was a spontaneous invitation and not a prompted one, and that Ron hears and agrees with the chairman of his board when he assures the members that Ron would not be going to organize but to stand with the Aborigines and demonstrate the board's support for their struggle. Of all the objections raised in the meeting, that which touches on this issue is the only really serious one. Assuming that the chairman has answered correctly, Ron must go and the members of the board should vote to allow him to do so.

A third possible reaction is to do nothing. This reaction may be prompted neither by coldness of heart nor apathy. Recognizing the error of denial but also witnessing the rejection of the liberal activists by the oppressed themselves, some self-acknowledged oppressors can see no role for themselves at all. They might argue that they can do no more than confess their sins and wait in hope that as Christ liberates the oppressed he will also liberate those responsible for oppression. There is some truth in this. As oppressors, we need to confess our sins and ask forgiveness. True, we cannot put things right by means of our program of activism. Yet this position is theologically inadequate. It could be characterized as an extreme justification-by-faith position. It does not take into account what Bonhoeffer called "the penultimate"— action taken for the sake of the ultimate and in turn constituted by it as penultimate. Secondly, it fails to recognize that confession of sin is cheap and shallow without genuine penitence, and penitence is bound to mean bearing of suffering.

Gary Wells's position is not exactly this one. His unwillingness to act or to be seen to be involved in any way springs more from the fear of the consequences in his own congregation than from any theological conviction. He raises the issue of protection of sites associated with a heathen religion, but this is a cover-up. He seems to be reflecting the views of those in his congregation whom he fears. If there is a principle implicit in his stance, it is that the church should not seek involvement unless it is already party to a dispute, as it was in the Aurukun case. It is at this point that his position has some similarities with this third kind of reaction. He regards himself as having a strong social concern, but that concern is empty unless he finds some way of translating it into meaningful action on behalf of the poor and oppressed, whether or not his church happens to be directly embroiled in the situation. In this case he is not called to travel across Australia to stand physically beside the Aborigines confronting the oil drillers, but at the very least he must be willing to bear suffering if necessary to represent the Aboriginal cause to his congregation, absorbing the hostility of persons such as Bob Croft, which may well be turned against him. If he fails to interpret their struggle to his congregation and seeks to change their attitude, he has copped out. This is the real issue; which way he votes in the meeting is relatively insignificant compared with this.

Gary must recognize that he stands in a very favorable position to effect change in the congregation at Glen Lea. He shares some of their theological outlook. If he has established his credentials at that level, he cannot be dismissed as a false believer. At the same time he claims to have a social awareness that many in his congregation lack. What is called for is not an all-out, win or lose, frontal attack. Nothing will be gained by achieving immediate dismissal, though in the end it may come to that, and Gary must be ready to sacrifice his hopes in the matter of the length of his settlement. The approach must be deliberate but gradual. The gospel will need to be preached not as though the church is filled each week with the unconverted, but in such a way that those who never doubt that they are Christians can be enabled to envisage, accept, and cope with change. Gary Wells's task will not be easy and he will need support. Ron Avery and others in similar positions will need to spare some of their time and energy to support persons such as Gary who have to work on the front line for attitudinal change.

There is still a more basic issue that the case seems to raise. It is clearly not enough for Ron Avery and his board simply to wait around for invitations such as the one they have just received. Nor has Gary done all that needs to be done when he has led his congregation into a more sympathetic understanding of the plight of Aborigines in Australia. I believe that those who are aware of their involvement in oppression have a responsibility to lead their group in a quest for self-liberation. It may be true that liberation is a matter of grace and not of works. It may be that as the oppressed find liberation, they liberate their oppressors. But neither of these points rules out the fact that there are things that oppressors can and should do for themselves if they are serious. And it is also likely to be true that as oppressors are themselves liberated and acquire a fuller humanity, they contribute to the liberation of others.

This assumes, of course, that in some sense we are all oppressed. I believe this is true in Australia. However, it must be said very clearly that most Australians are not oppressed in the quite gross and obvious way that Aborigines are. To claim otherwise is false and hypocritical, or at least demonstrates how ignorant we are of what it means to be grossly oppressed. Yet in another sense we do experience oppression. We are oppressed by our technology and by its demand that we avail ourselves of all its latest products. We are oppressed by the whole capitalistic superstructure of our society, which forms our opinions for us, shapes our politics, and even manipulates our desires. We are oppressed by our history and the axioms of our culture.

To take a specific and relevant example, it is not surprising that Australians, on the whole, have not a glimmer of understanding about what land means to Aborigines. Generally speaking, Australians have a poor attitude toward God's work of creation and a shallow relationship with that part of it they inhabit. This goes back to the origins of the colonies. For many of the first settlers it was a prison, and prisoners do not usually form a positive and happy relationship with their prison. Those lured here by the discovery of gold came to grab and get rich. Even the free settlers who came to settle on the land soon regarded it more as an adversary to be bullied than a friend to be tended lovingly, for it was a hard and difficult land that did not yield its blessings easily. Many never formed any relationship with the land because they were city dwellers. Early attitudes steadily hardened into a national characteristic. By the same token, the Australian stereotype of masculinity forbids any kind of sentiment or tenderness, even in relationship to the land. That is not to say that there are not country people who vow they love the land, but mostly it is "the land" as a way of life they love. It is a long way, for example, from Naboth's attachment to his land (1 Kings 21). The Aboriginal attachment to the land is quite foreign to this mentality. Aboriginal claims about their land appear sentimental, superstitious, and impractical. But is it not the attitude of white Australians that is defective? In this respect we are the unliberated ones, oppressed by our history and our stereotypes.

Here is a point at which the struggle for our own liberation would contribute to Aboriginal liberation and also a point at which Aboriginal life and culture can help us achieve a richer humanity. It is toward such a process of liberation that the issues raised by this case should direct us.

TERRY DJINIYINI AND DON CARRINGTON

COMMENTARY ON "SACRED SITES"

Australia is a land of great distances. The distance from Noonkanbah to the place where the board meeting is taking place is, in North American terms, equivalent to the distance from New York to Seattle. One is on the east coast of a vast continent, the other is in the far northwest. The distance to Aurukun is scarcely less, but this time the direction is north to south. Again in North American terms what is happening in this meeting is akin to Californians struggling to understand and to decide the part they will play in the destiny and future of Alaskans.

The real people in this story—Gary Wells, the Glen Lea congregation, Bob Croft, Ron Avery, and the committee—are the focus of our attention. We hear of their problems, we feel for them in their situation. Because they are persons who care, they are thinking about Aborigines in faraway Noonkanbah. But the committee is talking about persons and places that are not really part of their experience. It is difficult to get the picture clearly. Some misunderstandings creep in, again emphasizing the distances and making it difficult to feel the full impact of the human crisis of the Noonkanbah residents.

The proposal the committee is considering is a good one: the hope to send one representative to be with the Aborigines who are threatened. It will be expensive. A journey of so many hundreds of miles will mean a lot of church money for the airline ticket. In addition we are helped to see clearly that this will not be the only cost. There will be personal cost for Ron. If he goes, this expression of discipleship will need to be explained to congregations such as Glen Lea, which will have new opportunities to learn what it means to count the cost to take a stand for justice at a time of crisis.

This story helps the church to think through some of the implications of costly discipleship. When distances between persons and places are great, we are challenged to listen carefully to others in order to feel what they are feeling. And we are challenged to deepen our theological understanding of the way Christ acted in situations of this kind.

Jesus Christ was a person who went out to be with the people. He ate with

113

outcasts. He slept in their camps. He went into their houses not as an inspector from the health department but in order to be with those whom others called "rubbish." Christ accepted all persons. He built bridges between religious-minded persons and those who were called "rabble who knew nothing of the law." Christ's words and works were "good news" because he closed the distances between persons and identified with them.

Evangelism from a distance is not possible. Evangelistic words shouted across great distances may not be helpful "good news" to isolated peoples. Evangelism is not accomplished by shouting but by loving and by standing with a people. The "good news" for the people of Noonkanbah is that Ron Avery, a Christian and representative of the church, comes to *be* with them and to stand with them in a time of trouble.

English-speaking people call those in faraway places heathens and pagans. Pagans are not like us; they have strange customs and they follow strange non-Christian religious observances. The label "pagan" usually implies that we think they should change their ways to become more like our ways. But the ones who make these judgments have not listened very closely to the Bible or paid much attention to the customs of the people called Israel.

In the Old Testament particularly, the covenant people of God had special places of deep religious significance. We read of the special meaning of places like Bethel where meetings and struggles took place. Great importance is given to Sinai, the mountain of God where Moses received the law. Shiloh was another place of significance.

Some of these places were located within Israel, on promised land. Some were located outside and were places of pilgrimage into the wilderness. In many and various ways they were places sacred in the memory and life of the people—places associated with the teachings of the Torah and places to remember the law and covenant that the Lord God had made with Israel.

The focus of all sacred places became the law that centered around the ark of the covenant. When a temple was built in Jerusalem, sacred tables of the law came to be placed in the most holy of holy places in the very heart of the sanctuary. Those who, without permission, entered this most sacred place where the ark was kept were said to die. Only one person had permission and that was the high priest on only one day each year.

The people of the Bible understood the significance of a sacred place. Sacred sites in Israel were places where worship to Yahweh was deepened and personal renewal was experienced. Their understanding of places where the law was retained and remembered is very close indeed to the understanding the Aboriginal peoples of Australia have of "sacred sites."

We are sorry to report that in the history of Christian missions in Australia some missionaries came and saw the totems of Aboriginal people and jumped to the wrong conclusions. Encountering unfamiliar art forms of a sophisticated kind, some early missionaries wrongly decided that they must be idols. Theologians are today quite clear that idols are images of strange gods that some may worship. They are also clear that such worship is idolatry and is condemned in the Bible. However, it is also clear that "totems" are not idols as the Bible defines them and that both totems and sacred sites serve to retain the law in a way analogous to that of the ark of the covenant.

In Aboriginal culture, when persons approach a sacred site, a sacred object, or a totem, it is as if they are approaching the tablets of stone Moses brought down from the mountain. In special places in Australia a kind of law from long ago is thought to be retained. We would suggest that sacred objects that outsiders have called "totems" may be better compared to the tablets of stone enshrined in the ark of the covenant.

Christians seeing the winged creatures and exotic carvings of the ark of Israel will not conclude that it was an idol. On the contrary the ark reminded viewers not of false gods but of Yahweh himself and of the law that was a sign and seal of the ancient covenant between God and his people. Here the law is preserved. Here strong men tremble and learn again to relate to covenantal authority. Here the peoples learn the meaning of obedience and justice. Here the law is not dead but rather new hope is born and in significant ways persons renew their relationships for ongoing life. Here they recall whence they come and seek direction as to whither they are going.

Israel did not worship the ark. It was not an idol; rather, it was a sacred object placed in a sacred place to remind Israel of the law and of the mighty deeds of Yahweh in history. Moreover, Aborigines, if not all Christians, would generally understand the feelings of the Israelites if the ark were about to be crushed under the tracks of a bulldozer. In the Bible we read about the sorrow and sickness among the people when the temple was defiled. Christians who read the Old Testament with understanding of the spirituality of Israel will know and understand something of the genuine feelings of distress in distant Australian communities. At Noonkanbah the threat was a very physical threat. The heavy machines at Noonkanbah have been described as being involved in a militarylike operation: a calculated assault on someone else's "temple."

Is it carrying the imagery too far to ask members of the new Israel of God to imagine the Noonkanbah "convoy" rolling up to the gates of Jerusalem wanting to drill for oil in the temple itself? Even at a distance, and when dealing with the unfamiliar religious symbolism of *goannas*, it is certainly possible for Christians to feel empathy with those being so invaded. Thus we avoid the false "they-are-pagan—we-have-something-better" mentality and recognize as legitimate a deep spirituality with ancient roots.

It is also very clear that there is a legitimate way in which Christians may stand with Aboriginal people without compromise and agree that Aboriginal spirituality at least in relation to sacred sites is compatible with biblical spirituality and the law that Jesus Christ came not to destroy but to fulfill.

It is patronizing indeed to suggest that we "use" struggles for justice in order to put us on the right side with a people we want to evangelize later on. It is equally wrong to suggest that evangelism will later, in a kindly way, negate the primitive superstition of "sacred sites." This kind of pragmatism is hinted at in the case study when Ron says, "The church would have no right to evangelize these persons . . . if we do not stand by them now."

It is suggested that we stand by them now because they are seeking to protect something very precious given to them by God long, long ago. There are insights and spirituality here in relation to this place and this site that are precious to Jesus and may find fulfillment in him.

In another scene imagine being involved in a vital, attentive service of holy communion in an imposing cathedral when suddenly a crowd of engineers pushes in, breaks down a wall to make access for a rig, and commences drilling in the nave.

Of course it is impossible for worship to proceed under such circumstances. The spiritual preparation of the people for communion would be utterly disrupted. Considering what has happened in Australia, some feel much is irretrievably lost. Some feel that Christ has been affronted. Is it any wonder that many are afraid, saying that death has visited a place that earlier had such potential to affirm life in the Eucharist?

The point about the continuing pastoral relationship the protesters have with the church is well made. The point that is not made clearly is that many of the Aborigines gathered there were Christians. They are Christians who have come to see their traditional law in terms analogous to the Old Testament law. Theirs is a law that was given by God the Father of the Lord Jesus Christ. Theirs is an ancient law that is yet to be further deepened and fulfilled in Christ. In traditional Aboriginal Christian terms, theirs is a law that is not incompatible with the Spirit of Christ.

In Aboriginal tradition a ceremonial visit to a sacred site does not emphasize worship but rather focuses upon the traditional law. Mature persons who visit sacred sites in traditional ways are open to the law. They are open that they may receive wisdom and understanding in order to share with others who are ready to receive it. The parallels with the Old Testament Torah (teaching-law) are real. In the spirituality of the Aborigines, what happens at sacred sites is more like a recognition of ancient moral imperatives than a kind of worship.

For an "evangelist" to stop someone from visiting a sacred site is to stop someone from seeking personal and societal renewal. When thinking of the missionary activity of the church, we do well to remember the initial fellowship of Peter with gentile Christians. Then when members of the more conservative Jewish parties came, Peter drew back from gentile practices. It is Paul who challenges Peter, again emphasizing solidarity with outcasts and gentiles. It is Paul who shows that in Christ Jesus there is no distinction of persons and that Christ calls us to stand with minority groups. This is not a call to uncritically accept magic and idolatry but rather to recognize what are good gifts. It is a call to recognize in an ancient culture gifts that may have been given forty thousand years ago by God himself. This thought is humbling and, together with the biblical witness, helps us to cross the distance that separates peoples.

Following Jesus and Paul, the New Testament church is called to be fully involved in social affairs. Christian presence is not only to preach and teach but to struggle alongside others. It is to live with them, to suffer with them. In our experience, God is not somewhere floating over Australia; rather, God is revealed in the life of the people. God in Christ is with all human beings, especially those who are poor, outcast, and threatened.

When the church identifies in solidarity with the poor, we too will be called various names. Many of these names are uncomplimentary and are being spat out against the poor everyday. When these words hurt us, we remember that they are similar to words hurled at Christ.

In the experience of Aborigines, many of their friends who work with them are called "stirrers." This is a common label used by outsiders who are hoping that the Aborigines will stay quiet and docile. In our experience church workers with the people sometimes see an antagonist afar off and they act as watchmen to warn the people. Watchmen cannot keep silent; they must tell the truth about what is approaching. When the people then rouses itself, protects itself, and raises its voice in protest, those who hoped to approach by stealth will accuse the watchmen of being "stirrers."

From the point of view of the people, the real stirrers are the miscreants who are two-faced and have forked tongues—government workers who are supposed to be working for the community but who are deceitful, who withhold information, and mislead the community. They are "public servants" who think that they know best and they push the people in ways that they do not wish to go. These actions cause a stir because no one likes to be pushed, misled, or deceived.

Such trouble in the community is quite different from the way people "jump up" when they see or hear danger approaching. The Aboriginal people today want workers to tell the truth, to be people of integrity, to fulfill the biblical role of watchmen at the gate. When the cry "stirrer" is heard, it is well to ask who is using this label and for what reason. Are the people "astir" because of manipulation and lies, or are they on their feet because the truth has not been hidden from them?

There is no doubt in the Noonkanbah story that the local residents have been alerted. Resistance has already been organized. The issue to which this church committee is addressing itself is how it can side with the disadvantaged. As we discuss this story, we may well discover that, as the "church in committee" struggles to get its act together, Christ is there already:

He has sent me to announce good news to the poor, to proclaim release for prisoners and recovery of sight for the blind; to let the broken victims go free, to proclaim the year of the Lord's favor [Luke 4:18–19].

If Christ is in fact there, way ahead of us, may he in fact not be calling us from thousands of miles away? Is he saying to us what he said to the rulers of his own day, "Come, follow me?" The struggle of this committee is the struggle of someone who has possessions.

Christ is offering an open invitation to break down barriers, to discover that we are but one people, and that we belong together. This is the prayer of the Aboriginal people for Australia: "Father, make us one." It is a prayer that is being realized as justice is being realized in our land. It is a prayer that is being realized as the people of God learn to act together responsively.

JOHN MBITI

COMMENTARY ON "SACRED SITES"

Although the title of the Australian case study is "Sacred Sites," the issue behind it is of far greater importance than the geographical sites of the Aborigines that are under threat of desecration. The issue is that of genocide of the indigenous peoples of Australia by the European immigrants who began to arrive there only two hundred years ago.

Russell Rollason, information officer of the Australian Council of Churches, provides this background sketch:

> For at least 40,000 years prior to British settlement of Australia, the Aborigines hunted and gathered in a nomadic lifestyle across the vast island of Australia. It is estimated that before the white invasion, there were 300,000 people in this land, speaking 500 languages. Today, there are upwards of 160,000 Aboriginal people surviving (1 percent of the population), speaking 200 extant languages.
>
> In 1770, Britain took possession of Australia without the consent of the Aborigines and without any payment of compensation. Since then, the effect of colonization on the Aboriginal people has been catastrophic. White contact, pastoral farming and more recently mining activities have devastated Aboriginal society. . . . [Here the article refers to an international church team that visited Australia in mid–1981, at the invitation of the Australian Council of Churches. We shall return later in these comments to the findings and recommendations of this team.]
>
> For team member Quince Duncan, from Costa Rica, the destruction of Aboriginal society, which continues today, amounts to genocide. . . .
>
> The land, for Aboriginal people, is a vibrant spiritual landscape. "It is peopled in spirit form by the ancestors who originated in the Dreaming, the creative period of time immemorial," writes Aboriginal woman Marcia Langton. "The ancestors traveled the country, engaging in ad-

119

ventures which created the people, the natural features of the land, and established the code of life which we today call 'the Dreaming' or 'the law.' "

Thus land rights are basic for Aborigines and white Australia's failure to recognize the land rights of Aborigines has been a fundamental cause of destruction of Aboriginal values, culture and society. . . . One Aborigine described his feelings to the team about the white invasion of the land: "When the land is raped we feel like a man whose wife has been raped. We still love her but we feel ashamed that we could not protect her."

The most telling example of the destruction of Aboriginal society is that revealed in health statistics. . . . Life expectancy is an average of 52 years—20 years fewer than for members of the white Australian community; infant mortality is three times as high as that of the white race; anemia is 10 to 12 times more common; trachoma, a blinding eye disease, is 15 times more common; and hearing loss among Aboriginal children is up to 80 per cent in some communities. . . .

The poor health of Aborigines results primarily from their alienation from traditional food sources and adequate water supplies. Robbed of the means for their survival, and without sufficient land to establish a new economic base. . . .[1]

What the article does not touch on is that the Aborigines who lived on the island of Tasmania for twelve thousand years after the island had been severed from the mainland were completely exterminated in the last century by European settlers. In an article published in a Melbourne newspaper it is noted that Tasmania was colonized in 1803, and that the last full-blooded Tasmanian Aborigine, Truganini, died in 1876.[2] The article goes on to say that within her lifetime "the whole society was removed from the face of the earth" by the settlers and colonizers.

A documentary film, "Truganini: The Last Tasmanian," was released in 1978. The documentary information on which this film is based is an appalling example of genocide, bestiality, and criminality against human beings. There were an estimated four thousand to five thousand Aborigines from nine tribes occupying Tasmania (just over twenty-six thousand square miles) when the first British convict-colonizers arrived in 1803. Between 1820 and 1830, mass killings of the Aborigines accelerated; the government organized hunting parties and expeditions that wiped out Aboriginal groups. The last three hundred Aborigines were taken to Flinders Island, where they soon died out. Truganini, the last full-blooded Tasmanian, was one of them. Many bones and skulls of these victims were shipped to England, mainly to Oxford University, for anthropological, physiological, and anatomical studies. The building where these remains were housed was reported to have been bombed by the Germans during World War II.

To what extent the details of this background information are accurate, I have no way of ascertaining. But absolute accuracy of detail is not the issue here.

It is against this grim background that the case study of the sacred sites has to be seen. I feel deeply pained when I read about the demonic decimation that has been visited upon the Aborigines. They are God's children for whom our Lord Jesus Christ died and rose again. It is the sacredness of the human person that has been attacked and desecrated by the genocide of the last two hundred years.

Thus, the issue in this case is not so much one of "sacred sites" being destroyed, but the destruction of the people themselves who created these sites. The Aborigines have not been treated as human beings, as "sacred." Instead, they have been dispossessed; many have been hunted and gunned down; others have been put in reservations like animals, and their human rights have been violated sometimes with governmental sanction and initiative. Where does the gospel come into the picture in this case study? Is it at the end of the story, as Gary Wells sees it, or is it at the very fundamentals behind the story?

In 1770 "there were 300,000 people in this land. . . . Today [1981] there are upwards of 160,000 Aboriginal people surviving." But where are the other Aborigines and their descendants? "Then the Lord said to Cain, 'Where is your brother Abel?' Cain answered, 'I do not know. Am I my brother's keeper?' The Lord said, 'What have you done? Hark! your brother's blood that has been shed is crying to me from the ground' " (Gen. 4:9-10).

The sacred sites of the Aborigines are places where Abel's blood is crying to the Lord.

When citing Russell Rollason's article in *One World,* we mentioned the international church team that visited Australia in 1981 at the invitation of the Australian Council of Churches. The team was composed of two women and three men. Their report was published by the Australian Council of Churches under the title "Justice for Aboriginal Australians."[3]

The team traveled over six thousand miles visiting Aboriginal communities and churches, with the purpose of assessing the situation of those communities, consulting the churches in Australia, and bringing greater international attention to the plight of the Aborigines. The report was discussed by the Central Committee of the World Council of Churches at its meeting in Dresden, East Germany in August 1981.

Among other things, the report isolates seven major concerns of the Aborigines—namely, land rights, mining activities, the legal system, health, housing, education, and employment. It draws attention to the responsibility of the federal government vis-à-vis the Aborigines. The report includes a list of some seventy recommendations touching on all areas of Aboriginal life and calls for international action, Australian federal government action, state government action, and the action of the churches. Recurrent in these recommendations is the question of the land rights of the Aborigines, which obviously is the key to other concerns. It remains to be seen what will come next, in the wake of this team visit and its report. The visit may hold a promise for the betterment of Aboriginal life.

The issue of sacred sites is, therefore, to be subsumed under the much broader issue of the destruction of a whole people—together with all that pertains to them. The case study talks very much about Gary Wells, but does not tell us enough about the Aborigines from their own perspective. It does not sensitize us to their desperation. Something that touches me deeply and brings me to the brink of tears with the Aborigines are the two statements from the Aboriginal elder and the community, which come at the very end of the case study:

> . . . We got *goanna* inside sacred site. *That goanna been there from Dreamtime.* Long time before European came to Australia. That story come from grandfather to grandfather and now they still telling that story. . . . If Aboriginals give up their sites and special places *there will be no more law, no more story telling, no more initiation ceremonies. It will be like it has all gone out into space* [italics added].

These few words from the Aborigines themselves expose the whole issue in a moving way. The sacred sites symbolize the wholeness of the people—its law (socio-ethico-spiritual order), its story telling (its whole culture), initiation ceremonies (its humanness, hopes, continuity, and survival as human beings). The sacred sites symbolize and sum up the total worldview of the people, the worldview without which it cannot exist, cannot relate to the rest of the world, cannot affirm its consciousness of its own existence, cannot embrace the world. These sacred sites have been from Dreamtime, from time immemorial, the symbol and focus of the people's existence—its beingness and humanness. The *goanna* lives there, the *goanna* that they eat and hence which gives them life, continuity, and survival. The *goanna* lives there, which links them to their environment, to the world of nature, of animals, of the spirits, of the Dreamtime. If the sacred sites go, so goes also the *goanna*; if the *goanna* goes, so goes also the Aboriginal people. The people in their totality vanish "into space." There is no more Dreamtime, and with it goes the whole cosmology of the Aborigines. What is so painful is that the process of destroying the *goanna*, the sacred sites, the Dreamtime, has been taking place since the arrival, two hundred years ago, of European settlers.

The destruction of the sacred sites means that the gospel of Jesus Christ cannot come to the Aborigines. The gospel must reach them through their Dreamtime in order that they may hear it clearly, understand it without obstruction, and interact with it through the mediation of their worldview. Once this Dreamtime is destroyed, they will have nothing that speaks to the depths of their heart about the gospel of Jesus Christ. They cannot hear the gospel in empty space or through foreign languages.

It is only when Jesus says to the Aborigines "I am the *goanna* of life" that they can listen to him, understand his message, and accept him as the source and giver of eternal life. The *goanna* of the sacred sites is the language of their cosmology, of their Dreamtime. To destroy their sacred sites is to eat away their soul; it is cannibalism. The destruction of the sacred sites carves out a chasm between them and the gospel.

I do not know much about the depth of this Aboriginal worldview, Dreamtime (or Dreaming). Therefore I may stand to be corrected both in the comments I have made in the preceding paragraphs as well as in a parallelism to which I feel drawn. I am inclined to see an exciting and meaningful link between the Prologue to John's account of the gospel and the Dreamtime worldview of the Aborigines. "When all things began, the Word already was. The Word dwelt with God, and what God was, the Word was. The Word, then, was with God at the beginning, and through him all things came to be; no single thing was created without him. All that came to be was alive with his life, and that life was the light of men" (John 1:1–4). The Aborigines look continually to their Dreamtime. It is the beginning and center of everything else. They tell stories, starting with "in the Dreamtime. . . ." Is it not in this framework that the Word speaks to them first and foremost, from Dreamtime onward?

But, if that Dreamtime is desecrated, destroyed, will they still hear the Word that created them in the Dreamtime? How then will they embrace the gospel, how will they be saved by the gospel, and how will they celebrate the gospel? Because at that time ". . . there will be no more law, no more story telling, no more initiation ceremonies. . . ."

Is this "your brother's blood that . . . is crying out to me from the ground"? Is not Australia big enough for both brothers? But, immigrant Australians: "Where is your brother Abel?" Do you know?

NOTES

1. "Black Australia's Fight for Rights," *One World* (Geneva: World Council of Churches), 69 (1981): 12 ff.

2. *The Age*, Aug. 17, 1978, p. 21.

3. Sydney, Aug. 10, 1981, 91 pages.

Case Study 5

U.S.A.:
THE EYE OF THE NEEDLE

"How do you get people not only to sign a covenant for low income housing, but to seal it with their commitment and their funds?" Sue Edwards was speaking to a colleague during the monthly meeting of HOPE, a loose coalition of church leaders working for adequate housing for the poor of Springfield.

"Hope" was not what Sue was feeling as she left the session a short time later. Six months earlier, following a hotel sit-in crisis, a gathering of the newly formed organization HOPE (Housing Opportunities for People Ecumenically) numbered thirty with a good representation of bishops, executive secretaries, and presidents of church groups. However, as a Puerto Rican friend said when discussing HOPE the week before, "It looks like the power has put it to the poor again. The 'city fathers' and the 'bishops' are off the hook on housing while the Blacks and the Hispanics get co-opted." At the meeting Sue had just left, she was one of two whites. The other seven present were black clergymen.

Sue Edwards knew that the agenda of the next meeting of HOPE was for each member to make specific strategy proposals. As she drove home, she decided she would telephone some of the key figures in the drama. Many persons seemed able to share freely with her, perhaps, she thought, because she had no clout of her own.

As an elder on the governing board in the Presbyterian Church of Chesterton, Sue had become involved in the struggle for low-income housing

This case study was prepared by Robert A. Evans and Alice F. Evans as a basis for discussion rather than to illustrate either effective or ineffective handling of the situation. Copyright © by the Case Study Institute.

The names of all cities and the names of all case characters are disguised in order to protect the privacy of the individuals actually involved in this situation.

through a telephone call from the associate pastor of her suburban church of seven hundred fifty members. Acknowledging her current involvement in the city as a volunteer English teacher for Hispanics, he had urged her to join a demonstration at the Springfield Sheraton to protest the eviction of eighteen Hispanic families from the temporary shelter provided by the city. She had little idea then how her acceptance was to affect her life. She reflected now on the last six months, which were so much more involved with the problems of the inner city than the previous seven years when their family of four had lived in suburban St. Louis. In 1977, four years ago, they had moved to Chesterton, a suburb of Springfield. Sue's husband's business required him to travel a good deal, their two teenage sons were fairly independent, and her own career as a writer allowed time for volunteer involvement.

Background to the Crisis

The background to the housing crisis of Springfield, with a population of two hundred thirty thousand, was effectively summarized by a series of articles in the *Springfield Daily News*. Fifty percent of the city's population was black; 35 percent Hispanic. Springfield had one of the highest infant mortality rates of any city its size in the U.S.A., unemployment was double and triple the national average among the black and Hispanic communities respectively, only one-third of the city students who entered high school graduated, and many of them with only a fifth-grade reading level. All these conditions existed in stark contrast to what the executive director of the Council of Churches called the "white noose" of affluent suburbs that ringed the city. Among these was Chesterton, where the Edwards family lived.

The Springfield Housing Authority reported in the fall of 1980 that five thousand families were on the waiting list for public housing—nearly twice the number waiting eighteen months earlier. Another fifty-five hundred families were waiting for federal rent subsidies provided through the city's Public Housing Corporation. Another fifty families had been forced out of their apartments by fire, housing code violations, or redevelopment projects.

Gentrification

The 1980 census showed that over thirty-three hundred housing units were lost in Springfield during the past ten years. Despite the fact that this was the only major city in the state to have a decline in housing units, there was no shortage of housing for those who could afford more than $300 a month for rent. There was general agreement that the housing crisis was primarily limited to the poor.

A major factor appeared to be the relatively new phenomenon of "gentrification": developers were buying numerous units of low-income housing and turning them into large, luxury housing units for the middle class. Sue recalled a report that fifty old brownstone homes in the North End were purchased by a developer for $50,000 total; these were to be converted into condominiums with each apartment selling for more than the total original sale price. Sue also recalled reading an analysis of the process by the manager of a low-income housing project: "The huge profits go to the speculators and investors. The City Council praises the increase in the tax base, and other landlords raise their rents or convert to condominiums or abandon the buildings as not economically viable. In each case, the poor are the ones who lose."

Sue's husband Frank had openly disagreed with parts of the analysis. Though affirming the need for adequate housing for the poor, he said that "ultimately the poor will win if the city can regain a stable, middle-class base. Not only does Springfield desperately need the added tax revenue from the apartments, this kind of 'gentrification' restores fine old buildings that would otherwise be destroyed and is the only thing so far to turn the tide of 'white flight' to the suburbs. And I assure you," Frank added, "developers won't take the risk of this kind of project if there is no promise of a comfortable profit."

Sue had shared with Frank at the time that his "crisp profit logic" clashed with her understanding of social conscience. She added, "Are you sure you should be a deacon in the Presbyterian church? After all, they are committed to service."

City Hall Sit-In

Several Roman Catholic priests of Springfield held a news conference in September of 1980. Through their leadership, which included the suffragan bishop, they called upon the populace, in the name of the Christian gospel, to examine its attitude toward the poor and to support low- and moderate-income housing. The priests' statement reminded Greater Springfield residents that in Luke 16, "Jesus tells the parable of Lazarus and the rich man, who was condemned because he did nothing to help the destitute beggar [Lazarus] at his doorstep."

Not long after the priests had taken this public stand, a group of eighteen homeless Hispanic families, in cooperation with the Puerto Rican Center, decided to protest the lack of emergency housing for the homeless. Their strategy was to occupy the public meeting room of the City Council in City Hall. The "City Hall occupation" ended after city and state officials agreed to house the families temporarily at the Springfield Sheraton Hotel.

The Sheraton Hotel was owned by two prominent city corporations, which were then negotiating its sale for $4 million. The interested buyer was Fred Wilson, a millionaire developer who planned to redesign and renovate the building.

After a week, the city had not located permanent housing for the eighteen families. At this point, the corporate owners of the hotel took legal action to have the families evicted. Individuals at the Puerto Rican Center then made appeals to the priests of the diocese, to the ecumenical coalition of churches serving the city, and to suburban church members to resist the eviction and stand in solidarity with the homeless and suffering.

Sue responded to this appeal issued through her associate pastor and drove the fifteen miles into downtown Springfield to stand in the street outside the Sheraton with about twenty other supporters of the Hispanic families.

That same day a superior court judge issued a temporary restraining order barring the eviction of the forty-seven homeless persons and urged the parties involved to reach a settlement. There then followed daily demonstrations outside the hotel; Sue was involved in some of them. This picketing action drew from twenty to over a hundred participants. The situation was regularly covered by television news, and each day's happenings appeared on the front pages of local newspapers.

The Call of the Spirit

During these demonstrations Sue had become acquainted with Norman Thompson, who headed Urban Ministries, Inc. (UM). This coalition of a Roman Catholic and six Protestant congregations sponsored inner-city programming in areas of hunger, housing, health, education, and counseling. In learning about the UM mission to the city, Sue acknowledged that this innovative yoking of churches accomplished for the city what no single congregation could achieve alone. On the other hand, Norman admitted that all too often members of the seven congregations allowed the paid professional staff to "do the city ministry" for them.

When Sue asked Norman about his involvement in the present hotel confrontation, he had responded that the original request from the director of the Puerto Rican Center was "a genuine call of the Spirit, a call to action. However," Norman added, "I've got some real conflicts about this situation. The media have characterized some of these families as 'freeloading newcomers' who want to use the confrontation to jump past the five thousand people already waiting on the subsidized housing rolls—some waiting for over two years. They're being portrayed as phonies not concerned about adequate housing for everyone—but only placement for themselves.

"Now, the black city manager who placed the families in the Sheraton is related to one of our sponsoring congregations. He is already infuriated by accusations that the city is trying to avoid the issues being raised, that it cannot—or will not—find permanent homes for the families and is unable to develop a comprehensive housing plan. We ultimately need him on the side of the poor—and not as an antagonist, if that is at all possible. Then look at another side of this: the two corporations that own the Sheraton are major contributors to our UM budget. UM staff involvement in this thing is embarrassing not only to these institutions but perhaps to all of those members of our sponsoring churches who live in the suburbs. The main reason all this is so threatening is not the financial base, but that the staffs of the UM churches have been asked to give up not only power but control of the situation to these families. We have no idea what they may say or do. An invitation to solidarity means here that the families who are caught by the system will determine the strategy. We are agreeing to follow their directives—not those of their lawyers, the clergy, or leaders of the Puerto Rican Center. When we put our lives in the hands of others, it becomes more than a demonstration. It calls us to live out 'homelessness' ourselves for a moment. If this situation comes to arrest and jail, as was true in the sixties, I'm not sure if we have the commitment or the courage to hang in there. Will I release control over my life even though I'm sure of the cause—but not sure of all the motives?"

Sue recalled being startled by Norman's confession. His own lifestyle dramatically illustrated his concern for the poor. When he had become head of UM six years earlier, he and his family moved from the suburbs to the inner city. Norman, his wife Fran, and their own two children had opened their home to three racially mixed children, some with severe social problems. They were not only committed to economic change in the city but had become a strong force in the reform of the city school system. Sue acknowledged to Norman that she was only beginning to understand the complexity of the situation.

Second Sit-In

By Thursday morning, some two weeks after the eighteen families had entered the Sheraton, four families had still not been placed in permanent housing as promised by the city. Sue knew that many of the apartments made available had been found by UM staff, not by the city housing department. In anticipation of the arrival of the police to process the eviction notice, a group of a hundred persons, most of whom were church-related, gathered at the hotel entrance. A joint statement was issued by the suffragan bishops of the Roman Catholic and the Episcopal churches, by Norman Thompson as the director of UM, and by a professor of theology at the interdenominational seminary in Springfield. These representatives called on all persons in Greater Springfield to take responsibility for the housing crisis and in the name of human dignity to stop the discrimination against the defenseless poor and elderly in the city. A request was made for a new coalition between the government, business, and the churches to combat the problem.

At 12:30 P.M. it seemed apparent to Sue that the police were not going to confront the crowd, of whom about one-fourth wore clerical collars. Some UM staff members were inside with the families. It was rumored that the police were going to wait until that night when the crowd and cameras had retired. Suddenly, the closely guarded doors of the hotel burst open and it was announced that there would be a march to City Hall four blocks away; the families during the last thirty minutes had slipped out the back of the hotel and quietly reassembled to reoccupy the council chambers of City Hall. All those present were invited to join in a confrontation with the mayor and city manager. They were asked to commit themselves not to leave City Hall until all the previous promises were met. Sue joined the parade not quite sure where this action might lead.

About fifty persons occupied the city council chambers from 1:00 P.M. until about midnight. With the exception of reports of Hispanic persons "hassled" by the police for entering City Hall, the events had what one participant called an atmosphere of "empowerment and celebration" for the families involved.

Several things happened during this seven-hour period. The leaders of the four families who had made the decision about the surprise return to City Hall stated they had barred the press from the council chambers because of what they believed was "unfair coverage of events at the Sheraton." There was, however, a news conference with a statement by Hector Hernandez, who described himself as a militant Hispanic leader speaking on behalf of the families. Hernandez condemned the city, business, and media for "their neglect of all poor residents and for inadequate housing, education, and employment opportunities." Puerto Rico was described as a "colony of the U.S." used for American profit and as an "American defense base in the Caribbean." Hispanics in the U.S.A. were "expected to do menial jobs others will not take," yet they "pay more taxes, proportionally, than the wealthy." He stated that Hispanics "had inferior educational opportunities, discriminatory employment policies, and, most of all, no respect as human beings." Hernandez continued, his voice shaking with emotion: "U.S. capitalism makes profit, not people, the value. All the poor—black, white, Hispanics—are treated like animals; it only happens Hispanics come last and are the least respected." He charged the media with responsibility for "telling the whole story" not just "protecting interests of the [radio and television] stations and newspaper owners."

From her vantage point in the crowd, Sue thought the five clergymen who were asked to sit beside Hernandez looked uncomfortable at several points in the statement and during the heated exchange between Hernandez and the press that followed.

Negotiations with city officials followed, which resulted in promises of acceptable apartments for all families. This led to a celebrative, prayerful adjournment of the crowd of supporters about midnight.

In the elation that followed, Norman had shared with Sue his reaction to the outcome: "Moving the principalities and powers is what we were about. The church of Jesus Christ has been visibly present on the side of the poor and oppressed at this moment in 1980. It is for me the incarnational presence of Christ with those who suffer. The ecumenical church took on the role of suffering servant for this moment in history. It declared to the powers-that-be 'if you do it to one of the least of these my brethren, you do it unto me.' The city manager backed off. There were no arrests or handcuffs. Our presence helped humanize the process. That is what the church is for."

Mission to the Corporate Boardrooms

Sue knew, however, that others had serious reservations about what some described as the "victory" in the confrontation at the Sheraton.

For eight years Father John O'Shea had played a role as a leader of UM as well as a city pastor who held key positions in housing coalitions and regional foundations. Sue suspected that John knew his way around the city bureaucracy as well as any of the local clergy. John had what he described as "basic reservations" about the style of the hotel confrontation. "I would have wanted to know more about what was going on in the corporate world. What compromises were possible before the confrontation? The corporations that owned the hotel may have been willing to compromise and defuse the situation in a way that would have benefited the ultimate goal of housing for poor people. Some want just a fight. I want to win."

"There is danger in compromise," John admitted, "for it may allow one to avoid militancy when it is needed. I think the advent of the official church into the dialogue is extremely important. We must make a serious effort to integrate economics and theology. Many of my colleagues are shocked by my basic principle: the greatest mission of our time is the corporate boardroom. I don't automatically see business as the enemy. Business has the resources to solve the problems. We must compromise as well as confront. However, we have to make people in power aware of the problem in terms they understand.

"The Springfield priests experienced the housing problem in their own terms through contact with 'Mi Casa,' the very successful 'sweat equity' housing project in which Hispanics contribute time and labor toward acquiring adequate housing. Priests were just beginning to understand the basis of Latin American liberation theology—to be for the poor as Jesus was. However, the central factor in the priests' new awareness was a decision for each man to donate $1,000 from his personal income to establish a symbolic role for the church in the housing problem. When you add to the priests' personal sacrifice the additional promise of a $150,000 gift from the Catholic Campaign for the Development of People, you have the most important act for the social gospel in the diocese in this decade."

John emphasized, "You must remember the church is against change. Clergy are stabilizers, not confronters. Experiential theology is a big jump for priests. That is why ultimately the City Hall and hotel events were important. Catholics are authority-conscious and they saw a bishop putting himself on the line for poor people. We clergy have to learn to read the newspaper like a theology or prayer book. The confrontation became a consciousness-raising event for Catholic priests, which led to an ecumenical act in solidarity with the poor. Ultimately the conscequences may be important, but I have concerns about what the confrontation itself directly accomplished for the poor."

Public Response

Sue was perplexed when she found the bulk of the public response to the sit-ins negative, particularly to the Puerto Ricans. She made this judgment based on newspaper letters to the editor, radio talk shows, and conversations at dinner parties, grocery stores, and even church coffee hours in Chesterton. The strongest negative voice was that of the vice president of the City Council, Leonard Cohen, who attacked the Puerto Rican Center for organizing the event, and the families and clergy for participating. Cohen declared, "It is most important that we stress John Calvin's ideas . . . about the work ethic." Cohen suggested that, "If housing and welfare benefits are too generous, we will have all the homeless in Mexico City moving to Springfield." Cohen went on to introduce a resolution in city council that cited the four clergymen who had issued the joint statement of responsibility at the second sit-in. Cohen proposed that religious institutions help solve the housing crisis in the city by freeing millions of dollars they received in bequests from wealthy benefactors. Cohen referred to specific funds in the Catholic and Episcopal dioceses and accused the interdenominational seminary of destroying existing housing units to construct a new building. He concluded the statement by declaring: "Being in the housing business is not the city's function."

The city manager joined Cohen by suggesting the families' own inability to manage their welfare grants was partly responsible for their difficulty in obtaining decent and affordable housing.

Suburban Anger

Sue found a number of middle-class suburbanites angered by a remark of one of the Hispanic mothers housed at the Sheraton: "Who'll take care of us?" The response of one of Sue's friends was, "Who has the right to demand that the city take care of them?" On another occasion Sue encountered Sam Barnes, an irate Chesterton storekeeper who said that he had once rented two of his Springfield apartments to Puerto Ricans. "I'll never do that again," he declared. "Those people didn't pay the rent and then got legal-aid lawyers—supported by *my* hard-earned taxes—to take me to court when I tried to evict them. Those people don't even care enough about our country to learn English. They only want Spanish newspapers and even demand expensive bilingual school programs taken out of my tax dollars. It's about time we stopped the 'gravy train.' "

Sue felt that most of the middle-class citizens were not as angry as Sam. But on the other hand most were deeply concerned with paying their own mortgages and fighting inflation. She thought, "If you are worried about yourself, it is hard to hear the needs of others." Chesterton folk also seemed to believe what President Reagan declared, that social programs for the poor are "good intentions run amok."

Sue's husband Frank's assessment paralleled a number of the responses from her friends: "There has been a slow deterioration of the cities ever since the massive welfare programs began, as far back as the thirties. The handout system has evolved as ridiculously costly and cumbersome, open to absurd misuse by both white-collar clerks and welfare recipients, and, I believe, is ultimately destructive of the people it was intended to help. We must reverse this trend. The federal government simply can't be a cure-all. We need to find an alternative, and I believe Reagan's budget cuts will give corporations and the private sector a chance to respond to the needs of the people in a more responsible way. However, confrontations like the one in which you participated at City Hall and the Sheraton drive away potential sources of support."

Sue had retorted in frustration, "Can't you see, Frank, programs like legal aid, food stamps, and housing subsidies, which you—and Congress—seem to think are superfluous, are understood as the only means of survival by many of the poor in Springfield. How can we ask them to sit around and wait until big corporations or affluent citizens decide to toss them a few crumbs?"

Sue and Frank had gone to church that morning with the mutual promise not to discuss the issue again until they had "cooled off," only to hear the associate pastor preaching on Matthew 12:31 and relating the passage to the housing issue.

Sue recalled that Frank and other members of her congregation were disturbed when the associate pastor called on Christians, in the name of Christian love, to support low-income family housing in the city of Springfield and to initiate a low-income housing program in Chesterton to help bear the burdens of the city. During coffee hour a deacon muttered to Frank and Sue, "It is clear our associate pastor has never been a landlord. We spent the weekend cleaning up an apartment we had rented in an attempt to be helpful to a Hispanic family who recently moved to Springfield. The filth in that apartment was unreal. It may not be their fault, but these island people don't have the experience or resources to maintain a modern apartment. Low-income family housing in Chesterton would only concentrate a slum here and isolate Hispanics from their own people and language. The church should not meddle in social policy—especially if it is ill-informed."

Sue responded as best she could to interpret the need of those inadequately housed in Springfield, but felt patronizingly ignored. She regretted that Orlando Gonzalez was not present to give a more persuasive response.

Economic Structures

The Rev. Orlando Gonzalez had been one of the persons Sue had come to know during the demonstrations. He had told her, "We are not foreign people in a foreign country." Gonzalez was pastor of a Hispanic congregation that shared the facilities of one of the UM member churches in the city center. Born and educated in Puerto Rico, he had come to Springfield in 1975 to serve as the pastor of a small Hispanic congregation. Several of his family members were already residents of Springfield. Serving as a bridge between the Anglo and Hispanic communities during the hotel encounter, Gonzalez moved from a retiring position to a more active role in ecumenical city ministry. Several months after the sit-ins, his congregation became an official UM member.

One cold November morning when Gonzalez and Sue were standing outside the Sheraton, they discussed the negative media image Gonzalez felt had been portrayed of the Puerto Ricans in the hotel. He asked, "Why do people refuse to understand that Puerto Ricans are American citizens and that Puerto Rico is a commonwealth of the U.S.A.? Puerto Rican and other Hispanics contribute in a significant way to Springfield. We pay taxes far beyond our fair share."

Gonzalez's comment reminded Sue of a study by the state university that showed that those who earned $5,000 a year in this state, paid 18.4 percent of their income in taxes. However, if they earned $50,000 a year, they paid only 7.6 percent in taxes. The study concluded that the burden of taxes in Springfield and in the state was on the poor.

"If we did it, why can't they?" was the question Sue found raised again and again by the affluent middle class. Professor Lopez, a Puerto Rican at the state university, agreed that, "People assume poverty is a matter of lack of incentive, determination, or aggressiveness." He, however, argued that "poverty is systemic. There are elements of our economic system that maintain poverty. For instance, in the U.S., 20 percent of the people earn 50 percent of the income; 60 percent of the people earn 45 percent of the income; 20 percent of the people earn 5 percent of the income." Lopez suggested that it was no surprise where the Hispanics and Blacks fell on this scale: "Whereas the annual median income for all U.S. families was approximately $17,000, for Blacks it was $10,000, and for Hispanics only $8,000." Lopez indicated that the statistics were even more startling if one considered control of U.S. wealth: "6 percent of the people control 57 percent of the wealth, and 44 percent control only 2 percent."

Queuing

Lopez indicated that an integral part of the whole economic picture was the system of "queuing." Sue did not remember all the details of the theory, but essentially it held that the last immigrant group "queues" behind the social power and economic control of the former groups in line. The historical control of income is modified slightly, but poverty is maintained for the low-skilled, low-educational level immigrant group. They are needed by the affluent to do jobs—"dirty work"—that the more affluent resist. Also the new poor carry a disproportionate tax burden because they do not have the funds or knowledge for tax write-offs, loopholes, and exemptions. The tax exemptions for home owners and landlords are prime examples of how even the middle class benefits from their place in the system.

Sue thought about the historical queuing pattern in Springfield with successive immigrant groups: Irish, Jews, Italians, southern Blacks, and Hispanics. When economic times are hard, the last group to queue suffers unemployment and deprivation of even minimal social benefits offered to keep them reasonably content doing physically demanding, low paying, often seasonal work. However, in Lopez's words, "If local labor gets too expensive, then businesses ship out manufactured goods to be assembled in Hong Kong or Taiwan. The queuing system thus effectively maintains poverty, because one keeps alive the myth, especially for new groups, that if new arrivals try hard enough, they too can break through and make it big in the system. So we highlight the token millionaires, professionals, or government representatives from the queuing groups."

To counter this understanding, Sue could hear Frank declaring that the present federal programs of high taxes and a welfare state were hindering the normal process and "preventing the lower classes from entering the mainstream." In his words, "A healthy economy *will* create more jobs. Puerto Rico itself is a prime example. Because of the tax advantage on the island, numerous companies are now building plants. Jobs are being created and the immigration tide is reversing, with many Hispanics returning to Puerto Rico. In the same way, as businesses move to the suburbs, we will have a slow but steady stream of minorities moving out to find jobs. This way they will be absorbed by the community in a nondisruptive way."

Sue had understood that 70 to 80 percent of Puerto Ricans in Puerto Rico made use of food stamps and that jobs were scarce, with low wages. But this conflicted with Frank's ideas, and so she did not raise the issue with him. She decided she needed to do more research.

The Challenge

In Sue's judgment it was Cohen's public challenge to the churches following the sit-ins that initiated the formation of a loose coalition or, as members preferred to say, "a movement" of religious leaders for human dignity through housing. In his role as the vice-chairman of the City Council, Cohen issued a public statement to the institutions linked with four of the protest leaders to the effect, "put up or shut up." All four, without prior consultation Sue understood, responded to Cohen's challenge as if it were a genuine call for cooperation between the city and the churches to solve the problem.

An ad hoc informal group of about twenty persons who had been involved in the demonstrations gathered in the Episcopal House to chart a response to Cohen a few days after his statement and about a week after the second council chamber occupation. The group agreed to attempt to meet on a monthly basis.

HOPE

There were three turning points in Sue's mind that shaped the formation of HOPE. First was the decision of this group of twenty to seek more significant cooperation with the black religious community inasmuch as only two black leaders had been involved in the occupation. The move to join with the Black Clergy Association (BCA) expanded the composition of the group and moved their meeting location into the inner city. According to the chairman of BCA, black and white church leaders prior to this had had little history of sustained communication or cooperation.

Secondly, the organization now called HOPE arranged to be on the agenda of the next City Council meeting to respond to Cohen's challenge. Almost a hundred Christians from city and suburbs attended this meeting and stood in solidarity when the Catholic bishop read a statement. He rejected the direct use of church bequests for housing because "these had legal restrictions." However, he pointed out that the leaders of HOPE sought concrete forms of cooperation with the City Council and its committees. Following the council meeting, one council member interviewed by the press stated that the conversations had "opened up new lines of communication and established a more cooperative stance." However, no specific programs emerged.

Thirdly, the members of HOPE developed a statement of theological rationale based on a draft by two seminary professors. This document was discussed and revised by members of HOPE. A letter accompanying the document stated it was intended as a guideline statement as a basis for bonding, not a confessional statement to be exegeted line for line. The focus was on the God-endowed human dignity that makes adequate housing a human right. However, the statement pointed out that the problem of poverty was larger than that of housing, which was only an entry point to the systemic issues. The document called for an advisory board composed of a variety of affected persons and groups, ranging from the poor to business, labor, and government representatives. The document also summoned commitment from religious institutions in the form of (1) expertise based on a number of low- and moderate-income housing projects previously sponsored by churches, (2) personnel, and (3) funds. The document appeared in January.

It was now May, and except for the Roman Catholic gift from the Campaign for Human Development projected before the formation of HOPE, there had been no major, concrete contributions toward low-income housing.

No Serious Commitment

Following the May meeting of HOPE, in which members were challenged to construct concrete strategies, Sue began to call key church leaders whose opinions she valued.

"Rich churches in America will not do anything on their own about housing." Sue was listening to the Rev. James Phillips, pastor of St. Luke Methodist Church in Springfield's North End. Phillips had spent fifteen years as a black pastor in the inner city. "Those highly endowed city churches put a little change in UM, but they aren't going to do the big project until they are forced to. When you moved the HOPE meetings to the North End and out of Episcopal House, and the bishops and executive secretaries started sending their representatives, we should have known we were in trouble. That took the pressure off the power. Did you see how much respect the bishops got at the City Council meeting? If only ordinary black or Hispanic pastors are present, the disrespectful attitude is shameful. The one black member of the council pointed out the same contrast."

"If we really want to affect housing, before the developers buy up the North End," Phillips continued, "then the churches, the rich churches, need to do a *real* model low-income housing project. Our previous George Washington Carver project simply concentrated our poor people and their problems.

"We must also fund such services as health, social work, and welfare as a part of the project. People move into Springfield from the Caribbean Islands and the deep South. They need assistance and training to adjust to an urban setting. The people cannot be blamed for deteriorating housing. The church's pattern of partially funding and then abandoning people in these projects is worse than patterns in public housing. If we are really serious about housing for the poor, then we need a model project to dispel the doubts of those who use the negative argument as an escape. It is always too complicated, too slow, or too something, to demand a priority decision."

The Search for Allies

Phillips continued to reflect on the current situation: "Those in the ghetto don't have full-time allies. You can be 'ghetto' or 'middle-class'—but not *both*. Most city employees and officials live outside Springfield, in the suburbs. There are no real alliances inside the city. Blacks and Hispanics aren't closely related. It is no surprise there were few Blacks involved in the hotel occupation. They didn't see it as their fight. Puerto Ricans don't want to be identified with Blacks, and Blacks look down on Puerto Ricans. We just introduced a Spanish-speaking pastor and service at our church and the resistance among my people has been high. Five break-ins have occurred at our church in the last few weeks. Our people suspect Puerto Ricans.

"You add to all this the impact of the Reagan administration on the black community and it is devastating. Survival services are being abolished. Also cut is international development aid, which means many black brothers and sisters around the world will suffer. We talk about being a generous nation, yet we give in aid less than one-fourth of one percent of our gross national product. In terms of percentage-sharing, this puts us next to last of all the industrialized nations of the West. Yet I don't hear the church responding to any of this. Many of my people have now become so middle-class they are home owners and tenement owners. If they talk about the Reagan administration at all, it sounds like good old white folks talking about protecting their property and their investments. I don't think the church has a serious commitment to transform the problems of the poor. Strategy is almost impossible if you are counting on the middle-class black or white churches to help."

Occupation Strategy

Feeling discouraged about how she or the middle-class white church she represented could respond to the housing issue, Sue then turned to her new friend, the Hispanic pastor Orlando Gonzalez. Gonzalez linked the Sheraton and City Hall occupation strategy to the black protests of the 1960's by quoting the former president of the State National Association for the Advancement of Colored People: "It won't solve any problems, but it does attract attention."

Gonzalez noted that in recent years Hispanics had "become more outspoken than Blacks in pursuit of goals like better housing because many Blacks have become too comfortable."

Orlando declared, "Next to acceptance as full contributing human beings with a right to dignity and respect, the priority for Hispanics is housing. Springfield really wants to be a model city—one with no poor Blacks or Hispanics. We embarrass the city, but unfortunately for them we do necessary work.

"The most obvious result of the Sheraton sit-in," Orlando continued, "was that the Puerto Rican Center lost all of its federal funds. City Councilman Cohen not only managed to cut off all federal community development block grant money of those agencies that were critical of him, but he also tried to get United Way to cut off funding. If you fight the powers, they will silence you. The problem is we lack unity and understanding between Blacks and Hispanics. Blacks look down on Puerto Ricans as new immigrants who compete with them for funds and jobs."

Need for Unity

Gonzalez continued, "Hispanics relate to white bosses in 'rebellion with fear.' Hispanics are afraid to use their vote. The Hispanic population is divided among different candidates. So rather than choose one who represents the interests of our people, we choose one with personal political ambition to make it in the system. Then he can't help us because he becomes too indebted to that system. Unless we unify our vote, which we must decide to do for ourselves, we will not be able to put into power candidates who have a commitment to our causes.

"The only good thing that came out of the Sheraton event was HOPE. The church has some unity here, and because of this we may have a chance to affect the city. The only enemy the church has is itself. If it fails to act for the poor, this will be out of self-interest for its own institutional survival. The trouble is, the leaders don't really trust each other enough; perhaps God will give us trust as a gift of the Holy Spirit."

On the Brink of Social Chaos

As she began to prepare her family's evening meal, Sue decided to make her last call one to Dr. Curtiss Wilmore, an African Methodist Episcopal pastor who was now in education work and was one of the blacks present on the Sheraton picket line and present at the last meeting of HOPE. "Those struggling for survival can't see others' views, can't applaud the gains of others," Wilmore proposed. "Blacks felt the hotel occupation was a Puerto Rican issue and therefore did not identify with those who could be natural allies. The powers in the city cultivate this lack of cooperation. If people can be kept divided by fighting over a limited number of grants, jobs, or houses, it keeps them off the back of those in control. I am not sure whether community leaders self-consciously discourage coalitions or whether that just occurs.

"Look what has happened with HOPE," Wilmore continued. "In the hotel and city chamber occupation, the church showed concern for the poor. In fact it put itself on the line to get shot at and Cohen fired. HOPE has brought an offensive posture to the encounter and that is important.

"However, look at our last meeting of HOPE. There are too many different agendas. This is still a fragile ecumenical coalition. More important, where are our white and Hispanic brothers? Is it bad communication and too many personal agendas, or is it more than that? In housing we don't need conversation, we need houses for low-income people of all races. The priority is to lobby business and government and to get them involved in specific projects.

"In my opinion," Wilmore continued, "the government scene is a disaster. Reagan's actions on the budget will be devastating for the poor. The energy companies raise prices and profits while Congress cuts controls and fuel assistance. People are out of work and unable to pay rent and utility bills. UM has been swamped with calls for help over the past three months. The growing pressure may crush the instinct to survive. The present government attempt to turn back the clock," Wilmore predicted, "will lead us to the brink of social chaos."

The Church Must Agitate

Wilmore added, "The church must agitate, not just consciousness-raise. Reagan claims he has a mandate. The church must test that mandate. If Reagan does indeed have one, then 'Lord have mercy on us.' But the white church has never been revolutionary. Maybe that is why our white brothers, especially the bishops, are so busy lately. Let's face it; the poverty program is dead!

"However, middle-class anger may enter the picture. When people learn the Reagan tax cuts are no help to the poor, little help to the middle-class, and extremely beneficial to the wealthy, then the middle-class may revolt with the poor. Reagan says that business will reinvest in social programs and the state will take up the federal slack, but that is a fantasy with no basis in history.

"The white church," Wilmore warned, "has a chance in HOPE if it becomes a community in solidarity with poor people. If we act as a group to take a prophetic stance, we may be able to take the shots. No significant impact of the gospel as a social phenomenon has had an individualistic base. Civil rights and anti-Vietnam war movements were not based on personal salvation, but on God's will as perceived by the community. Blacks learned that to save souls one-on-one means your body still belongs to the oppressor. You may be saved but are not whole. You can't have freedom on the installment plan."

Arms Stampede

In trying to assess the impact of the Reagan policies on the poor of Springfield—an issue raised by Phillips, Gonzalez, and Wilmore—Sue's mind kept returning to the administration's target to receive the bulk of the $68 billion that would be saved by the cuts: the defense industry. This issue had been raised during the UM-sponsored conference on peacemaking last March. Sue now recalled some of the data as she sought to envision how a strategy for peacemaking might affect the Springfield housing situation.

It was clear in the presentations that the social service cuts would ultimately supply arms to support procapitalist governments such as those in Brazil and El Salvador or to build SSN nuclear attack submarines to add to the U.S. firepower capable of destroying the USSR eight times over. Sue also learned that the world spends $450 billion a year on armaments and the U.S.A. represents one-third of the total. The major powers manufacture weapons so deadly and sophisticated that they have moved from deterrence to preemptive first-strike capacity.

The figures always overwhelmed Sue, but what she had learned was that there was a direct relationship between armaments and the issues of urban ministry. Was the cost of that one trident nuclear submarine—$1.2 billion—worth eliminating all the food stamps, school lunches, and rent subsidies in Springfield for the next several years? If the Reagan budget, with social service reductions and defense increases, went through, it could mean that the number of Americans living below the poverty line would go from 7 to over 20 percent, with malnutrition in the U.S.A. likely to be on the rise again.

When Sue came home with euphoric reports on the conference and the call to peacemaking, Frank challenged her with the reality that their state had the highest per capita dependence on the defense industry in the U.S.A. The clear implication of peacemaking for their state was that of a direct challenge to job security for thousands of workers.

Strategy for HOPE

The conference on peacemaking and the conversations with community leaders had raised what Sue felt were critical questions, yet ones she was reluctant to face. Was the issue really the system and not housing? If persistent discrimination against the poor maintained the self-interests of the affluent, then was there any real possibility of change coming from the middle class? Sue could not imagine her affluent neighbors abdicating either their comforts or their power. Was it not fruitless to even attempt to change the historically established economic patterns Dr. Lopez had illustrated?

In the same way, if the churches were also captives and promoters of the system, there seemed to be no acknowledgment of it and certainly no attempts to change. The status quo worked too well for established churches. As Norm Thompson had said at the last HOPE meeting, "It's back to business as usual. We still have no long-range plan. The bonding we have established won't impact the powers. We're not tithing, not sacrificing—not even challenging our own institutions."

Sue felt the drain of energy and the resistance of her family and friends. Everyone agreed there was a housing crisis. Even the mayor could say that without fear of rebuke. The issue was strategy for change and at what cost. Wilmore reminded her that "everyone, including the clergy, is still thinking more about what is fiscally feasible, not what is best for people at any cost. Poor people are considered ultimately transformable or expendable."

A simple, comfortable, gradual solution of the problems for poor and middle class is what Sue confessed in her heart she wanted. No one else should suffer needlessly. She wanted O'Shea to be right about negotiation in the corporate boardroom as the real mission field of the church. It seemed more constructive and yet more distant. Wilmore's prescription of agitation in social chaos was more threatening and yet seemed dangerously futile. HOPE was *becoming* a community, but was not one yet. Could it really be a Christian community in solidarity with the poor and oppressed? Was the better strategy to agitate or negotiate?

As Sue thought about the next meeting of HOPE, now only a week away, she was a little overwhelmed. The problems were so massive, complicated, and systemic. How could one take concrete, practical action in the name of the gospel to feed and house the suffering? Who should she believe, or support? Or should she just retire for the summer?

Norm Thompson kept raising the most uncomfortable issue for Sue by his own lifestyle as urban-centered, autoless, in an interracial family, struggling with the city and the church. The "eye of the needle" was Norm's question. "Do rich men and women, which most Americans are in the global context, really want to pass through the eye of that needle to enter the kingdom of heaven? Jesus said, 'Sell everything and give to the poor.' "

Sue was tempted to answer, "Not everything Lord—not yet anyway. First we've got to think about the kids' education, retirement plans, and institutional continuity." Maybe she had been co-opted during the last six months or had she been converted? Is this what Wilmore and Thompson meant by solidarity with the poor?

Just then Sue Edward's sixteen-year old son, yelling from the outdoor grill, broke into her thoughts. "Mom, the steaks are burning!"

TEACHING NOTE ON "THE EYE OF THE NEEDLE"

The next meeting of HOPE is one week away. Sue Edwards confronts several issues as she discusses the housing situation with a number of friends and acquaintances and seeks to develop a strategy for community support and action.

A. *Housing:* Various church and international organizations have declared that equality in access to housing is as fundamental as the rights to food and education. The process of gentrification and special tax concessions to corporate builders highlight the conflict between the rights of the middle-class to economic gain versus the right of the poor to affordable housing.

B. *Racism:* Within this case racial stereotypes are expressed by suburban home and apartment owners; there is also racial tension between ethnic minorities competing for the same jobs and funds. This raises the issue of minority rights and equality of opportunity.

C. *Corporate Strategy:* The strategies of confrontation, negotiation, and evolution are all introduced, raising the issue of how political and religious groups bring about change.

D. *Individual Responsibility:* Individuals such as Sue Edwards are challenged to examine their responsibility for making personal life-style changes as a response to the need for justice and equality for the poor.

CASE PLAN

1. Enter the case by outlining the sequence of events from the November City Hall occupation to the May meeting of HOPE. Discuss the situation which precipitated the original sit-in. What factors appear to have led to the present impasse within the organization?

2. List the key persons with whom Sue Edwards speaks. (Be sure to include Sue's husband Frank.) Develop the position each takes and examine the preconceptions and implications of differing positions.

In order to focus on the question of strategy, invite participants to become members of a lay and clergy meeting of Urban Ministers, headed by Norman Thompson. A member of the group has proposed another sit-in to stop the city's condemnation of a large privately owned tenement building and subsequent eviction of its residents. Divide participants into small discussion groups of three or four persons with the task of returning to the larger group in a specific time (e.g., 10 minutes) with specific recommendations.

142

3. In order to focus on another aspect of individual responsibility, develop the group's understanding of Sue Edwards. (What has the group learned about her from her actions and reflections in the case?) Sue asks her church study group to help her think through her role in the inner city and to help her consider any changes she could or should make in her own lifestyle. Ask participants to offer specific advice to Sue out of their understanding of the Christian faith.

SUGGESTIONS FOR ADDITIONAL READING

The Affordable Community: Growth, Change, and Choices in the '80s. Washington, D.C.: HUD, 1981. Write to U.S. Department of Housing and Urban Development, Washington, D.C. 20410. Ask for publication HUD-PDR-675.

Goodman, Robert. *After the Planners.* New York: Simon and Schuster, 1971.

Hartman, Chester; Keating, Dennis; and LeGates, Richard. *Displacement and How to Fight It,* 1981. Write to the National Housing Law Project, 2150 Shattuck Ave., #300, Berkeley, CA 94704.

Housing Choice: A Handbook for Suburban Officials, Non-Profit Organizations, Community Groups, and Consumers, 1981. Write to Metropolitan Action Institute, 424 West 33rd Street, New York, NY 10001.

Noyce, Gaylord B. *Survival and Mission for the City Church.* Philadelphia: Westminster Press, 1975.

People Who Care: Making Housing Work for the Poor. Write to Prentice Owsher Associates, 1522 Connecticut Ave., Washington, DC 20036.

Sternleib, George, and Hughes, James W. *America's Housing: Prospects and Problems.* New Brunswick, N.J.: Rutgers University Center for Urban Policy Research, 1980.

Taking Charge: A Process Packet for Simple Living, Personal and Social Change. Can be ordered from Simple Living Program of the American Friends Service Committee, 2160 Lake St., San Francisco, CA 94121.

Tonna, Benjamin. *Gospel for the Cities.* Maryknoll, N.Y.: Orbis Books, 1982.

ORLANDO E. COSTAS

COMMENTARY ON "THE EYE OF THE NEEDLE"

As a Puerto Rican who lived for many years in a city like Springfield, I can empathize with the struggle of the eighteen families for decent housing. Indeed their plight is not only representative of the urban poor across the nation, but is unquestionably an American variant of the world struggle for human rights.

Likewise, the response of the mainstream sectors of the Greater Springfield society is reflective of their counterparts in other cities. On the one hand, a majority with deep-seated prejudices based largely on their own economic interests and plain socio-cultural ignorance; on the other, a minority with a sincere concern for and a growing awareness of the roots of the problem, but almost incapable of making a deep-level response.

I can even understand the cool reaction from the black community. It reflects the growing need for improved relationships between racial minorities throughout the major urban areas of the country.

Lastly, I am not surprised at the ambiguous and impotent response of the church. It is a tragic and telling reality, considering the challenges that the church faces in urban American society.

These are the issues that in my opinion are raised by "The Eye of the Needle." In the following paragraphs, I want to comment on each of them in the hope of clarifying the meaning and challenge of human rights in the U.S.A.

Traditional approaches to the question of human rights have focused on individuals and their political rights. Thus, for example, both the American Declaration of Independence (1776) and the Universal Declaration of the United Nations (1948) "defend the interests of citizens as free individuals, free producers, free proprietors."[1] Such has been in fact the emphasis of Western capitalistic nations.

For the socialist/Marxist world the focus has been on the collective rights of human beings. For these nations the traditional approach is too restricted,

144

abstract, and ideologically conditioned. They put their emphasis on "the creation of conditions in society which make it possible for all human beings . . . to practice their personal, political, and cultural, but also economic and social rights."[2] Thus they give greater weight to the International Covenant on Economic, Social and Cultural Rights than to the International Covenant on Civic and Political Rights, both of which were adopted by the UN in 1966.

Interestingly enough, however, both the capitalist and socialist blocs have been reluctant to apply any other category than "political" to the problem of refugees. To be sure, each has a way of dealing with refugees; they treat them from either their individualistic or collectivistic point of view. But both recognize *political* refugees only, and refuse to acknowledge as such those who become exiles because of economic or socio-cultural conditions.

This is why in most sectors of the Third World the question of human rights is not dealt with in either capitalist or Marxist terms. Indeed for the Third World human rights have to do with the right to survival in the face of famine and national disasters, and liberation from colonialism, poverty, and cultural overpowerment. Jan Milič Lochman is thus correct in stating that in such a world human rights means "primarily a demand for life-sustaining conditions for work and nourishment, for an improved balance of life-opportunities between the poor and the rich, for elimination of exploitation within national and international frameworks."[3]

It is well known that not only has the American government restricted human rights to individual and political rights, but has been unwilling to accept the fact of Third World-like situations on its own turf. Although it has received with open arms Cuban, Laotian, Cambodian, Vietnamese, and Eastern European refugees (political refugees), it has refused to legalize the Mexican, Haitian, Dominican, and Central American undocumented workers (socio-economic refugees) on its territory.

The case in question presents a socio-economic/cultural human rights situation. It highlights the reality of a poverty-stricken people in an American city. Puerto Ricans have been American citizens since 1916, but their homeland is one of the last vestiges of colonialism in the western hemisphere. The eighteen families were most likely established in Springfield for many years. They probably settled in the area during the two decades following World War II, having been brought in as hired hands to work on nearby farms. After their contracts had expired, they settled in adjacent cities and towns. The situation in Springfield is typical of the entire eastern seaboard and the midwest.

We are not dealing simply with latecomers and foreigners, but with American citizens and low-income residents in an urban setting where society has failed to meet the housing needs of a minority. As a result, these persons have had to live at the mercy of absentee landlords who exploit their meager financial resources with badly kept, rat-infested apartments. Some of them simply had nowhere else to go. The eighteen families acted out of desperation.

All of this takes place at a time when city after city is making adequate housing provisions for the well-to-do (the "gentry"), believing that the urban future lies with the creation of affluent neighborhoods. If cities can be in the "housing business" (as developers, promoters, or investors) for the "gentry," why can they not do the same thing for their poor citizens? Could it be that American cities are reverting to a neo-Hellenic concept of democracy where only certain persons are citizens with rights? Indeed they are! The urban poor in Springfield and elsewhere appear to have no rights, because "rights" are defined politically and individually, but are *determined* socio-economically and culturally. Thus everyone has the right to invest and own property. Governments make it easier by easing the tax burden and the legal red tape. But the only ones who can take advantage of such a right are the wealthy who have the resources to invest in commercial housing and those whose education has allowed them to compete for higher income-bracket jobs that enable them to buy or rent expensive housing in exclusive neighborhoods.

The fact of the matter is that government serves the interests and needs of the majority in the Springfield area (and indeed all over the U.S.A.), not those of the poor and disenfranchised. Hence, the question of housing for the poor is in fact dealt with in terms of *class interests,* not *ethical responsibilities*—a response reminiscent of the greedy majority in Judah and Israel (Jer. 8:10) "who oppress the poor and crush the destitute" (Amos 4:1).

The plight of the urban minorities is not simply one of economics, but also of racial stigma and cultural chauvinism. In the U.S.A., class conflicts have tended to pass through the "color line." It is therefore no surprise to hear representatives of the dominant sectors of society talk about Puerto Ricans in disgusting terms. Their language reveals a racist attitude, characteristic of mainstream American society throughout the last century and a half. What is said, directly or indirectly, of Puerto Ricans (they are "dirty," "irresponsible," "lazy," "free-loaders," "intruders") has also been said about Blacks, other Hispanics (especially Mexican-Americans), Asians, and native Americans. Indeed this color bias represents the most fundamental difference between contemporary urban minorities and the minorities of past decades.

Several years ago Eduardo Seda-Bonilla, a Puerto Rican anthropologist, pointed out that for European migrants the process of adaptation to North American life and culture started at "a point in which the group boundaries, the 'differences,' were drawn according to ethnic or cultural characteristics in contrast with the surrounding 'American way of life.' " As a means of cultural survival, there flourished Little Italies, Germantowns, Irish shantytowns, Scandinavian and other similar neighborhoods in the major cities of the nation. When the inhabitants of these slums had become "American" enough—that is, when they had adapted "the American way of life," when they had become part of the American melting pot—"most of them moved away leaving their golden streets for the racially discriminated group, who [remained] to inherit the filthy, overcrowded, crumbling tenements left behind by the 'ethnics.' " Whereas the only thing European ethnics had to do to be part of the mainstream was to discard their old way of life, for the non-

European minorities "adaptation" makes no difference. Once the European migrants' "cultural identity subsided under the American cultural identity, the door to the 'silent' or socially invisible world of the majority was open, because they were 'white.' " For the other minorities,

> . . . identified on the basis of "racial" stigma, shedding the cultural items that distinguished [them] from the American culture and taking over [its] identity made no difference whatsoever. If anything, it made things black with a foreign accent styled after an alien way of life more attractive than the "native son." . . . Perhaps deep in their hearts majority Americans want to racially stigmatize groups to remain alien, to feel alien; out of sight, out of mind—with a memory of a home somewhere else where "white" Americans hope [these groups] will eventually return.[4]

In Springfield and surrounding communities, the reaction of the majority to the City Hall/Sheraton incident was blatantly racist. But it was a racism that passed through the "linguistic" line. The reaction was not motivated simply by the fact that Hispanics were, in their mindset, "nonwhite," being *mestizos* (that is, brown, or a mixture of Amerindian, African, and European peoples), but also that they were *non-English-speaking,* or at best bilingual.

Behind the ideology of "manifest destiny," language (English) has been almost as important a component as the "ethnic/racial" (White Anglo-Saxon) and "American national experience" variables. Indeed, the monolingualism that has characterized mainstream American society stems from the fundamental belief that English is a language superior to Spanish, French, or any other. Hence there has been a traditional distaste for Hispanics, whose very cultural identity is defined by language. (Hispanics are those who trace some aspect of their cultural roots to *Hispania* [the Iberian Peninsula] and speak Spanish or Portuguese, which became the leading languages of the peninsula and Latin America.) This explains why Puerto Ricans in New York and surrounding communities were first called "Spics."

Given the historical reality of racism (and linguistic chauvinism) in mainstream American society, it is all the more admirable to see Sue Edwards, Norman Thompson, John O'Shea, and the other white representatives of the Urban Coalition standing in solidarity with the eighteen families. In so doing, they did not just show human compassion, but prophetic courage. They became countercultural, a disturbing sign of protest that earned them the dislike of their class peers, but also the appreciation of the eighteen families.

Yet the problem in Springfield was not simply between the Anglo majority (which controlled the means of production, political power, and cultural institutions), but also between Blacks and Hispanics. The lack of solidarity on the part of the black community is very telling. Blacks either saw it as a Puerto Rican issue or as a questionable, suspicious move to gain advantage over the many black families that also needed housing.

That Blacks and Hispanics have not had close working relationships is a well-known fact of contemporary urban life. On the one hand, Hispanics feel intimidated by the capacity of Blacks to articulate eloquently and forthrightly their protests. Because they have to communicate with the majority society through a "borrowed" language, it is natural that many Hispanics would feel threatened by a rhetoric they neither understand nor can match. They further complain that when Blacks have gained some power, they have been slow in sharing it with other minorities. Hispanics fear that Blacks may simply want to "use" them to get ahead in the struggle for a better way of life. Accordingly, Hispanics have sought to develop their own strategies and carry on their struggle independently.

Blacks, on the other hand, have been suspicious of Hispanics. For them, Hispanics seem to court "whitey" too closely. Indeed, for many Blacks, Hispanics appear unwilling to be associated with "people of color"; Hispanics see themselves as "white." Moreover, the fact that Hispanics speak a "foreign tongue" makes Blacks uncomfortable—it intimidates them. Hispanics are also competing with Blacks for similar jobs, houses, schools, and other crumbs that the majority society deems fit to throw them. In the ghetto, it appears as if the law of life is the "survival of the fittest." Most of all, many Blacks feel that they have been struggling against the system for some three hundred years and that Hispanics, as newcomers, should join their cause, not compete against it.

Thus, each group has been suspicious of and a threat to the other. Yet, both are victims of the same oppression. They share a common experience, even if they have different cultures. Moreoever, the fact that they have not been able to join forces has put a tremendous strain on their common struggle. Ultimately, failure to work together has benefited the system. Therefore, if they are ever to be emancipated from the ghetto, they have no choice but to learn to work together.

One would have to be blind not to see how much Hispanics have benefited already from the black struggle of the 1960s. The process of reverse acculturation initiated by Blacks has had a tremendous impact on other racial minorities, especially Hispanics. Hispanics owe them the courage to take dramatic measures (such as the City Hall/Sheraton incident). Blacks have been pioneers in "pressure tactics" in the city.

On the other hand, Hispanics are not totally helpless. They are conscious of their numerical (and thus political) strength. Nor are they inexperienced newcomers. They bring to the city a history of revolutionary struggle in their Latin American homelands. Accordingly, they have their own unique ways of doing things, and insist on being treated as equal partners in the process of human liberation in the city.

Both communities have a lot to give each other; they also have a lot to prove to each other. But the challenge before both is that either they "clean up their act"—settle their differences and start working together—or there is not going to be anything left for anybody!

Caught up in the dialectic of the Springfield City Hall/Sheraton incident is the church. It reflects the same class, racial, and interethnic reality outlined above.

The majority church, represented by Sue Edwards and her husband, the members of their congregation, all those who supported the Urban Ministries, Inc., Norman Thompson and John O'Shea, expressed its class commitments by its ambiguous attitude and impotent response to the eighteen Puerto Rican families. By and large this church reacted *against* the homeless families, though some of its leaders sought to help without understanding how or, even worse, without having the power to do something significant. The minority church, represented by Orlando Gonzalez, Curtiss Wilmore, James Phillips, and the Black Clergy Association, though advocating the cause of the poor and outcast, reflects, nevertheless, a middle-class mentality. It limits its presence to ministers (paid professionals); its membership does not appear anywhere.

Apart from the fact that the minority church is a sign of social and cultural marginalization (and therefore a protest against a racist mainstream church), it is no different than the majority church when it comes to class: both are middle-class institutions and express, consciously or unconsciously, its interests and values. Is it any wonder why so few individual Christians and church bodies in HOPE committed funds to low-cost housing? Or is it any wonder why so many poor persons seem to have lost hope in the institutional church?

Middle-class churches have been increasingly alienated from the urban poor. They have become, directly or indirectly, agents of the middle class's economic interests and value system. Yet these churches have had to contend with the gospel commitment to the poor and the oppressed, its passionate denouncement of personal and social sin, and its anticipation of a new order of life where justice, peace, and freedom will prevail. In this context, they have been torn between their vested class interests and values, and the gospel.

This dilemma comes out quite vividly in the Springfield case study. The church, as a prophetic institution, finds itself perplexed and embarrassed by the "witness" of the eighteen families. They represent the poor, the powerless, and the oppressed of the city, the state, the nation, and the world. They are prophetically knocking at the church's door, calling it to a bold and courageous stance vis-à-vis the powers that be. This challenge is received with indifference, even anger, by the greater part of the institutional church. But some of its leaders and a few local churches feel morally, theologically, and missiologically compelled to respond affirmatively to the cry of those on the fringes of society. They create HOPE, a coalition that seems promising for black, Hispanic, and Anglo church involvement, but with relatively little success in mobilizing the resources of the church for the solution of the housing problem.

For all the good intentions of the members of the coalition and of persons such as Sue Edwards, the challenge of the wretched of Springfield proves to be too circumscribing—indeed "the eye of a needle"—for the middle-class churches and Christians of Springfield to squeeze through! Do we not find here a parable of the tragedy of the institutional church in the U.S.A.? Yes, indeed! Has not this church betrayed the gospel (theologically *and* socially)? Of course it has! Can there be any hope for such a church? Only in God's grace! "What is impossible for men is possible for God" (Luke 18:26).

This fact keeps us from becoming victims of pessimism and despair. Indeed amid the seemingly gloomy atmosphere of the case, we can see several rays of hope.

The eighteen families represent a courageous, positive effort in the Hispanic community, which has a track record of social passiveness and political inertia. These families bear witness not only to their own community but also to all oppressed minorities that human liberation requires fearless and implacable struggle. They might not have won the battle, but they managed to dramatize their plight and make the cry of the oppressed in Springfield heard in the centers of power. In so doing they helped to advance the struggle for human rights.

The case also demonstrates the need for racial minorities in the U.S.A. to work together. It challenges the leadership to move beyond past differences and find ways for their respective communities to join hands and struggle together for a just and peaceful world.

Finally, the narrative shows that even among oppressive majorities, one can find committed prophetic minorities that dare to cross the boundaries of racial prejudice and class interests to stand in solidarity with the oppressed and to work for their liberation. And as long as there are such committed Christian minorities among oppressors, there is hope for the humanization of society, the liberation of the institutional church, and the respect for the right of every human being to enjoy the basic necessities of life.

NOTES

1. Jan Milič Lochman, "Human Rights from a Christian Perspective," *Christian Declaration on Human Rights,* Allen O. Miller, ed. (Grand Rapids: Eerdmans, 1977), p. 15.

2. Ibid.

3. Ibid.

4. Eduardo Seda-Bonilla, "Ethnic Studies and Cultural Pluralism," reprint from *The Ricans: A Journal of Puerto Rican Thought* (1969), pp. 2–3. See also Seda-Bonilla, *Requiem para una cultura* (Rio Piedras, P.R.: Editorial Boyoam, 1974), p. 251.

J. DEOTIS ROBERTS

COMMENTARY ON "THE EYE OF THE NEEDLE"

Many inner cities in the United States are on the verge of strangulation. Springfield, which is the city of our case study, is a sterling example. Eighty-five percent of its people—the black and Hispanic communities— are concentrated in the inner city. Unemployment and poor housing have intensified infant mortality, inadequate education, and other ills that afflict the young. Left to itself, the result can only be a self-perpetuating situation of hopelessness and abject poverty.

Chesterton, on the other hand, is described as one of the affluent suburbs that ring the inner city. Sue Edwards, who is the main character in our case, is a concerned church leader who favors better housing for the poor of Springfield. It is to be noted that she lives in Chesterton. Her involvement may be traced to the fact that she is an elder in the Presbyterian Church of Chesterton as well as volunteer English teacher for Hispanics. Her involvement came gradually. The real beginning seems to have stemmed from a suggestion by the associate pastor that she join a demonstration to protest the eviction of eighteen Hispanic families.

Springfield's housing crisis is severe, with thousands of families on the waiting list. The matter is made worse by the process of gentrification: developers buy up low-income housing, which is then turned into luxury apartments for the middle class. Huge profits go to investors. Landlords raise their rents or convert to condominiums. In some cases buildings are abandoned. In all cases the poor lose out. Sue's husband, Frank, who is a businessman, takes a rather pragmatic view of the situation. He sees the movement of the middle class back into the city in terms of increasing the tax base. Frank also bows to the need for developers to realize a comfortable profit. Sue, however, reminds him of his deaconship and the requirements of a social conscience. The dialogue reminds us that correct ethical decisions are not always easy.

What we see clearly is that the poor cannot entrust their welfare to the hands of the establishment, even the religious establishment. Key church

151

leaders are, too often, more interested in pronouncements and press conferences than in taking a stand with the poor. Grassroots movements are crucial in such instances. The eighteen homeless Hispanic families occupied the council chambers at City Hall.

The decision to house the homeless families at the Springfield Sheraton Hotel adds fuel to the drama. The corporate owners of the hotel were on the verge of selling the building for $4 million. The potential buyer was a millionaire developer who expected to renovate the building. These same corporate owners contributed to the Urban Ministries (UM) group, which is to take a bold stand with the poor. This entanglement of loyalties and commitments demonstrates again the ambiguities in which Christians must sometimes make decisions.

Even in joining coalitions of Christians who strive for the alleviation of social ills, one must choose carefully. In Springfield there appear to be two types of church organizations concerned with better housing. One is HOPE (Housing Opportunities for People Ecumenically). It is made up of bishops, executive secretaries, and presidents of church groups. This organization seems to be primarily the powerful in the church speaking for the powerless. Although they say the right things, there seems to be a lack of solidarity with the poor. It is easy for this type of organization to make trade-offs and compromises. Siding with those in power, such organizations usually end up against the poor.

There is another organization in Springfield that appears to be more "with it." The UM, headed by Norman Thompson, is more congregation-oriented. Its director lives among the inner-city poor. It is an ecumenical body, but is consciously grassroots in composition. Sue Edwards rightly perceived this group to be more effective as a witnessing agent.

Sue discovered that the poor had made a decision that called upon her for a commitment to their cause. The families victimized by the system were to determine the strategy. She was being called upon to join them in their struggle. She experienced a "homelessness" herself. She was sure of the worthiness of the cause, but could she go so far as to give up control over her life for it? This was perhaps the most profound insight into the gospel she had ever experienced. She had discovered what it means to stand in solidarity with the oppressed.

Four Hispanic families remained homeless. Eviction was a continual threat. The UM stood solidly with the families. The police were called in to evict the families. But even they were reluctant to take on the crowd. The demonstration moved back to City Hall, after the families had quietly slipped out the back of the hotel. By this time Sue had joined the movement and felt called by the Spirit to follow the action to its resolution. After a seven-hour sit-in at City Hall, the families were relocated in apartments. Sue experienced an "empowerment and celebration" for the families.

Norman Thompson's reflection on the situation puts the incident in theological perspective:

Moving the principalities and powers is what we are about. The church of Jesus Christ has been visibly present on the side of the poor and oppressed at this moment in 1980. It is for me the incarnational presence of Christ with those who suffer. The ecumenical church took on the role of suffering servant for this moment in history.

Unless Christian social action is to be limited to crisis-response episodes, there must be a serious study of each situation. Father John O'Shea's concern for dialogue is not to be ignored. Theology does need enlightenment from economics, political science, and sociology. Business ethics must be considered. Churches need to become concerned about the social responsibility of major corporations. City Council member Leonard Cohen correctly points to the need of wealthy congregations to share their wealth with the poor. The poor need to become more responsible in job seeking and the care of property. There is a need for pastors to become more "worldly-wise" and better informed, in order that their sermons might be more effective in dealing with such matters as inadequate housing for the poor. Our seminaries must go deeper into pastoral care if we are to be effective in these matters.

As Sue returned to her husband, her fellow suburbanites, and the power structure, she became aware that she was not prepared for the task she faced. The homework she assigned herself after the City Hall confrontation should have been part of the preparation for her involvement. The facts she gathered from Rev. Orlando Gonzalez, Fr. John O'Shea, and others are necessary prerequisites for effective social witnessing. We see the need, therefore, for ministers and laypersons alike to be well informed as well as dedicated in this ministry of liberation. The reason why it was so easy for Councilman Cohen to issue a counterchallenge to the churches ("put up or shut up") was that the churches were ill-prepared to take on the housing crisis.

There are very important reasons why Blacks and Hispanics must learn to work together. In conversations with Pastor Orlando Gonzalez and Rev. James Phillips, a black pastor, Sue discovered the tension between the two oppressed communities. One reason for this tension is that they must compete for the means to survive. Racism and greed in the power structure are destructive to both. Reaganomics will tighten this economic noose. It will be up to the leadership in these two oppressed communities to gather their people together around a common struggle for liberation.

The revitalized HOPE in Springfield should dedicate itself to this task. It is good that it included more Blacks, made a theological statement, and decided to meet the Cohen challenge. The task of Black-Hispanic cooperation is fundamental to the solution of the housing crisis and other social ills in Springfield. There needs to be not only solidarity *with* the oppressed, there needs to be solidarity *among* all oppressed groups for their common freedom. Blacks who have a measure of creature comforts must not alienate themselves from the black masses or other powerless groups. The gospel read and pondered in the black churches will support this general concern.

Dr. Curtiss Wilmore, an African Methodist Episcopal pastor, sees promise in HOPE. It has shown its concern for the poor. He is aware that federal funds were lost, but an important moral victory was won. The churches had taken an offensive posture. But he was correct in assuming that most white churches are reactionary. HOPE gives these churches a chance to identify with the cause of the poor. The gospel, he urges, must take on a prophetic role. It will not be effective socially if it has only an individualistic base. He says: "Blacks learned that to save souls one-on-one means your body still belongs to the oppressor. You may be saved but are not whole. You can't have freedom on the installment plan."

Sue learned that much of the money being cut from social services by the Reagan administration was to be plowed into the defense industry. She then observed that peacemaking might affect the Springfield housing situation. Upon further reflection she noted that her state was deeply involved in the defense industry. To cut back on that industry would upset the job security of thousands of workers. It was clear, however, that the system—not housing— was the real problem. It was also apparent that the status quo worked only too well for the established churches. The poor were considered expendable; the better-off, including church leaders, were mainly concerned about what was financially rewarding. There is a housing crisis today, but what is the better long-range strategy: to agitate or negotiate?

For Sue, as for most Christians, the matter comes down to individual soul-searching. It is symbolized by the "eye of the needle." Norman Thompson raised the issue for Sue in concrete form through his family lifestyle. He moved into the inner city and added children of another race to his family. The question is, Are you willing to pass through the eye of the needle to enter the kingdom of heaven? Jesus' question haunted her: "Are you willing to sell everything and give it to the poor?"

Sue Edwards' answer, "Not everything Lord," is the honest answer of most well-off Christians. We must first consider our family security and the continuity of our institutions. And yet we are also called to solidarity with the poor. As we face the hard decisions that our faith demands, our cry must always be: "Lord, I believe; help thou my unbelief!"

This case study deeply probes the awesome demands of the gospel of liberation. It is a call to decision, action, and transformation of one's own lifestyle as well as the social order. We discover how difficult and involved decisions can be. There is no room for self-righteousness. In these matters all have sinned. We are challenged to study as well as to act. Quick action is sometimes the needed response to a crisis, but there is also a need for action with long-lasting repercussions. Dialogue as well as confrontation, negotiation as well as agitation, may be what is needed. The all-important thing is to accept the challenge of the gospel of liberation in solidarity with the oppressed.

Case Study 6

SWITZERLAND:
I WAS A STRANGER

Swiss pastor Hans Keller looked up from the open Bible and the notes he was preparing for Sunday's sermon and gazed out the window of his study. He simply could not concentrate. The visit with Pierre Gauvin yesterday afternoon continued to disturb him.

Pierre, an old friend from university days, now worked in another Swiss canton for the social service arm of the Reformed Church of Switzerland. He was in town on business for a few days. In the course of their conversation, which centered on Pierre's present ministry, Pierre had strongly urged Hans to speak from the pulpit about the plight of the migrant worker, saying that the issue was a veritable "time bomb" not only in Switzerland but in all of West Europe where "every seventh person is a migrant." Pierre had concluded, "As Christians we have no choice but to denounce our government's policies, which are as blatantly restrictive as South African apartheid."

Hans recalled his own angry rebuttal of Pierre's stance. He told Pierre that he sounded "more like a Marxist every day! We can't help it if we attract these people. They need work which we offer; they need the food, shelter, and money that we supply. Switzerland is a tiny country with few natural resources. If we do not protect our borders, thousands of uneducated, unskilled immigrants will flood in, destroying the very stability on which their jobs depend. The gospel does not call us to sacrifice the rights of a whole society for the needs of a few."

This case study was prepared by Alice F. Evans and Robert A. Evans as a basis for discussion rather than to illustrate either effective or ineffective handling of the situation. Copyright © by the Case Study Institute.

Hans Keller, Pierre Gauvin, and Alfredo Maletta are names disguised to protect the privacy of the actual persons involved.

Background

As Hans worked through his feelings about the encounter with Pierre, he thumbed through a sheaf of pamphlets his friend had left behind. One article traced the background of the present Swiss immigration policies. Statistics indicated that in 1850, when Switzerland had a number of reciprocal "friendship, commerce, and residence" treaties with other nations, only 3 percent of the resident population was foreign-born. Foreigners exercised the same rights as Swiss citizens: freedom to enter and depart from the country, and freedom to work and select housing. However, following World War I the foreign population rose to over 40 percent in border cities such as Basel and Geneva, and over 14 percent in the country as a whole. As the job market tightened with the subsequent depression years, laws were written to regulate the flow of foreigners.

A 1931 law established various work categories. A foreign worker could apply for a permit as a daily worker (*frontalier*) and enter the country each day from the border states of Germany, France, Austria, Italy, or Liechtenstein. This type of permit also covered those who were given short-term contracts—of one or two years. A second category was that of the seasonal worker (*saisonnier*), who was allowed to enter the country for a period of nine months and had to return home for the other three months of the year. In 1954 the period of residence was extended to 11½ months for certain jobs. These persons worked under Permit A. Under this permit a man's wife or family were allowed to visit briefly, but could reside in the country only if they were of age and had their own work permits. Even then, in some situations, husbands and wives had to live in separate quarters with set visiting hours. As of 1972 wives of migrants who had underage children were not allowed work permits at all.

The law also stipulated that migrant workers must work in the same canton and at the same job. A 1974 updating of this law stated that application to change jobs would be authorized "only if no Swiss citizen or resident alien can be found" for the position. Migrants were not allowed to rent their own apartments but had to live in barracks or furnished rooms chosen and rented by the employer. At the beginning of each "season" the worker had to undergo a health examination at the border.

Another category, introduced later, allowed a worker to apply for a Permit B after four consecutive years of work in the same job. This would allow a worker to change jobs and to live year round in Switzerland. After fifteen consecutive months of work, one holding a Permit B was then allowed to apply for a permit to bring in family members. A Permit B had to be renewed annually. After ten years under this permit, a person could apply for a Permit C, which guaranteed one's right to remain in Switzerland. The years one worked under a Permit A, whether consecutive or not, did not apply to the residence requirement for a Permit C. However, workers from Belgium, Holland, France, Great Britain, Iceland, Liechtenstein, and Scandinavia were given only a five-year waiting period.

In checking another pamphlet, Hans learned that in 1978 the majority of the migrant foreign workers in Switzerland came from Italy (98,302), Spain (42,052), Yugoslavia (29,421), France (41,961), and West Germany (27,377). An additional three hundred thousand foreign workers had by now received residence permits (Permits B and C) and lived year round in Switzerland with their families. These added up to nearly seven hundred thousand foreign workers in a work force of three million.

Looking at statistics on different years, Hans realized that the total of migrant workers was currently some three hundred thousand less than it had been prior to the recession of the early 1970s . In contrast one chart indicated that in 1974 only twelve thousand Swiss were unemployed. Hans knew that there had been three national referendums on the issue of foreign workers between 1970 and 1974. Sponsored by the National Action Party, the proposals sought to apply more stringent limits on the entry of foreigners, to expel a percentage of those already living in Switzerland, and to increase the percentage of migrants (Permit A). Though all of the proposals failed, Hans noted that in the past few years the number of workers allowed a Permit B was lower than before, now averaging only ten thousand a year. Hans recalled Pierre's point that in an "economic crunch" the current system allowed the Swiss to "export" their unemployment. Employers who needed to cut back their work force could simply refuse to renew migrant workers' permits.

It was mandatory for all Swiss and foreign workers to pay dues to an unemployment fund. However, in case of a bankruptcy, those under Permit A would receive benefits only up to the time when their contracts would end. By law they must then return home, with no further compensation. Those holding a Permit B could receive benefits for a longer period, but risked having their annual application revoked if they did not find another job.

Hans tossed the pamphlets back on his desk and reached for the telephone. He smiled to himself as he realized that he was responding to his unrest just as Pierre had jokingly predicted he would. Pierre, still in conference at the central church offices, agreed to meet Hans for lunch and indicated he would like to bring a friend.

Two hours later as they settled into the back booth of a modest neighborhood restaurant, Pierre introduced Hans to Alfredo Maletta, an Italian who had worked in Switzerland for over eleven years. After the men ordered, Pierre encouraged Alfredo, who spoke understandably but with a distinct Italian accent, to share his own story with Pastor Keller.

Alfredo Maletta

Alfredo's family had lived in the mountains of southern Italy. When the arid, rocky land was no longer fertile, his parents left their small farm and moved down to the plains. Alfredo stayed behind in their mountain village and from the age of six worked as a farmhand and shepherd. He later moved to the city with his sister and her husband. There he worked as a painter, a waiter, and a construction worker. He also attended school until he was eighteen. Alfredo added that he had been very lucky; these had been years when the government "put a great deal of money into education."

In September of 1970 Alfredo came to Switzerland looking for work. He entered the country as a tourist using his Italian identity card, found a place to sleep, and became a "black worker" in a meat cannery. In Switzerland there is no set minimum wage. Rather, the pay scale is established between the union, if there is one, the individual employer, and the employees. Alfredo accepted a salary of 1200 Swiss francs a month (in 1970 approximately U.S. $300). Though low by Swiss standards, Alfredo said that this was more money than he had been able to earn in Italy. The average monthly salary of the Swiss workers in the plant was 2,100 francs. Alfredo estimated, however, that as many as one-half of the workers in this particular plant had no working papers.

When Hans expressed surprise at this information, Alfredo smiled and said that "even now in 1981 there are more than 10,000 'black workers' in Switzerland. The workers dare not complain or organize for fear of expulsion; their employers benefit from the low salaries."

The following spring Alfredo searched for outdoor manual labor for which he had some training. He located a construction company that agreed to hire him based on his previous experience. The company provided him with the necessary papers to procure a Permit A. Alfredo added that many of the larger firms send "middle men" particularly to Spain, Italy, and Yugoslavia to enlist seasonal workers. These workers then arrive in Switzerland with papers in hand. By law they must live in housing provided by their employer.

Alfredo continued, "I have seen some of this housing. Often these are large dormitories or barracks where one has no privacy. There are often as many as four men in one room. They have inadequate plumbing and cooking facilities. They have enough rent deducted from their salaries by the employer for these facilities that together they could afford a much better place to live. Instead, they must live in these conditions. Even some of those who have a Permit B continue to live in these barracks though they are free to rent an apartment."

When pressed by Hans for reasons why those with permission would not seek better housing, Alfredo continued, "It is very hard to find housing and the rents are enormous. Many do not speak the language and are afraid to venture into the cities. Consequently, they stay in 'safe' but inadequate housing, becoming increasingly dependent on the employer. Though it is not allowed, many of the migrants bring their families and hide them in these squalid barracks and apartments. They live like rats.

"It is often the women who suffer the most. They seek undocumented jobs to supplement the family income and they are often exploited beyond belief. Neither they nor the children have medical benefits, and the children who are undocumented cannot attend school. The women who do have work permits receive lower salaries for the same work.

"The children are another matter. There are more than ten thousand undocumented children in Switzerland. They are not sure what world they belong to. This is also true of the tens of thousands of registered children of foreigners. Many become more at home with Swiss culture than with that of their parents' homeland, but they are stamped as foreigners with no right to remain if the parents' permits are cancelled. This is true even of migrant children who are born here. But marriages in which family members do not live together suffer from the strain of months and even years of separation. The children grow up not knowing their father or mother. This is not right."

When Hans asked why the migrants did not organize to seek better living conditions for themselves, Alfredo responded that less than 10 percent of them were organized in any way. By Swiss law migrants are restricted from any political activity, and many local Swiss trade unions "want nothing to do with them" even though membership dues to the trade unions are automatically withheld from the migrants' salary whether they are members or not. "Many migrants are uneducated; they speak only their native tongue. Even those who want to learn the other language must do so at the end of a long day's work, and on their own time. Many jobs do not require the language of the employer, and the workers live and work almost exclusively with other migrants. Most also come to the cities from a rural life and are afraid to speak out or even join a group for fear of losing their work permits."

Alfredo continued, "I worked for one construction company for over three years. There were several layoffs of migrant workers. An employer has a right to dismiss workers without giving any reason. I also found the working conditions to be harsh, even dangerous at times. A friend and I tried to organize the workers to protest. In late October, during a hard rain that made working on the structure hazardous, about fifty of us refused to work. The following week the Spanish migrant who had worked with me to organize the workers—both of us were fired. We got no support from the Swiss union. I had only a few months of work left before I could apply for a Permit B. It was late in the building season. I returned to Italy and knew I would have to begin all over again on my four consecutive years if I wanted any assurance of regular work under a Permit B. You ask why migrants don't organize? Those who struggle for their rights must pay for it personally."

Pierre, who had nodded his assent to Alfredo's statements of the restrictions that bind migrants, urged him to continue his story. "When I returned to Italy I had very mixed emotions. The pay in Switzerland was good, but I was angry about the inequality between workers. During those years of work, my pension payments, taxes, medical insurance, and union dues—all were deducted from my salary by the employer. This was about 25 percent of my salary. The same amount is deducted whether I have no family or six children at home to support. Yet Swiss citizens can have deductions based on the size of the family. If I am injured on the job and I cannot work at all, and I then return to Italy, I will receive no benefits. Though there is a health examination as we enter the country, there is no examination when we leave. If we have contracted an illness related to our work, we are not entitled to health insurance benefits after we return home. And if I work all my life in Switzerland, paying the same pension as a Swiss, when I am sixty-five and I return to Italy, I receive my pension based on the much lower pay scale of Italy, not on what I actually contributed. Someone pockets a handsome profit." Alfredo added that the pension payment differential was sanctioned by a mutual agreement between Italy and Switzerland.

"I feel that we are used by the more affluent countries of Europe. They need us to do the jobs their citizens do not want. We are the street sweepers, house servants, hotel help, and manual laborers. Our labor brought great prosperity to Switzerland in a booming economy after World War II. But when times are not prosperous, we are shunted back home with less regard than unwanted baggage gets. Even after ten years of living in Switzerland on a Permit B, it can be revoked in some cantons by a local official who thinks you have been involved in anything suspect. Only in Jura, the youngest of the Swiss cantons, can migrants vote on community or cantonal issues. And this is only after ten years of living and working there.

"I was very discouraged by these facts and decided I did not want to return to Switzerland, yet I also realized once again how difficult it was to get work in Italy." Alfredo recalled the strong pressures on many friends with families who felt they could not provide adequately for their families in rural Italy. Husbands, fathers, or mothers would migrate to northern Europe to send back money to support the family. He had also learned from co-workers from Turkey and Portugal that their home governments even subtly encouraged workers to leave. These countries relied on migration not only as a remedy for unemployment but needed the funds sent back home from abroad. Without this money, Turkey's deficit spending, in particular, would be much greater than it is. "The governments of rich and poor nations have placed migrants in an unrelenting vise."

Alfredo said that after several months at home he became determined to return to Switzerland and become actively involved in establishing unions for migrant workers. He said that he did not want to become a Swiss citizen or be "assimilated" into Swiss culture. This would imply that his Italian heritage was somehow inferior. Alfredo concluded by asserting his commitment to migrants who live, work, and pay taxes in Switzerland, yet live in constant insecurity with limited, unequal rights and have no voice even on issues that concern their work.

Pierre told Hans that since Alfredo returned in 1976 he had worked at several jobs in the construction industry. When his political activity became known, he was often fired, but he stayed with friends who then helped him procure other jobs. Alfredo had been extremely active in the formation of a new nonnational trade union and was now working half-time as the secretary of that organization. Alfredo added that last year after he had married a naturalized Swiss-Italian woman, he had applied for and received a Permit B.

He had fulfilled the four-year requirement earlier and applied for the permit when he and the woman were living together, but it had been denied with no reasons given. Alfredo indicated, however, that even with the Permit B he still had to be very careful. If he broke the law or if he was considered to "endanger national security," he could still be expelled from the country.

Hans then asked Alfredo if he saw the role of the church in any way connected to the struggle for migrants' rights. Alfredo replied, "To many in the church my concerns smack of socialism and Marxism. I must admit that some of my most dedicated workers understand their struggle from a Marxist perspective. The established church often reacts so violently to these ideas that it is a hindrance, not a help, to us. I feel there are priests and pastors such as Pierre who are concerned for us on humanitarian grounds, but I do not think the church wants in any way to become involved in economic or political causes. The work I am involved in is not theological, it is practical. I am on a practical search to respond directly to problems. My work with the new union is important because I am fighting for the rights of workers who have no voice. We are committed to the whole picture of seasonal workers, to help them develop initiative through solidarity and to fight for new and more just laws. Our goal is to mobilize general opinion to put pressure on Parliament. None of this is on the theological level of the church."

Role of the Church

Alfredo needed to return to his union job; Hans and Pierre, however, agreed to stay and talk a while longer. The men all shook hands and both Pierre and Hans expressed their appreciation to Alfredo for coming. As Hans watched Alfredo leave the restaurant, he turned to Pierre with a smile: "You see, even Alfredo believes the church has no role in the issues of migrant workers. He neither wants nor seems to need the church's help. He is also a perfect example of the fact that in our free Swiss society a migrant—even one with an illegal job record—can make it if he's willing to put in the effort!"

Pierre was silent for a few moments as he stirred his coffee. He looked at Hans and spoke slowly. "Hans Keller, I can't believe you really feel that way. Alfredo is an exceptional man with exceptional ability. I believe Christ calls us to be for those who cannot help themselves."

Hans replied, "All right, in all seriousness, Pierre, that was a glib response and one that clearly doesn't reflect my awareness of the depth of the problem. But it still has a lot behind it. I really do believe in the democratic process we have; I believe that as citizens and as Christians we have a right and an obligation to vote for issues that protect the common good. I am also genuinely caught between some new insights on the migrant issue and the mind of the people to whom I minister.

"I can just hear my parishioners responding. Look at some of the individual issues Alfredo mentioned. If we do away with the migrant family restrictions, an uneducated, untrained southern migrant is free to bring in his wife and ten children. In all likelihood the family would soon be overwhelmed.

They are not aware of the cost of living here, or of the cold of our winters, or how to function in our society. When the head of the household is unable to support them, must we assume this responsibility? Even with the high level of our taxes—the 25 percent Alfredo mentioned as taken from his salary—our social services are strained. It is more responsible for us and more loving to insist that family members remain in their homeland until a worker has established a home and is adjusted to our culture.

"Should we have unrestricted entrance by workers? Look at the angry racial conflicts in Germany against the Turks and the atrocious attacks by teenage toughs in Sweden against the Iranians. In London there are open riots in the streets led by thousands of displaced migrants. When there is a recession, those who are on the lowest economic rung are the first to lose their jobs. If they go on welfare, they are accused of laziness; if they continue to work, they are accused of stealing jobs from the Germans or Swedes. It's a vicious circle we've so far avoided by not opening the floodgates. I believe the racial tension created is much more dehumanizing to both sides than are the policies that control entrance. Whether it is sinful or not, this 'protection of our turf' is a natural human reaction when a country's citizens fear they will be swamped by foreigners. No amount of legislation can force their acceptance.

"I must be honest with you, Pierre. There's no way I can convince my parishioners to grant voting rights to those who don't care enough about our country to seek citizenship. True, Alfredo pays taxes, but in return he receives the many benefits of Swiss stability. He is willing to take from our society, but this refusal even to seek citizenship implies he is not willing to give in return. I suspect one of his primary reservations is the mandatory annual military commitment of all Swiss male citizens.

"Now you and Alfredo have clearly educated me about the living and working conditions of some migrants, which seem to be deplorable. I agree that as Christians we must be concerned for these persons, but the Christian church is a collection of individuals, and as a pastor I need to respond to them on an individual basis. In our suburb there are only a few migrant workers. I believe it is my role as pastor to speak to the conscience of my parishioners to care personally for those who work for them. My wife gives clothes and food to a woman who helps her clean once a week. But would it be loving to encourage this woman to join some socialist group that would get her deported? I may be able to gather a group of women in the church who are willing to work with a language program to help our migrants adjust more easily. If these migrants come to us seeking food or shelter, I am also convinced that as Christians we must help them. These kinds of things are possible. On the other hand, the migrants who work for the neighboring chemical companies are predominantly Roman Catholic or Muslim and have no relationship to our parish whatsoever."

Pierre interjected, "What about your ministry to those managers of the chemical companies?"

"It is true that some of the managers are in my parish. But as you well know, our parish units coincide with our political units. Consequently, I have ten thousand official members of my church. Because the church is supported through a system of national taxation, neither my salary nor my position is jeopardized if I speak out on issues. However, 'speaking out' does not imply that I am able to reach any of these company managers.

"If I begin to espouse political solutions from the pulpit, that's the surest way of turning away those managers, if and when they set foot in the church. I am not personally threatened by the Marxist ideology or the Marxist support behind much of Alfredo's new union movement. But many of those in power in Switzerland, including those managers, are convinced that elements in this movement are counterproductive, even destructive, to the strength of the country as a whole. The members couldn't turn me out if I addressed these issues; they'd simply turn me off.

"Pierre, it is as a citizen that I vote and it should be as a citizen, not as a pastor, that I speak out on concrete political and economic issues. In all honesty I believe my voice is much stronger when I speak as a citizen. You have convinced me that as citizens we may need to work to see that the laws of this country are more just, particularly in terms of unemployment benefits, migrant housing, and pensions. These are all issues for the voters. But it is impossible to legislate full equality. We are not born equal—by aptitude, ability, even income. And we can't make it so even if we want. God never intended us to be equal in this way. Jesus himself said, 'The poor you will have always with you.' So in my sermons I can give examples of issues dealing with the migrants to sensitize my parishioners to the needs of the poor around them. But I believe it is not right for me to suggest political solutions from the pulpit. I just don't see how that can be the role of the pastor. In contrast, you, Pierre, have a special role and office to speak for the church on these issues and you do it well."

Pierre smiled at his friend. "Hans, think carefully about what you're saying. Aren't you really suggesting that the church can use me and my office to buy off its conscience? Is your response to individuals rather than to the system based on your critical analysis of your effectiveness as a pastor or on your timidity to tackle the system? I am convinced that the issues we are discussing go right to the fiber of our nation and strike at the heart of the gospel. This means every Swiss and every Christian must respond on much more than a 'sensitizing' level to what I perceive as a diabolical, systematic violation of human rights.

"As a country we prosper at the expense of brothers and sisters in Christ who are born in less fortunate circumstances. We have created laws to lock them into those jobs and into stations in life that serve us best. True, at birth we are endowed with certain abilities and aptitudes. But as Christians, isn't it our responsibility to try to enable everyone to develop those abilities to the fullest?

"I believe our faith calls us to be *un*democratic; it demands sacrifice on the part of those who have for those who have nothing. The church has been silent too long. We need to shout the relevance of our faith to the Alfredos, and to the plant managers, and to the housewives. Together we must denounce a system of profiteering and privilege. Hans, we are not a collection of individuals. We are the body of Christ. And Christ calls us to serve the people of God—not just those of one nationality.

"I have always been moved by a quote from St. Ambrose: 'You are not making a gift of your possessions to the poor. You are handing over to them what is theirs. For what has been given in *common* for the use of all, you have abrogated to yourself. The world is given to all, not only to the rich.'

"Now it *may* be correct to assert that our government needs to exercise legitimate authority to care for the good of its people and its institutions, and I add as a footnote that our prosperity should not be at the expense of the basic human rights of those from poorer countries. I say 'may' because St. Ambrose—and my growing understanding of the gospel—are pushing me. Do we as Christians have a right to set up *any* barriers? Granting others 'entry permits' and 'work permits' implies that these can be withdrawn. I have been impressed by a treatise on human rights and migrant workers by Daniel Perrin. He notes with some skepticism that we are not nearly so restrictive with foreign permits for multinationals and investors as we are with permits for those who are powerless. We open our doors to those who add to our coffers. The root issue, however, is to question not only our selection process but our right to limit the freedom of others in any form. I've even been pushed to ask if citizenship itself isn't a fundamental discrimination of human rights."

Hans glanced at his watch and murmured that he needed to return to his study for an appointment. He then paused and looked at his friend. "Pierre, I hear your struggle. But you are an unrealistic idealist who looks for the coming of the kingdom right here and now. I feel the suffering of others and the injustice of elements in our society, but that doesn't mean we dispose of the society. As Alfredo would say, 'Your concepts are theological not practical.' What you seek is not only impractical, it is impossible."

Pierre reached out and warmly gripped his friend's hand. He responded slowly, "Human rights is not a matter of practicality, economics, politics, or laws. It is a matter of basic human dignity, and this is a matter for the church. I have a feeling you have heard some of what I have said. I noticed in your study yesterday that you are preaching Sunday from Matthew 25:35. 'I was a stranger and you welcomed me. . . .' I should like to know how you interpret this passage. Can you in all honesty interpret it only to imply limited, practical service to those 'strangers in our midst'? I believe the gospel asks for much more."

As the friends parted, Pierre called out, "I'll see you on Sunday."

TEACHING NOTE ON "I WAS A STRANGER"

Though the clear legal regulations for Swiss migrants provide a solid background for discussion, this case raises issues of migrant workers far beyond the borders of Switzerland. Several themes for consideration could be:

A. The rights of a migrant minority to work versus the rights of a national society, or, in terms of the Introduction, survival rights versus individual, political rights.
B. The unique dilemma of migrant women.
C. The role of the church in political and economic controversies.
D. The responsibility of governments of both rich and poor nations for their own citizens and those of other countries.

CASE PLAN

1. In order to clarify the current Swiss migrant worker policies, list the basic regulations which Hans and Alfredo raise. Identify those areas where the labor policies differ for Swiss residents. What is the rationale for this discrepancy?

2. Develop the character of Alfredo Maletta. What were his reasons for entering Switzerland? Why did he remain? Probe his possible feelings as he moved between Italy and Switzerland. Move the discussion to the general living situation of migrants under Permit A. What were Alfredo's particular concerns about the role of migrant women?

3. Develop Alfredo's and Hans's contrasting positions on the rights of migrant workers. Discuss how their concepts have been shaped by their life histories.

What is the basis of Pierre Gauvin's understanding of migrant rights? Outline the major points of his position. Consider a role play between Hans and Pierre as they discuss Hans's statement: "The gospel does not call us to sacrifice the rights of a whole society for the needs of a few."

4. Alfredo declares that "economic and political causes" are not "on the theological level of the church". Would you agree? If not, why? If so, what should the role of the church be?

5. Consider the role of a specific congregation such as Hans's. Should the congregation be limited to the role designated by Hans? To what extent is his response based on the environment of the Swiss church? (To what extent

should the role of any church in society be determined by that society?) Should a Swiss congregation have a role in interpreting a national referendum, or should this be left to the political sphere of the citizen as voter? (To what extent would this question apply to any church or citizen?) Consider the voice of factory managers within the Swiss congregation. What might be the basis for their resistance to policies espoused by Alfredo?

6. What does Alfredo mean when he says that "the governments of rich and poor nations have placed migrants in an unrelenting vise"?

Consider a role play of a study group faced with Pierre's question, "Is citizenship itself a fundamental discrimination of human rights?"

7. Read aloud Hans's sermon text Matthew 25:35. What are some of the implications of this text for the church as it deals with the worldwide issue of migrants? Consider what Hans might say on Sunday morning.

SUGGESTIONS FOR ADDITIONAL READING

"Migrant Workers and Human Rights: A Selection of Documents for Study and Action," Dossier Number 8. Geneva: World Council of Churches, February, 1980.

"Migration Today: Current Issues and Responsibility." This magazine is published by the World Council of Churches. Write to Migration Secretariat, World Council of Churches, 150 route de Ferney, 1211 Geneva 20, Switzerland.

Padrun, Ruth, and Guyot, Jean, eds. *Migrant Women Speak.* London: Search Press, 1978.

Perrin, Daniel. *Human Rights and Migrant Workers.* Geneva: Centre Europe—Tiers Monde, 1978.

THERESA MEI-FEN CHU

COMMENTARY ON
"I WAS A STRANGER"

With Hans lies the burden of decision: should he or should he not preach the cause of the migrant workers from the pulpit? He seems to have decided in the negative. But the difficulty he has in arriving at the decision is indicative of the depth of his doubt and of his realization of how complex the issues are.

Pierre's arguments must have affected Hans greatly. There are facts regarding migrant workers that he had not known before. Hans is perturbed. His uneasiness speaks of a blurring of the horizon of his moral conscience. The line of demarcation between good and evil, or between the greater and the lesser good, is no longer so clear as before. In a way, God was awaiting him in the migrant worker. But, whereas Hans can easily recognize God incarnate in the poor, who meekly endure sufferings, he seems to have a hard time including the poor who rise to fight for their own cause in the sphere of the holy or the religious. Is Hans going to accept the challenge and think things through? Does he welcome his new awareness as an opportunity to deepen his faith? Is he going to welcome the stranger?

Obviously, there is much in what Pierre says that causes resistance in Hans. The reality set before him by Pierre and Alfredo has moved his heart and he can feel the element of injustice in his society. Yet, reasoning things out, Hans quickly justifies his own position. He brands Pierre an idealist to show that his own direction is rational and therefore right. But it is interesting to note that in the end Hans uses an argument of feasibility rather than desirability against Pierre's proposal.

It is also interesting that Hans assumes that the goal of union organizations such as that undertaken by Alfredo and supported by Pierre is a *total destruction* of the present social order. Although acknowledging the existence of deplorable injustice, Hans says, "that does not mean we dispose of society." Perhaps this is partly due to his conviction, as reflected in the conversations, that behind Alfredo's union there is Marxist initiative and support. To him

167

the question becomes—unnecessarily—one of choosing between the existing order and a Marxist society.

Pierre and Alfredo also reveal interesting personality traits. Pierre's insistence that Hans take up the cause of the migrant workers reveals how much he values the institutional church, and how he trusts the basic good will of church-goers. It also indicates that his religious faith is inseparable from his social involvement. It is quite understandable that, as a church social worker, his effort should begin with members of the church. Pierre's insistence and his patience in dealing with Hans, however, reflect his conviction that, the situation being what it is, sincere believers will not fail to support the cause. Truth has persuasive power for persons of good will. However, the way one defines truth is conditioned by particular elements in society. Hans does not appear to take this fact into account. He is, therefore, somewhat naive in his belief.

As to Alfredo, circumstances helped him to grow in the eleven years he has been a worker in Switzerland. At the beginning, he left his country in search of ways to meet his basic economic needs. He was willing to put up with any hardship in order to make a living. Now, economic motivations are no longer the dominant factor in his life. Perhaps because his basic needs have been satisfied, even though on a day-to-day basis and with no guarantees for the future, other concerns have taken possession of him. He is organizing unions at great personal risk.

How did this change come about? One wonders if he would have left Italy at all if eleven years ago he was the person he is now. One also wonders what could happen in Italy if his kind of energy and effort toward social change were poured out there. His unwillingness to become a Swiss citizen, with all the privileges that would entail, suggests that he can still be useful to his own country. It might even be true that he has learned to love Italy more by being an Italian in Switzerland.

On this point, one notices what is perhaps one of the saddest parts in the whole account. Alfredo's refusal to be "assimilated into Swiss culture" is misunderstood by Hans to mean pride or irresponsibility. In the context of the case, it is clear that Alfredo is not a person who shirks responsibilities. How could Hans fail to see this? Alfredo might have been proud, but it was justifiable pride. He might have been angry, but not with irrational anger. It is indignation in the face of injustice in society that prompts him to harbor negative feelings regarding the possibility of gaining Swiss citizenship. This indicates he cares for fair treatment much more than he cares for personal economic advantages. Hans's critique of Alfredo in this respect implies, if not a view of the poor as purely economic beings with no sense of dignity, at least a shallow understanding of the human person, generally speaking.

Whatever the motivations of the three main persons in this case study, however, it is perhaps more important to take a look at the issues touched upon.

First is the issue of the immigration laws. The responsibility of any government is first and foremost toward its own people. If foreign workers threaten to deprive Swiss citizens of jobs, it is understandable that there be laws limiting the number of foreigners coming into the country. Pierre recognizes this need as well as does Hans. However, the way the Swiss government handled the situation did not serve the cause of disinterested justice for all. In the face of a sudden increase of foreigners in the postwar years and a threatened depression, Swiss legislators reacted by making a series of regulations to safeguard the interests of the Swiss economy, to the disadvantage of foreign workers. The new laws enabled Switzerland to benefit from the cheap labor of foreign workers, while helping industrial management to sidestep its responsibility toward the human beings who provided the labor.

For the Swiss economy, foreign laborers constitute a buffer zone protecting Swiss workers against unemployment in extraordinary circumstances. In normal times, the existence of such a zone does not bring down the wages of Swiss workers. Nor does it lessen job opportunities for the Swiss. Cruel though these laws are toward foreign labor, they at least have the merit of protecting Swiss laborers against management that might otherwise be tempted to use cheap labor exclusively. At least this is the case in theory. What constitutes injustice is not so much restrictions on immigration as the unfair treatment of foreigners working within Swiss society.

From the viewpoint of the lawmakers, the inhuman conditions imposed on the foreign worker seem to be justified by the fact that, these impositions notwithstanding, significant numbers of foreigners still wish to come. Does this imply that conditions in the migrant workers' countries of origin are even worse? Is the Swiss system generous, handing out work and bread to those who otherwise would be deprived of both? Is exploitation justified because the victims are willing?

An attempt to give fair answers to these questions may lead beyond the horizons of a strictly legal worldview. One is forced to ask why—why are millions upon millions of persons today seeking to leave the land of their birth? Is this due simply to the fact that some countries are rich and others poor? Hans rightly states that men and women are not born equal. However, he is wrong in drawing the conclusion he does from this fact.

In terms of justice versus egalitarianism, Hans takes the cause of Pierre and Alfredo as a kind of egalitarian movement. Arguing from the principle of inequality of birth, Hans implicitly condemns their actions or at least discourages them from continuing. In the context of the case study, however, there is the issue of actual abuse of the poor by the rich. This is then a question of correcting serious abuses of power rather than an idealistic pursuit of equality. It is all too easy to discard responsibility for such correction in the name of a God-given inequality of birth.

Moreover, this issue of justice versus egalitarianism must be viewed in the context of the world economy. It will not do to dismiss the issue by saying some countries are too poor. One must ask once more the "why" of the given situation. It may take ages before social scientists arrive at a clear explanation of the causes of hunger and poverty. But even now we have enough information to know that a new economic order exists. (The United Nations Conference on Trade and Development has annual estimates on Corporate Control of Global Commodities. This might serve as one source of information.) There have emerged, since the early 1960s, economic structures that reach out to control both the production and the distribution of primary and manufactured commodities on the global market. Taken seriously, available data would lead one to conclude that the responsibility of the "haves" towards the "have-nots" is a case of justice, not of charity alone. Openness to information on this score becomes all-important, and it is here that the nature of one's faith comes into question. Perhaps another look at the different perspectives held by Hans and Pierre will make this clearer.

Whereas Hans and Pierre have both received the same information, their reading of the situation is quite different. Pierre finds Jesus in the stranger. The imperative to welcome that stranger is at the very heart of his faith. The unjust practices toward the migrant workers are intolerable to him. He has grasped the direct relationship between the profit reaped by Swiss and other industrialized nations on the one hand, and the restrictions suffered by the stranger on the other. It is his devotion to the God incarnate that opens his eyes more fully to the horror of human sinfulness, which in this case takes the shape of the more powerful exploiting the less powerful. Nothing short of repentance could satisfy Pierre. Perhaps he does not believe in the possibility of perfect and lasting social structures identifiable once and for all with the kingdom of God, but that does not prevent him from seeking the kingdom in this world. For him, there is no need to come out of the one in order to enter the other.

As for Hans, he might also see Jesus suffering in the stranger. He might even agree with Pierre that there is a direct relationship between the profit made by big businesses and the sufferings of the stranger. But for him, the world is one thing and God another. This basic attitude prompts him to minimize the gravity of the situation and to take a defensive and pragmatic attitude toward these inhumane laws. He implies that the theological and the practical are two different things. In actuality, this means he has recourse to a different set of principles—all good in themselves, to be sure—to take care of his secular life. He does not have to relate everything directly to his religious faith so long as the abstract principles he relies upon are acceptable in the light of the gospel. As a result, the stranger is viewed in the light of unchangeable moral principles and assigned to the realm of charity rather than justice.

Paradoxically, Hans's "God-beyond-this-world" binds Hans to human institutions. He has to have two faiths mutually supporting one another. He is almost irrational when he confesses his faith in the democratic process. In spite of the fact that he knows the process was not effective for Alfredo, he still believes in the "free Swiss society." Even knowing that workers live like rats within that society does not shake his faith in the system. On the contrary, he blames the workers for their lack of commitment to Switzerland.

Hans also shows his confusion when he speaks of the relationship between his status as a citizen and as a Christian. "As citizens and as Christians," he says, "we have a right and an obligation to vote for issues that protect the common good." When there is a question of his voting in support of the migrant workers, however, he is adamant that he would do so only as a citizen, not as a pastor. He may have said this out of consideration for his congregation. However, it seemed clear to him that he could *support* the system from the pulpit—that would not have been political. Yet he should not *criticize* the system, for that would be political, and therefore beyond the limits of his duty.

Hans's separation of the theological and the practical—presumably because the former is so very high above the latter—ends up having him "selling out to the system." In contrast, Pierre's "God-in-this-world" enables him to be free from the human systems that sustain his being. He dares to be "undemocratic," perhaps because he is closer to the spirit that first brought about the democratic system. In other words, the system that had become an end in itself for Hans was for Pierre an open-ended thing into which he continues to put substance. For Pierre, it is the spirit, not the letter of the system, that is crucial.

The different faith positions also have their consequences in the broad cultural sphere. Relatively speaking, Pierre's understanding of fellowship is much more universal than Hans's. The latter found ample reasons to congratulate his own country for not being in the plight of some other nations where ethnic minorities are causing social unrest. His statement points to the real difficulties that emerge when different ethnic groups live together. One cannot deny these difficulties. But it is also true that, following the logic of Pierre's argument, he could be subject to charges of racism.

The sign of hope in Hans is his state of being perturbed. If he continues to look at concrete reality, perhaps his faith in God will lead him to a greater integration and then he will better recognize who the stranger is.

SELECT BIBLIOGRAPHY

Haberman, Jürgen. *Toward a Rational Society: Student Protest, Science and Politics.* Boston: Beacon Press, 1970.
Miranda, José. *Communism in the Bible.* Maryknoll, N.Y.: Orbis Books, 1982.
Tillich, Paul. *The Socialist Decision.* New York: Harper & Row, 1977.

HEINRICH OTT

COMMENTARY ON "I WAS A STRANGER"

Switzerland has two main churches: the Reformed and the Roman Catholic. Active, representative, leading groups from both churches were basically in agreement over the political question of equal rights for foreign workers—a question of great importance to our country. In this situation, Pierre Gauvin's position was not at all that of an outsider. Quite the contrary, the church groups on the whole argued as he did.

In the spring of 1981, the Swiss people voted on the so-called *mitenand* referendum (*mitenand* means "together"; the intent, as is always the case with Swiss referendums, was a constitutional amendment). The referendum was staunchly supported by the church groups. The bill called for stabilization of the number of alien residents, but also for reform of their legal status, especially the abolishment of the seasonal work permits (Permit A). The referendum was overwhelmingly rejected by the people and the cantons, even though the church groups argued strongly in favor of it. Various types of criticism were levied against the churches: they should not get involved in politics, they did not understand the real needs of the people, and so forth.

Pastor Hans Keller's line of argumentation in our text corresponds quite closely to the position of the moderate opposition to the *mitenand* referendum. The majority of the electorate declared itself to be in agreement with this position. Hans would not have had to summon up much civil courage in order to preach on the Sunday following his conversation exactly what his friend Pierre expected him to: Hans represented the prevailing trend in the churches. Paradoxically, he would have needed much more courage to represent the cautious, moderate view of the situation in a political sermon, a position for which he had taken up the defense shortly before in talking to his friend.

This commentary was translated from German by Eileen Fitzsimons.

172

I am writing this in October 1981. The vote of last spring on the *mitenand* referendum was the fourth in a series of such plebiscites concerning the political status of aliens in our country. I myself, as the only theologian in the Swiss Parliament and as a representative of the democratic left as well as the union movement in the parliamentary debate that preceded the plebiscite, had taken a stance in favor of the referendum in question—a decisive liberalization of the legislation on foreign workers. I had appealed to the golden rule and the ethics of Immanuel Kant, especially in regard to the rights of the foreign workers with respect to their families: Would we, the members of this Parliament, not protest and feel that our personal rights had been violated if we were to accept work in a foreign country, and that country would then demand that we leave our spouses and children behind? "Whatever you do not wish to have done unto you, do not do unto others."

Nonetheless, the left was defeated, albeit not as devastatingly in the Parliament as in the plebiscite. A calculated political judgment kept the upper hand, in combination with economic and demographic concerns (fear of being overwhelmed by foreigners), and throughout it all—though not prominently—there were humanitarian considerations. In place of the *mitenand* referendum, which sought extensive legal equality for foreigners, a new law for aliens was approved in Parliament. It introduced isolated, not totally insignificant, improvements for the "guest workers," as they are called in Switzerland and elsewhere. In the parliamentary debates I heard dedicated Christians (I would never dare to question the authenticity of their personal belief) speak in favor of this compromise and argue against the draft of the *mitenand* referendum, which was inspired by concern for human rights in Pierre Gauvin's sense.

It must be kept in mind that the form of democracy in effect in Switzerland is the so-called concordant democracy. All cantons, political parties, and other groups interested in a bill in question are asked for their opinions in what is called a "procedure of consultation." The discussion is acknowledged by the administration and continued in the Parliament. The two houses of Parliament—as in the USA—must agree with each other in order for a bill to become a law. It is at this point that the citizenry has a say: it can demand a referendum. Thus Swiss democracy is like flea-market bargaining: you talk and haggle until everyone arrives at an acceptable compromise. True, nobody is completely satisfied as a rule, but on the other hand everybody, or at least the majority, can reach an agreement. This structure of bargaining— "concordant democracy"—is at the basis of the extraordinary stability of the Swiss state, and is the reason why, in spite of everything, so many Swiss can identify so completely with their country, at least to a greater extent than is found elsewhere. One has to keep this ideational and political landscape in mind in order to be able to evaluate accurately this battle over an important issue of human rights in Switzerland—a battle that has lasted for years and is by no means coming to an end.

Here is the situation at the time of my writing: the political right, under the leadership of the National Action Party, petitioned a referendum against the new law for aliens, with its moderately liberal measures—the law that Parliament had passed instead of the more radical *mitenand* referendum. Apparently even this law, which represents a compromise, goes too far for these groups. They evidently wish to retain the severe treatment of foreigners that has prevailed until now, with its occasional abuses, which Alfredo Malettá describes so impressively. Members of the National Action Party again and again refute the accusation that they are motivated by xenophobia. They insist that they are acting solely in the interest of protecting the Swiss citizenry (that is, protecting Swiss identity from being overwhelmed by foreign elements) and protecting Swiss workers (from losing their jobs to the competition of foreign, less costly, and less qualified workers). The vote on the draft of the new bill will probably take place in the spring. As far as numbers are concerned, the National Action Party is minute. Nonetheless, it is frequently successful in mobilizing a large portion of the electorate in favor of its causes. The leftists and the moderates, the Pierre Gauvins and the Hans Kellers, so to speak, who are opponents in the parliamentary debates, will then have to work together to defend the compromise, the new bill, against attack from the extreme right.

This filling in of the details of the contemporary situation from the viewpoint of an insider can help us, perhaps, if we now turn to the central problem. The major theological-political issue of this case study, the substance of the intellectual debate between the two friends Hans Keller and Pierre Gauvin, is, in my opinion, not so much that of an isolated right—the right to employment—but much more the manner in which the church of Jesus Christ can and ought to get involved in issues of human rights at all. This is the substance of the discussion between Hans and Pierre, not the particulars of an individual human right.

In this discussion Pierre speaks from a viewpoint of the gospel as a whole. For him, the particular human right at stake is viewed within the total picture presented by the gospel. Therefore, Pierre wants to influence—radically and directly—decisive political questions concerning human rights. And he wants Hans to preach just as radically from the pulpit. Hans, on the other hand, mainly presents arguments of a tactical and ecclesiastical nature—tightly interwoven! The church must first of all minister to those who belong to its own community—the foreign workers are mainly Roman Catholic or Muslim! But the church has to minister to and be responsible for *all* who belong to its community, and that includes employers as well as employees. Finally, the church must guard the credibility of its message: it cannot make politically unrealistic solutions the theme of a sermon.

The discussion held by Hans, Pierre, and Alfredo is presented as a case study. The decision to be made is: How should Hans Keller preach on Matthew 25:35 the following Sunday? Should he allow himself to be won over by the caution, the "realism," and the considerations of his parishioners, which characterize his position in the discussion, and concentrate on, or even limit himself to, sensitizing his parishioners to the individual needs of the poor? Or should he give the overtly "political sermon" that Pierre urges? Should Hans take the structure of society and thereby human rights as his theme? On which side are the weightier theological arguments?

My advice, as a matter of principle and also from my own knowledge of the situation, would be that Hans ought to give a political sermon, as many other Swiss ministers and priests have done. In my opinion, Pierre definitely has the stronger theological reasoning on his side when he says "we are not a collection of individuals. We are the body of Christ. And Christ calls us to serve the people of God—not just those of one nationality." Indeed, we must carry Pierre's argument further and deeper: the basis of Christian action and Christian responsibility for human rights lies in the belief that the body of Christ, the "people of God," is to continue to expand until it embraces the world. According to Vatican II, the church, through its relationship with Christ, is a kind of sacrament—that is, a sign and instrument of intimate union with God, and of the unity of all humankind (Dogmatic Constitution on the Church, I, 1). Through Christ, not only those who believe in him, but all human beings are to become brothers and sisters. And among brothers and sisters there can be no exploitation, no discrimination. Granted, we are certainly un*like,* but it is just as certain that we are not un*equal.*

This is a basic approach and in fact grounded in the incarnation as the fundamental Christian truth of christology, ecclesiology, and anthropology, and, therefore, it can and should be preached and explained from the pulpit in exactly this way, and clarified in the political context where such a context is deemed to be important and current. If Hans is politically active "on the side," whether it be as a member of the government or simply as a citizen in a community meeting, he will have exactly the same thing to say, even though he will sometimes use other words, words without biblical roots, entailing a "nonreligious interpretation of the gospel."

To be sure, even when Hans speaks in a directly political manner from the pulpit or in a community meeting on a political issue, his words, in any case, cannot have any effect other than that of heightening consciousness, if indeed they have any effect at all. For in a democratic country he is not an autocrat who, by himself, on the basis of his own convictions and by the strength of his own will, can bring about a new political order that will enshrine human rights in a pure form. He will have to make an effort to build up majorities, which is a long-drawn-out process. For the time being, he will have to content himself with majority decisions, even though they do not entirely correspond to his own vision. For this reason, much depends on *how* he proclaims his politically articulated gospel.

Although in general I am astounded at his reluctance to speak out politically, individual thoughts of his in the discussion seem to have merit. Perhaps his friend Pierre is indeed "an unrealistic idealist who looks for the coming of the kingdom here and now." Perhaps Pierre, if he were to preach, and to preach in his own style, would not achieve very much by pronouncing the democratic system in which he lives—and to which he must be grateful for much of what he is as a person—guilty of "diabolical, systematic violations of human rights." Hans probably is right when he says, "in all honesty, I believe my voice is much stronger when I speak as a citizen"—that is, as one who knows the problems, the practical needs, and as he also knows the prejudices and narrowness of his fellow citizens, and not as an idealist, as a representative of a "pure ideology" of a "pure ideal," who believes one can ignore the human, all-too-human, factors.

Human rights have their own history. They arise from specific historical contexts. They do not exist from the beginning, like immutable mathematical laws. They are not static norms, but dynamic processes. Human rights can be established only with the help of persons who gradually arrive at the insight that these rights are just and reasonable.

Human rights are intimately related to the process of consciousness raising. The politician must recognize this, as well as the church representative who, after all, wishes to enliven and change the conciousness of the church. The perspective of the church ought to be, above all else, prophetic. The church ought always to sense and point out—ahead of others—human problems, needs, and developments as they arise. And the church should be sensitive there where no one else has become sensitive.

Case Study 7

PROPHET OR PROVOCATEUR?

Alan Johnson's chain of thought was momentarily interrupted as the Boeing 747 began its approach to John F. Kennedy Airport, New York. He was returning from a three-week business trip to Brazil, and he had been mulling over the meetings with businessmen and church leaders in São Paulo, one of the largest cities in the southern hemisphere. A company conference awaited his report on Monday, and, perhaps equally troubling, the Social Concerns Committee of his local United Methodist Church of Stamford, Connecticut, expected a recommendation from him. Should Brazil be their mission focus for the next year? Were human rights and the oppression of the poor really the central issue, or were improved relationships with the Brazilian government and more money through the church for food, medical facilities, education, and evangelism, the critical needs?

Could Alan recommend that his company expand its business investments in Brazil and at the same time argue that the church should oppose the present violation of human rights by Brazilian military leaders? Alan's recommendations had seemed clearer before this visit; he was now confused by conflicting additional information. The words of Carlos de Carvalho still rang in his ears: "When will the church in America have the courage to be a prophet and not just a provocateur?"

Social Concerns

On Tuesday evening Alan was scheduled to share his findings during this trip to Brazil with the other members of the Social Concerns Committee

This case study was prepared by Robert A. Evans as a basis for discussion rather than to illustrate either effective or ineffective handling of the situation. Copyright © by the Case Study Institute.

The names of Fred Morris, General Ernesto Geisel, General João Baptista Figueiredo, Cardinal Arns and Archbishop Hélder Câmara are actual. All other names are disguised to protect the privacy of the individuals involved.

of his 1,500-member church. The congregation was composed largely of the families of business executives and professionals, many of whom commuted each day to New York. The committee in recent years had been involved in promoting charitable causes on a local level, such as a children's home, family counseling services, meals-on-wheels, and some mission interpretation for the national church. The year before, in the autumn of 1978, a new chairperson, John Andrews, had urged the committee to take an active position on national and international issues of justice, drawing on the expertise and knowledge of several members of the congregation. John declared that the committee's mandate was set by Jesus himself at the beginning of his public ministry. John had read from the prophet Isaiah:

> The Spirit of the Lord is upon me, because he has anointed me to preach good news to the poor. He has sent me to proclaim release to the captives and recovering of sight for the blind, to set at liberty those who are oppressed, to proclaim the acceptable year of the Lord [Luke 4:18–19 RSV].

Andrews personally recruited Alan for the committee, knowing that he was committed to issues of civil rights and that he traveled widely for International Electric as a vice-president of the international division. Although initially reluctant to serve because of a heavy work schedule, Alan found the committee work exciting. It was in his judgment, however, too scattered; there were reports to the congregation on everything from drug abuse to world hunger. Alan urged the committee to make an impact upon the congregation through the identification of a specific mission priority for the new year. Given the human rights concerns of the Carter administration and the growing significance of South America for both U.S. government and business interests, this area was selected by the committee.

The Morris Incident

For researching problems in Latin America, a seminary professor suggested to Alan that he read an article by Fred Morris in the January 25, 1975, edition of *Christian Century*. Morris, a former Methodist missionary in Brazil, had testified in December 1974 before a subcommittee of the House Committee on Foreign Affairs.

In the *Christian Century* article Morris described his arrest and torture by the military authorities in Brazil. His mistreatment was a result of his association with Roman Catholic Archbishop Hélder Câmara of Recife, the economic capital of the impoverished northeast of Brazil. Because he believed he could serve the mission of the church as effectively in a "tent-making" ministry and because of a financial crisis in the Methodist Board of Global Ministries, Fred took secular employment in Recife. He indicated that another factor in his decision was his recent divorce. Working as a part-time correspondent for *Time* magazine, he was accused by the Brazilian army intelligence of supplying information for articles in *Time* that praised Archbishop Câmara for his efforts to aid the oppressed masses of the northeast despite the repressive activity of the military. Despite Morris's claim to have stopped sending dispatches to *Time* and discontinuing contact with Câmara, he was detained on September 30, 1974, and subjected to four days of physical torture and threats of death. His torturers repeatedly pressed for a confession of his subversive activities. After thirteen days of solitary confinement, Fred was released through the energetic efforts of the American consul in Recife. He was then expelled from Brazil by orders of President Ernesto Geisel and declared a person "prejudicial to the interests of Brazil." Formal charges were never filed.

Morris, testifying before the House Committee on Foreign Affairs, asked why: (1) no assurance was sought by the government for the protection of human rights of U.S. citizens living in countries with oppressive regimes; (2) the government continued to give massive financial aid and to guarantee private U.S. investment in and loans to countries that abuse their own citizens and violate their own legal systems; (3) the U.S.A. did not take an active stand in the United Nations organization and in the Organization of American States on protection of human dignity rather than acting from political expediency; (4) U.S. foreign policy should be determined solely on the basis of military and economic policies rather than on the promotion of human values and welfare.

What struck Alan about Morris's testimony, which became a controversial case in Brazilian church life still discussed in 1979, was not only Morris's call to terminate aid, prohibit guaranteed investments, and discourage loans for countries such as Brazil, but the clear implication that for those in the church these responses should be supported on the grounds of Christian love and responsibility. Morris implied that to confess belief in the communion of saints means to share the suffering of brothers and sisters in Christ in every section of the earth including the developing nations—even though it may be done only in small or symbolic ways, by limiting profits or by sharing resources. Anything less would be to avoid Christ's mission to set at liberty those who are oppressed and to deny Jesus' own proclamation that when we feed, clothe, and visit those in prison we are doing this for him.

Call for Nonconfrontation

This visit to Brazil and the conversations he had on the Morris issue caused Alan to question the strategy of persons such as Fred Morris, even if one believed in the revolutionary nature of the gospel message that Alan professed. Doubts were seeded by Doug Williams, another American missionary who knew Fred Morris slightly: "Missionaries are the guests of the country and the Brazilian church. They are not free to speak out as natives. Fred Morris was very imprudent!

"It is presumptuous for outsiders to think they know how the structure of Brazilian society should be changed," Doug declared. "The task of the church is conversion. Its role is to change people and then they are liberated to change their own situation. Only intellectuals and the upper class have the luxury of reflecting about changing society. Those of us in the church are called to minister to the immediate needs of the lower- and middle-class poor. We will drain our energies and resources fighting the government or the rich, and will neglect the power of the gospel to change lives.

"Of course I don't approve of torture," Williams continued. "However, as foreign nationals, we have to understand the position of the government trying to survive in a nation with an enormous gap between the rich and poor, and with political controversy always being stirred up from the outside. The communists are seen by the generals as a threat to the survival of Brazilian life. It is like going into the *favela* [slum area] and being challenged to a fight. We have been taught in our protected society to fight fair. But if the boy who challenges you has sand to throw in your eyes and a broken bottle to cut your throat, to fight fair would be to die. The government must sometimes take extreme measures to survive these foes. Who are the Fred Morrises to challenge that on individual grounds?

"Some strategies of confrontation hurt the mission of the church and even the cause of human rights. President Carter sends his wife to visit personally the radical priests working in the *favelas* at Recife. Then, when Carter visits Brazil, he not only meets with Cardinal Arns, one of the most outspoken critics of the government, but invites Arns to ride in his limousine to the airport. All of this was an enormous insult to the president, General Ernesto Geisel.

"And what was the result," Doug asked, "of all this intervention? A greater pressure put on those advocating change and the recognition of human rights. Also a change in policy: no missionaries or church personnel are presently being granted resident visas. How are we to support the Brazilian church on tourist visas? Yes, the Morris strategy is very imprudent."

Call for Liberation

It was difficult for Alan to believe that Doug Williams was describing the same country as the churchmen he met at the headquarters of the Inter-Faith Task Force for Liberation. "Identification of the church with the poor, not the powerful," the Rev. Paulo de Souza declared, "is the only hope for the Catholic or Protestant churches in Brazil." A dedicated group of church persons, including priests and lay persons, Protestants and Roman Catholics, men and women, had formed the task force to demonstrate the need to "labor together across ecumenical and geographical lines in the name of the universal church of Jesus Christ." They were often criticized by members of their own church bodies, sometimes harassed, arrested, and imprisoned by the government when they sought to "denounce and expose the violation of human rights and dignity of all God's children."

Father Antônio Cardoso, a Dominican priest and teacher, reminded Alan that over 60 percent of Brazilians were hungry, living far below the poverty line as defined in the United States. "There is enormous wealth in Brazil, concentrated in a tiny proportion of the population that exerts power to maintain the status quo. Staggering estimates suggest that up to one-third of the total population might be in migration from the north to the south simply for economic survival. What does it mean to follow Jesus' command to preach the good news to the poor? The critical issue is: How can a people be free? How can the church as church be free? Conscientization of the church would mean to move from the Mass to the community in Christ's name."

Paulo de Souza was clear about the major issues that faced the church in Brazil, and what was required of those seeking to be faithful:

"(1) The church must become a true companion in favor of justice—an advocate of justice, not in principle only but in concrete situations. Problems of poverty and violence can no longer be ignored by the church.

"(2) We need identification of the church with the populace. In the past the church has always been linked with the powerful. The church can no longer simply react; it must take its place in the struggle and initiate action.

"(3) Identification with the poor—the special concern of God in the Old and New Testaments—involves ceasing to spiritualize the problems of the poor. Poverty in Brazil has a social structure that is a direct result of the capitalist system. This system—nurtured by the U.S.A. and protected by the rich, which includes the present church—breeds injustice.

"(4) There is a built-in relationship between creative pastoralization and politicization. The church is involved in the problems and must work at the issues. Politics is a form of faith for an institution seeking to be a church of the poor. Three elements required are: (a) practical alliance with the poor; (b) a methodology for the scientific interpretation of social reality; and (c) biblical and theological reflection resulting in the stress on action with the poor, excluding any compromises with power.

"(5) Local congregations are inadequate. There is need for a new form of church where believers are not domesticated, but take part in the decisions that affect their lives. Our hope is in the base communities [*comunidades de base*] in the Roman Catholic Church that are attempting to change the structure of an unjust society. The question is not so much individual rights as it is the social rights of a whole community. Although they may seem threatening to some priests, these lay groups provide new structures of hope for the church."

Father Antônio was in agreement that the new hope of the church was in those same base communities now numbering two million persons, with fifteen thousand new groups formed the previous year alone. "They have no sacrament and no priest, but are studying the Bible and politics in order to discover a way to liberate themselves and the world. The need is for an honest, aggressive, and compassionate world church that will be willing to suffer with us. Galatians says we are 'to bear one another's burdens.' Let us then do this for one another."

Following these conversations, Alan was convinced that Fred Morris was on the right track in demanding a new position from the American government and a new lifestyle from Christians in North American churches.

Call for Moderation

Some church bodies, Alan found, represented neither the commitment of the Inter-Faith Task Force nor the individualistic reservations subscribed to by more conservative Protestants such as Williams. "The mediators," as the Rev. Benjamin Villaca described them, "are the practical moderates present among Roman Catholics, Presbyterians, and some other Protestants. They call for gradual transformation of our Brazilian society. This nation, which occupies over half the land mass of the South American continent, has been characterized by evolution, not revolution. The Brazilians are a relatively gentle and tolerant people who have had such a stable development that even our coups have been relatively bloodless for Latin America. Realistically, social change will be slow and the church must be present and faithful. The answer lies in the responsible use of the God-given talents of individual Christians in the public service of their people."

"Education and evangelism are at the heart of the matter," Villaca continued. "Religious and secular education of the people provides the foundation for a renewed church and a developed society. Christians must devote their talents to providing better schools, more adequate housing, and medical facilities at every level of society. Evangelism programs will allow the Brazilians to see that the church has the key to a better life. The Christian message will take different forms in the *favelas* and on Copacabana Beach in Rio. The Christian is called to be responsible to God, neighbor and self. Catholics constitute over 90 percent of the overall population in this 'most Catholic nation of our times.' If only 5 percent of them, and the Protestants, who comprise a similar minority, are active, then the opportunities for evangelism are enormous.

"Ecumenical radicals are as much Marxist as Christian. They cannot really affect the government or the privileged classes despite their claim that 'only a revolution in the structure of society and the church will bring liberation.' Christians are entitled to the fruits of their labor if the gains are responsibly shared with others. The World Council of Churches has been simply ignored ever since it began to support terrorists and guerrillas who only bring violence and loss of life by preaching liberation, not reconciliation.

"The conservatives and Pentecostals are individualistic escapists, unwilling to face their societal responsibilities. Their refusal to dance, smoke, drink, gamble, or in general participate in society simply evades the reality of an evolving society. A few hours of ecstasy each week through baptism of the Holy Spirit is little different from our spiritualist cults. Moral rigidity that judges and condemns all practices except one's own builds enthusiasm for a righteous minority but will not attract those who need the Christian gospel of forgiveness.

"We need," Villaca concluded, "the support of the North American churches as we have usually experienced it, only to a fuller measure. We need more money and trained personnel for schools, hospitals, housing projects, and Christian education projects. Send us aid without strings attached. Help establish better relations with our president, General João Batista Figueiredo, who took office March 15, 1979. He promised liberalization in several areas of life, from press censorship to a more active anti-poverty program. This is a religiously oriented nation. The church could help us by private and governmental gifts. Let your church and companies know we need their continued support."

Double Dilemma

After circling for thirty minutes, the captain announced he was entering the final approach to New York. Alan's thoughts spun from his confusion on the church recommendations to the business advice he must provide. With over 450,000 color television sets sold in Brazil the previous year alone, and the promise of the U.S. government to guarantee the investment, it seemed good business sense to recommend expansion. However, the 90 percent inflation rate in Brazil, and the standard practice of private lending companies to finance television sets and refrigerators at an 8 percent monthly interest rate, made Alan hesitate. He was disturbed by the loan policies with which newly arrived immigrants in Rio were generally unfamiliar. They made little more than the $80 a month national minimum wage—if they had a job at all. The "buy low, sell high" attitude of retailers, coupled with aggressive debt collections, spelled tragedy for low-income consumers, though a boon to the appliance business. As the Interfaith Task Force had kept repeating to Alan, it was the excessive profits of multinational corporations such as International Electric in foreign countries (due to higher risk, twice the return on money expected in a domestic investment) that maintained oppressive regimes and flourished on the misery of the poor. On the other hand, Alan reminded himself, stockholders wanted a return on their money, not a speech about corporate social responsibility.

The church report was equally a problem. Should he recommend Brazil as a mission priority? If so, which request by Brazilians does one honor? What is most faithful and effective: political and economic intervention; lobbying at home combined with a new awareness of the world church; a campaign for major mission funds for education and evangelism; or not recommend Brazil as a mission project because the issues are unclear and involvement from outside is not wanted?

As the clouds parted over Long Island, the face of his host and old friend Carlos de Carvalho—an active Christian layman in Brazil—came to Alan's mind. After a lively discussion of the options on the last evening, Carlos had said: "It's a tough decision for you to make and I am not sure what you ought to do. I am convinced the world church must learn to make decisions in light of needs everywhere in the world. To make no decision is cowardice. A sustained strategy is needed. When will the church in America have the courage to be a prophet and not just a provocteur?"

"Fasten your seatbelt, please, Mr. Johnson," the stewardess said. "The landing in this wind may be a little rough."

TEACHING NOTE ON
"PROPHET OR PROVOCATEUR?"

Alan Johnson's interviews with religious leaders in Brazil reveal an ecumenically diverse spectrum of religious, economic, and political positions. The case raises several questions as Alan ponders his response to his church and his employer:

A. In relation to *mission* in Brazil: what is the appropriate role, if any, of the U.S. churches?

B. In regard to *human rights* and their violation: what responsibility does the church have because of its commitment to social concerns of world justice?

C. In Christian *business ethics* and the role of foreign investment by multinational corporations: what is the task of individual Christians and/or churches?

D. In considering theological approaches such as *liberation theology:* what implications and problems are posed by contrasting requests for support?

CASE PLAN

1. One approach to a case discussion might employ the categories from H. Richard Niebuhr's *Christ and Culture* (New York: Harper & Brothers, 1951) to examine the views reflected by the four principal participants. It has been suggested that the fundamental issue in the case is the relationship between Christ and culture from the "Christ above Culture" of Doug Williams to the "Christ Transforming Culture" of Paulo de Souza. Though this identification could be disputed, the Niebuhr schema may provide a basic systemic entry point to the discussion.

2. Another approach is an investigation from the perspective of any of the primary concerns noted above: mission, human rights, business ethics, or liberation theology. Acknowledging that these concerns overlap, one could nevertheless pursue such an outline using persons, issues, alternatives, and resources.

a. Persons: List the central characters: Alan Johnson, Carlos de Carvalho, Fred Morris, Doug Williams, Paulo de Souza, Antônio Cardosa, and Benjamin Villaca. How is a particular concern (i.e., mission or human rights) understood by each of these persons?

b. Issues: Possible responses from participants might be: nature of mission; meaning of evangelism; church and state; human rights and political pressure; method and means of liberation; policies of multinational corporations; how to fulfill basic human needs; international implications of interference and/or involvement; First and Third World dialogue; change in priorities and lifestyles in U.S. and Brazil. Discuss more fully at least two of these issues.

c. Alternatives for Alan Johnson. Urge a critical evaluation of proposed approaches.

Possible recommendations for the Connecticut church:

—avoid political issues and increase evangelism support for Brazilian church;

—engage in political activity to urge U.S. support of human rights and withdrawal of support to oppressive regimes;

—support identification of church with poor and new consideration of church/state issue;

—increase support of funds for food, medicine, and education and encouragement of better relations in Brazil;

—recommend no action or priority be set;

—seek alternative to or combination of listed options.

Possible recommendations for the corporation:

—expand company investment and operation in Brazil;

—expand investment with conditions concerning labor relations and loan terms;

—hold to present involvement;

—reduce involvement in Brazil with conditions;

—withdraw from business involvement in Brazil on ethical grounds.

d. Resources to be identified no matter what decision is reached. Some possible resources identified might be:

—theological reflection and biblical guidelines;

—information on social, political, and economic interaction;

—consultation and dialogue with Brazilians;

—prayer and sacramental sources of present history and present relationship between government and churches in Brazil and U.S.

SUGGESTIONS FOR ADDITIONAL READING

Antoine, Charles. *Church and Power in Brazil.* Maryknoll, N.Y.: Orbis, 1973. Historical analysis of church/state relations with prorevolutionary stance. Preface by Richard Shaull.

Brown, Robert McAfee. *Theology in a New Key.* Philadelphia: Westminster, 1978. A response to liberation themes from Latin America by an American theologian who pursues the implications from the American society and church.

"Doing Business in Brazil." *Financial Times of London,* 2:7, February 19–25, 1979. Short history of economic development and discussion of economic, labor, and loan policies.

Freire, Paulo. *Pedagogy of the Oppressed.* New York: Seabury, 1973. Politically provocative study of educational strategy for the Third World by a Brazilian.

Morris, Fred. "Sustained by Faith under Brazilian Torture." *The Christian Century,* January 22, 1975, pp. 56–60. This article by Morris contains excerpts from his testimony before the House Committee on Foreign Affairs. Neither the article nor the case implies that Fred Morris did anything to justify the Brazilian government action against him. Public documents are cited and responded to by others in the case according to their personal interpretation of events.

Segundo, Juan Luis. *The Liberation of Theology.* Maryknoll, N.Y.: Orbis, 1976. A careful and critical study of theological implications of liberation.

The Washington Office on Latin America, 110 Maryland Avenue, N.E., Washington, D.C. 20002. Supplies information as a nonprofit organization serving as a liaison between Latin Americans and U.S. institutions affecting foreign policy. This includes churches, press, professional organizations, trade unions, nongovernmental organizations, and executive and legislative branches of government.

The Embassy of Brazil, Washington, D.C., may provide information on request.

RUBEM ALVES

COMMENTARY ON "PROPHET OR PROVOCATEUR?"

It happened many years ago, when I first visited the United States of America. My English was worse than it is today. I could not understand most of the phrases that are not explained in textbooks. With my eyes wide open I tried to guess the meaning of tricky words. A rest room is not for taking a rest. I could not find the word "betcha" in any dictionary. But I wanted to understand the world that was hidden behind and showed itself through the symbols with which the whole country dressed itself. Those signs and symbols were parts of a dream that was there, alive, right before my eyes, demanding interpretation.

I remember that I was amazed to see, as I traveled from one place to another, how often the same kind of sign was posted on fences and trees, like an echo that reverberated in the valleys and from one mountain range to another, an unending cannon roll:

> WARNING
> Private Property
> No Trespassing
> Violators will be Prosecuted

This was a new meaning of the word "trespassing," which, in my vocabulary, was related to sin only. The gravity of the warning informed me that I was in a land where the importance of space was appreciated. Otherwise the Americans would not have spent so much of themselves in those fences and walls, all those interdictions scattered throughout the country. Yes, they knew that space was an extension of their body. And it was right that it was called "property": something that belongs to a person's essence, as if it were one with the flesh and bones. Property is something to be protected and defended, as part of one's life: my body, my property, my right, a human right, like food, air, freedom—something without which I would not survive.

188

But I also found signs to the effect that, in former times, Indians had used trails that are still to be found today through the woods—sacraments of a world that no longer exists, a world that was not divided by fences. . . . How different the body must have felt in those days, without the armor of real estate to protect it.

And I suddenly began to realize how ambivalent those fences were. True, they defined an inner, protected space, an extension of one's body, one's right. But outside was a different kind of space, threatening and unfriendly, which had to be resisted. Those fences were dams to keep the waters of chaos out. The signs of warning revealed, then, a double image. On the one hand, they were statements of rights; they defined and pointed to inner spaces. On the other hand, they were expressions of fear.

A curious idea came to my mind. Let us take for granted this inner space and its bodily extension, property, surrounded by fences. Let us take for granted that this space is one of my most sacred rights. Now comes the question: Is there not something basically wrong in a world in which one has to wear armor in order to be safe, even if we have legislated armor to be a personal right? Is it not true that, for one to have a right to this island of security, one must obstruct the space outside? The right to this inner paradise revealed itself, then, as a confession that the world beyond the fences was no longer felt as one's home.

The Indians, then, did not have the right to protect themselves, as isolated individuals, within the armored spaces of private property. They did not need it. Their world and their corporality were grander. Their fences were distant horizons, mountains, seas, the stars. . . .

These thoughts of warning signs and of Indian trails began to dance again and the memories started to reawaken when I read about Fred Morris. He was a lucky exception among thousands who did *not* survive to tell their story, who were killed without anyone's having ever heard their sighs. It is out of this situation that some—especially childless mothers and fatherless children—began to raise their voices. In the name of God and in the name of humanity, they cried prayers addressed to humanity and to God, and this universal groaning of creation was baptized with the name "human rights."

Gone is the hope of a social order from which fear would be banned.

Gone is the hope of open spaces for our bodies.

Gone is the time when fences were enough to safeguard one's life.

A time has come when nothing seems to be of any avail—the time of our final humiliation; a time when nothing else is left for us but to grovel before our torturers.

The torturers torture because they are stronger.

The victims are the sacrificial lambs; impotent, silent. The wolves wear badges of law and order. They always declare the lambs guilty without a trial, just as in the absurd, nightmarish world of Lewis Carroll, in which the queen demanded: "Sentence first, verdict afterward."

And we cry: "Human rights."

These are our impotent fences, made out of words, words only, because the victims are left with empty, useless hands. . . .

"Warning. Private property. No trespassing. Violators will be prosecuted."

Who will prosecute the violators, if prosecutors and violators are the same persons?

Max Weber once defined the state as the community that successfully exercises the "monopoly of the legitimate use of physical force within a given territory." The state has the right to use violence. Those who have power set down the rules of the game. They decide what is right and what is wrong. Indeed, Weber was not the first one to realize this. I remember Augustine:

> Justice being taken away, what are kingdoms but great robberies? For what are robberies themselves, but little kingdoms? The band itself is made up of men; it is ruled by the authority of a prince, it is knit together by the pact of the confederacy; the booty is divided by the law agreed on. If, by the admittance of abandoned men, this evil increases to such a degree that it holds places, fixes abodes, takes possession of cities, and subdues peoples, it assumes more plainly the name of kingdom, because the reality is now manifestly conferred on it, not by the removal of covetousness, but by the addition of impunity. Indeed, that was an apt and true reply which was given to Alexander the Great by a pirate who had been seized. For when that king had asked the man what he meant by keeping hostile possession of the sea, he answered with bold pride, "What thou meanest by seizing the whole earth; but because I do it with a petty ship, I am called a robber, whilst thou who dost it with a great fleet art styled emperor."[1]

Human rights: we demand that the holders of power do not trespass our fences.

Why should they respect this demand?

And suppose that they did. Would this make the game acceptable? Are we not simply asking them not to invade the narrow enclave of freedom that is still left, a space much smaller than the one circumscribed by fences? Today the space of our rights is no longer defined by fences. Its limits are our skin. Suppose that this space were left untouched. Suppose that bodies were not tortured and killed. But suppose, also, that the price of this survival were defined by a kind of treaty whereby the state would guarantee the inviolability of this individual, bodily space, whereas the citizens would acknowledge the right of the state over the space that it claims to be its own—namely, everything outside the confines of our skin. A very convenient arrangement. Our islands of freedom would be preserved. The cost? Our submission to the state, now recognized as the guarantor of the minuscule space still left. Something similar to *1984:*

I have to torture you until you love me. Once you acknowledge that your body belongs to me, you may sleep safe, knowing that nothing bad can happen to you. I, the State, will protect your rights. Everything will be yours, if you only fall down and do me homage.[2]

And I asked myself if this is not the hidden confession behind Doug Williams's rationalizations in the case study. He argues that one should not challenge the state. It is stronger than the individual. It can infringe on private rights. But the state can be benevolent also, he says, provided that you do not invade its areas of influence. "Fred Morris was very imprudent," and so was President Carter. The state has power. It can define what is just. Might makes right. Everything would be all right if only we play according to the rules of the Masters. Nothing can hurt you, then. Your rights will be protected. Big Brother will see to it. Williams's conclusion is easily discernible: If anyone's rights are violated, it is because that person challenged the rights of the state.

The state is an altar. On it individuals are sacrificed. These sacrifices are what *we* call "violations of human rights." It is strange that we speak for the victims but seldom speak against the monster. Is it because we still live under the protection of its shadow? Is it because it still protects our human rights?

There are states that demand fewer sacrifices than others. There are states that do not eat openly the bodies of those who are near; they find it safer to eat the flesh of those who are far off. There are good states and bad states. One state can even wave the flag of human rights against other states. This sedates it and its worshipers with the perfume of self-righteousness.

The stronger the state, the weaker the individual. And the confines of the body shrink and shrink, for the sake of . . .

national security,
national interest,
stability,
democracy,
prosperity,
even "socialism."

The colors of the flag do not matter. The arguments are always the same. The realities are always the same. Wolves, regardless of the color of their fur, are always fond of lambs. . . .

It is time to call the beast by its proper name.

It is time to question the rights of the state.

Leviathan, beast, dragon, monster, fiend, hellhound, vampire—take your choice of names.

It is time to question: In the name of what? With what right? For how long? At what price? And the squandering of resources? And the apocalyptic festivals? The end of the world? Weapons?

Individuals must be made weak for the state to be strong.

Individuals must be deprived of space for the state to dominate the world.

Individuals must be reduced to silence for the state to be the only one allowed to speak.

Individuals must be tortured for the state to savor the taste of its power.

Individuals must be killed for the state to live.

Let us stop mourning over our corpses. Let us chase the beast:

Only where the state ends, there begins the human being who is not superfluous. Where the state ends—look there, my brothers! Do you not see it, the rainbow and the bridges of the new man? [Nietzsche].

NOTES

1. *The City of God,* book 4, chap. 4, in Whitney J. Oates, ed., *Basic Writings of Saint Augustine* (New York: Random House, 1948), vol. 2, pp. 51–52.

2. George Orwell, *1984* (New York: Harcourt, Brace and Company, Inc., 1949).

KOSUKE KOYAMA

COMMENTARY ON "PROPHET OR PROVOCATEUR?"

Recently, in conversation with an influential Tokyo businessman, I was given a definition of "good and evil." According to him, "good" is "making money," "better" is "making more money," and "best" is an "unlimited possibility for making money." "Evil," correspondingly, is "losing money," and so on. What, I asked him, would he do with all the money? His answer was "invest it, to make more money."

We can understand this Japanese businessman because something within us is fascinated by the philosophy of greed. The great religions of the world—Judaism, Christianity, Islam, Hinduism, Buddhism, and Confucianism—warn of the destructive nature of human greed. "To be religious" means to be free from the clutches of greed in personal as well as social life. "You fool, this very night you must surrender your life; you have made your money—who will get it now?" (Luke 12:20). Our world does not have enough for everyone's greed, but it has enough for everyone's need, according to Mahatma Gandhi.

Baal is a fertility god. He represents our human pleasure in seeing possessions increased. It is particularly pleasurable when the increase happens to be the increase of *my* possessions. This pleasure of Baal, however, can introduce the annihilating Moloch, the idol that demands human sacrifice (Lev. 20:2–5; Jer. 32:35). When profit making takes precedence over human rights, the destructive Moloch appears on the scene. The church is not always aware of this demonic appearance. When the emperor-worship cult surfaced in the early part of this century in Japan, only a minority within the church realized that it was another appearance of Moloch.

Prophetic tradition fights against the power of Moloch. History as we know it is never free from this destructive power. Hence the struggle continues—the struggle of Isaiah, Jeremiah, Ezekiel, Amos . . . and of Mr. Alan Johnson, a member of a United Methodist Church in Connecticut. The central passage in Alan's Christian theology is Luke 4:18–19, which is taken from Isaiah 61: 1-2. What is going through his mind, as Alan returns to New York from Brazil, is a part of the great historical experience of listening to the word of God in a concrete historical setting. This kind of listening does not yield easy answers.

The contrast between Fred Morris and Doug Williams highlights the critical dimension of the issue. Both of them seem to be sincere and observant. Fred finds in the person of Archbishop Hélder Câmara the voice of the truth that emancipates the lowly from the shackles of poverty, of physical and spiritual malnutrition. So he is expelled from Brazil, branded as a person "prejudicial to the interests of Brazil." Fred's criticism of the elevation of military and economic priorities over the promotion of human values is in line with the teachings of the great religions of the world, and in particular the prophetic tradition of the biblical faith. He was "subjected to four days of physical torture and threats of death." This is the cost of discipleship. Witnessing for Jesus Christ, in whose name Fred Morris is a Methodist missionary in Brazil, has occasioned this suffering. His physical torture and suffering remind me of the ultimate sacrifice of Archbishop Oscar Romero of El Salvador, who said only a few days before his assassination:

> My life has been threatened many times. I have to confess that, as a Christian, I don't believe in death without resurrection. If they kill me, *I will rise again in the Salvadoran people.* I'm not boasting, or saying this out of pride, but rather as humbly as I can.
>
> As a shepherd, I am obliged by divine law to give my life for those I love, for the entire Salvadoran people, including those Salvadorans who threaten to assassinate me. If they should go so far as to carry out their threats, I want you to know that I now offer my blood to God for justice and the resurrection of El Salvador.
>
> Martyrdom is a grace of God that I do not feel worthy of. But if God accepts the sacrifice of my life, my hope is that my blood will be like a seed of liberty and a sign that our hopes will soon become a reality.
>
> My death will be for the liberation of my people and a testimony of hope for the future.
>
> A bishop will die, but the church of God, which is the people, will never perish.[1]

Fred Morris and millions of others know that the phrase "prejudicial to the interests of Brazil" means it is prejudicial to the interests of the few who enjoy power and a life of luxury at the expense of the masses. It is prejudicial to their high-flying lifestyle! If one visits the "walled city" of Makati, a section of Greater Manila, one understands what "prejudicial to the interests of the Philippines" means.

Doug accuses Fred of being imprudent. "It is presumptuous for outsiders to think they know how the structure of Brazilian society should be changed." It is presumptuous for a Briton to think he can speak Japanese without an accent. This makes good sense to me. But if apartheid were practiced in Japan, would we think it simply presumptuous for the British to study how the structure of Japanese society could be changed for the better. Have not there been many painstaking and erudite books written on South Africa by "outsiders" who sometimes know better than "insiders" how the structure of South African society should be changed? Outsiders can have a perspective that insiders never gain. How often do we see Alexis de Tocqueville quoted by our own social critics for his insights on American society! Outsiders see what insiders only look at. Besides, we are living today in a world in which races, cultures, religions, and languages coexist in such proximity that it is hard to tell who is an outsider and who is an insider. Who is an outsider to New York City or São Paulo? Everyone is an outsider and everyone is an insider. Doug was perhaps unaware of how much the world has changed.

Does not "conversion to Jesus Christ" involve criticism of any exploitative social system? Can Doug preach the gospel of Christ without making critical judgments on social injustice? Perhaps he can. Doug *says* he is an outsider. But can an outsider preach the gospel of Christ to insiders? Is Doug saying that the only danger to Brazil is communism? How about the inner forces that invite communism, such as destructive social injustice?

Are there only two possible positions for missionaries to take: limiting themselves to activities that promote conversion *or* getting involved in political participation in the struggle to change Brazilian society? Are there not many more possibilities between these two poles? In many oppressive countries in Latin America, Asia, and Africa, Doug's version of Christianity has been welcomed by dictators. They have given the missionaries who preach "conversion to Jesus Christ" a red-carpet welcome and escort helicopters. Why?

Let me quote from Jürgen Moltmann's "Open Letter to José Míguez-Bonino":

> In December 1974, thirty-two leading Protestant church officials greeted the power grab of the military junta in Chile as "God's answer to the prayers of all believers who see in Marxism a satanic power". . . .
> The God of Jesus Christ does not answer the prayers of those who believe in him through the execution of more than 10,000 poor people.

The shocking response of the thirty-two leading church officials forces us to recognize a serious problem. Here exploitation and the violation of human rights are "theologically" justified. Something that is routinely condemned in the eyes of humanity is justified in the eyes of God! This is a grievous situation that Christians can fall into.

"They exchange the glory of God for the image of a bull that feeds on grass" (Ps. 106:20). A demonic exchange. When such an exchange takes place, the human perspective on values is distorted. "Have they no knowledge, all the evildoers who eat up my people as they eat bread, and do not call upon the Lord?" (Ps. 14:4 RSV). This is the biblical message that comes to everyone, whether outsider or insider. To say "It is presumptuous . . ." may sound humble. Yet it can mean dulling the cutting edge of the gospel in the world today. Without the sharp edge of the word of God we shall easily settle down to a theological position that justifies human greed.

What Doug says about President Carter's inviting Cardinal Arns to ride in his limousine must be carefully considered. He points out that the insult to the Brazilian president, General Ernesto Geisel, resulted in greater pressure on "those advocating change and the recognition of human rights." It is true that well-meaning symbolic acts can effect a negative influence upon the very cause that the symbolism is meant to promote. This is a sample of the complexity that exists between symbolism and history. We recall the Lord's words of caution: "Be wary as serpents, innocent as doves" (Matt. 10:16). Perhaps President Carter was not as wise as the serpent. That the incident had a reverse effect is, however, Doug's interpretaton. It is not that of General Ernesto Geisel, nor is it that of the people or of those who are behind bars. It is the interpretation of an outsider. The symbolic act as a criticism of social injustice must be studied from many angles. In this case it is important to know how Cardinal Arns interpreted this symbolic ride with the American president.

There is one more subtle danger in Doug's viewpoint. It might inhibit all symbolic acts against social injustice. One can *always* emphasize the reverse effects of such acts. At the same time I appreciate Doug's words of caution about the choice of time, place, and form of symbolic acts. There, indeed, we must be as wary as serpents.

Whether change should come through revolution or evolution, it must come to any society that subsidizes the rich with resources taken from the poor, whether those resources be money, time, or the sweat of their labor. Benjamin Villaca places emphasis on "education and evangelism." He opts for gradual change. His advice to the church and the North American companies is to "send us aid without strings attached." His position is not that of the individualistic escapist. He is committed to change.

These three persons represent three possibilities for the church today. The first is to take active participation in the total life of a nation. The second is to concentrate church energy and resources on conversion alone. The third is a gradualist position. Each speaks with a sense of intellectual and spiritual integrity. I believe the discussion must go on among these three. The living church must be able to seek mutual corrections.

Alan is landing in New York. He is to make a report with recommendations to his United Methodist Church, and to his company. In obedience to the gospel of God, who is concerned about the poor, the widows, and the orphans, Alan must on both occasions relate his observations.

He must share this with the passion of his full humanity. That would be a preamble to what he has to say. I think he should read at both meetings Luke 4:18–19 and tell what this passage meant to him in terms of his visit. His company must be challenged by the Christian viewpoint. Alan must know that there is no easy solution to this painful situation. His observations must be shared with others.

The Christian faith is future-oriented. It believes that there is hope in this world in spite of all its darkness. Our world is not a world abandoned by God. Jesus Christ was abandoned on the cross in order that this world should not be abandoned. To say this is easy; to practice it is extremely difficult. That the world is not abandoned by God means that we are participating in the power that maintains and energizes this world in accordance with the will of God. The kingdom of God must be realized at every point of human history as much as is possible. Our sincere participation in this process is rooted in the deep sense of our repentance before God. It comes from our commitment to the God of the poor and the oppressed.

The Commission on World Mission and Evangelism of the World Council of Churches, meeting in May 1980 in Melbourne, Australia, acknowledged that when Christians pray "Your kingdom come" it does not mean that we may just sit down and wait. It is not a prayer of uninvolved bystanders. It is a prayer of responsible participation in the rule of God in this world and at this very moment. Christian eschatology demands our historical involvement. Our God is an ethical God, not a magical God. Alan is being confronted by this ethical God.

In this paper I have mentioned the other major world religions only in passing. The peoples of other faiths would be very much interested to know what Alan will say to his company and to his church. His report would provide an exciting moment of witness for Christ.

NOTE

1. Quoted in Plácido Erdozaín, *Archbishop Romero: Martyr of Salvador*, John McFadden and Ruth Warner, trans. (Maryknoll, N.Y.: Orbis, 1981), pp. 75-76.

SELECT BIBLIOGRAPHY

Anderson, Gerald H., and Stransky, Thomas F., eds. *Mission Trends No. 4*. New York: Paulist, 1979, pp. 71-76.
Brown, Robert M. *Theology in a New Key*. Philadelphia: Westminster, 1978, pp. 155-88.
Gutiérrez, Gustavo. *A Theology of Liberation*. Maryknoll, N.Y.: Orbis, 1973, pp. 101-19.
Niebuhr, Reinhold. *An Interpretation of Christian Ethics*. New York: Seabury, 1979, pp. 84-122.

Case Study 8

CHINA AND THE CHURCH

Chang Yao-chung was sixty-seven years old. Now retired from his occupation as a farmer, he received a modest pension from his rural commune in southeastern China. Chang spent several hours each day working in the plot of land given to him by the commune for personal use.

With a certainty that had been growing, he believed the hardships of the past years were behind him and his wife, Lin Mei-hua. Now, however, James Wong had traveled from Guangzhou (Kwangchow)[1] with an offer that deeply disturbed him and threatened to upset his quiet life. Chang had first known James in Shanghai over thirty years earlier. James had left China with his family before Mao's "victory of liberation," in 1949. He was now a successful businessman in Hong Kong and returned to China frequently to visit relatives who still lived in Guangzhou, long known in the West as Canton.

Chang turned from hoeing to greet his neighbor's young son returning home for the evening meal, having spent his day in school. Chang was suddenly reminded of his own son's youth and the drastically different life his family had led in the now distant past.

Twenty years earlier, Chang had been a prominent bank manager in Shanghai. He had also been an active lay leader in a major Protestant church. His home was large and comfortable; his only son—then fifteen—was already an accomplished pianist. Because of Chang's importance in the business world, his family had not suffered as some did during the early formation of the People's Republic of China (PRC), from 1949 to 1958, or even during the "three years of hardship"—1960 to 1962—which involved natural disasters and the economic upheaval following the withdrawal of all Soviet aid. However, with the launching of the Cultural Revolution (1966), his fortune drastically changed.

The violence and chaos brought by the Red Guards—groups of young militants who often assumed broad powers—burst into Chang's life with the death of his son during a riot at the university. Then, a few days later, when Chang was at the church, a large group of Red Guards, shouting against the "traitorous running dogs of the Western imperialists," descended on the church building. They ripped out the pews, broke windows, and gathered hundreds of hymn books and Bibles, burning them in a giant pyre in the street. The fire lasted for two days. Chang learned that the same thing was being done in Christian churches throughout the city.

Following a period of beatings and public ridicule to force them to confess to being traitors, the pastors and two lay leaders, including Chang, attended mandatory re-education sessions. These involved intensive study of the writings of Mao Tse-tung. The sessions continued for over a year. The men had no work and lived on a small monetary allowance. Then in 1968 Chang and his wife were sent many miles south to work on a farming commune. Chang later learned that one of his pastors had been sent to work in a ball-bearing factory. The church building was converted into a warehouse.

Though he was physically strong and quite fit for his fifty-two years, Chang remembered the first year on the commune as grueling. From dawn to dusk he stooped to plant acres of rice seedlings by hand. Possibly because of her frail stature, Lin was assigned to care for babies in the commune nursery. But Chang felt the change was no less difficult for her as they both adjusted to the meager rations and rough housing of the peasants.

It was known by the commune heads that they were Christians. Chang believed that as a consequence his first assignments were more menial and their living quarters more severe than those of others who had been forced to move to the commune. Yet he and Lin soon learned of other Christians there and began to worship regularly in secret. They met in one another's homes, whispered remembered hymns, quietly shared the understanding of memorized Scripture, and prayed with one another.

A New China

That harsh time was a part of the past; the commune leaders now tacitly acknowledged the quiet gatherings of Christians and did not interfere. Though it was not possible to talk openly with nonbelievers about his faith, Chang had found ways to communicate his Christian beliefs and values to others. He was convinced that his faith had not only sustained him through the commune years but had given him a chance to witness to others through his cheerfulness, cooperation, and genuine caring for those around him. As Chang and Lin had told others in their house meetings, there was "no way to suppress the joyous spirit of Christ that lived in them." They sought "to glorify God by doing their best at every task."

Chang had been elected six years ago to a position of responsibility in the commune. Even before this he and Lin had acquired their own small home and a fertile piece of land for vegetables. They shared a courtyard, kitchen, and outside toilet with another family. With money from the sale of their extra vegetables, and bonuses for good work, Chang and Lin had bought furniture, a radio, and a sewing machine. Throughout the commune Chang was aware of an incredible improvement in the general living conditions of the fifteen thousand persons who lived and worked together. They all had enough to eat; there was inexpensive basic medical care and basic education for everyone. Chang remembered the abject poverty, filth, and disease in which millions in China had suffered during his youth. Changes had begun after 1949, but he understood there were now even more dramatic improvements, with basic necessities assured for virtually everyone.

Though they had no son to care for them in their old age, Chang and Lin were grateful for the community in which they now lived. They were assured friends, a pension, housing, food, and medical care for as long as they lived.

Chang and Lin now felt little desire to return to Shanghai, but they were always eager to receive news about their former home and about national events. Reliable news about the church was especially difficult to get. Their best source was Chang's nephew, Chin Jun-an, who visited them on the commune every five or six months when his work as an engineer brought him from Shanghai to a city near the commune. Chin had been full of news on the last two visits about a revival of the church linked with a reaffirmation of the government policy of religious freedom.

Chang received the news from his nephew with pleasure and excitement, but he also expressed to Chin that he was still cautious about the government's promise of religious freedom. Chang had heard those promises before the Cultural Revolution and had experienced how quickly guarantees could be withdrawn under the influence of a group such as the Red Guards. His brother-in-law, Chin's father, like Chang's own son, had been killed at an early stage of the Cultural Revolution. Yet Chang listened with fascination to his nephew's account of the church's restoration throughout China.

"Uncle, the reports now indicate that by July of 1981, there will be at least one hundred fifty churches open again in the PRC," declared Chin. "This is not enough to serve the estimated one million Christians in China today. But given the fact that all places of worship—Christian, Muslim, and Buddhist— were forced to close during the persecution of religious believers, the recovery is striking. Some Christians even suggest that numbers of believers may have grown when institutional religion disappeared between 1966 and 1976."

Chang remembered asking his nephew with fascination, "How and when has the church begun to re-emerge?"

Reopening the Churches

Chin began to explain. "The Three-Self Patriotic Movement (TSM) has played an important role. The principles that gave this Protestant group its name—self-government, self-support, and self-propagation—have been strongly reasserted. The TSM joined with members of the Catholic Patriotic Association (CPA) and with Buddhist and Islamic leaders to petition the government for the reopening of churches and temples. This freedom is guaranteed first by article 88 of our 1954 constitution and again by article 46 of our 1978 constitution. As you know, the latter was written after the downfall of the 'Gang of Four' who supported the Cultural Revolution. The Protestants through the TSM also made a proposal to the government to allow them to reopen churches in Shanghai. The government responded positively and one of the first churches to be reopened was the Mo An Church in Shanghai. This was in September of 1979. The Rice Market Church in Beijing (Peking) had been open since 1972 serving foreign personnel, mostly from embassies.

"Where did the support come from to refurbish these church buildings?" Ghang inquired. "I heard they had been converted into warehouses, factories, and schools during the Cultural Revolution."

"The Mo An Church is a good example of the rebuilding process. For many years it was used as a school. The Religious Affairs Bureau of the PRC is responsible for implementing the government policy of religious freedom. The bureau has been empowered to implement decisions in favor of reopening places of worship. Thus the TSM had the support of the Religious Affairs Bureau in reopening the churches." Chin also noted with appreciation that this support involved no control of curriculum or policy decisions of the TSM.

"The process of reopening the Mo An Church was not easy," Chin continued. "First, space, which was extremely scarce in Shanghai, had to be found to relocate the school. The process began by freeing the sanctuary. As other space for the children can be found, the church will move into the rest of the building. Much of the money to operate and remodel the church is coming in the form of back rent for use of the church property during the Cultural Revolution. The terms for this repayment of churches have been negotiated with local building committees and sometimes rents run as high as 20 to 40 percent of the net income over these years. I understood the figures vary depending on the present condition of the buildings and the attitude of local officials. The church legally owns, for example, hospitals, schools, churches, and YMCA buildings. Even partial payments of back and present rents, plus the gifts of time and money from Christians, allow the churches modest but adequate resources to rebuild."

Out of Retirement

"Where has the staff for the newly reopened churches come from? And what has been the response of Chinese Christians?" Chang asked these questions remembering his own initially secret and then somewhat more open family gatherings for worship on the commune.

Chin, sensing his uncle's anxiety, responded to his questions with care. "As you well remember, in the turmoil of the 1960s we had few students in our

Christian seminaries. By 1966 most ordained members of the clergy were already middle-aged. Like yourself, they were sent to factories or communes during the Cultural Revolution and by 1980 many were of retirement age. Thus just under 50 percent of the men and women now serving as pastors have come out of retirement to serve the church while living on their pensions. This is the case with two of the pastors in my local congregation in Shanghai, the Gau-Ji or Community Church, one of five now open in the city.

"The only elder of this church still living who was on the pre-1966 governing council," Chin stated, "was sought out in retirement and asked to help reorganize the reopening of the church. This elder confessed to me that when he was first approached, he was afraid. He feared the possible return in the future of another Cultural Revolution. He shared his belief, however, that 'Christians must be patriotic to the government and trust in Christ.' So he agreed to supervise the repair of the building."

Chin spoke softly but firmly to his uncle, "I do not understand much of what happened in our country during the last decade nor can I see into the future. However, as an active member of the church in Shanghai, I am pleased with what is happening and I think you would be too, my uncle. Our church had been used since 1966 to house an opera company. Now six months after reopening, there are two services held each Sunday with over a thousand persons at each service. The sanctuary seats only seven hundred, worshipers often come at 6:00 A.M. in order to have a seat for the 7:30 service. We have just opened a chapel that seats an additional two hundred; it has loud-speakers from the sanctuary. One-fourth of our congregation is made up of young persons. We have a long way to go, but the TSM is helping us to rebuild our churches and urging the government to assist us in printing our own Bibles. This demonstrates that we are patriotic, loyal Chinese Christians."

A National Context

Chang asked, "What is the relationship between the historical Chinese Protestant church and the TSM? What influence have leaders of the TSM had on your perspective?"

"First, I now see the church within the context of our country's history," Chin declared. "Linked by language and history, our Chinese civilization is the oldest one in the world to have kept its shape into our modern era. The 'Eternal China' of our ancestors was shaken to the roots by the peasant revolts of the nineteenth century. The Beijing mandarin rulers could not reform their dynasty in time to halt the exploitation of China by foreign interests. The British, Russians, Japanese, and Americans all came to claim their shares. Even Hong Kong, I am reminded, began as the spoils of the Opium War and was lost through a mandated lease to Britain in 1842. China virtually surrendered its independence for a century after the Opium War. The very name of this conflict was a symbol of the means by which the outside world for whatever reasons corrupted and exploited our people, even as our own Chinese rulers had often done.

"The agony of the peasants, 80 percent of whom were underfed and oppressed, resulted in a revolution that sought to turn back all foreign influences. A Marxist revolution by the workers resulted in a class struggle in which Chiang Kai-shek's government, called the Republic of China, was overwhelmed in 1949 by Mao Tse-tung's army. And in the PRC under Chairman Mao it was promised that all things would be made new.

"Recent events, including the condemnation of Lin Biao (Mao's named successor at one point) and the 'Gang of Four,' one of whom was Mao's wife, are leading to a new official evaluation of Chairman Mao's role in the Cultural Revolution. Mistakes were made even by Chairman Mao, which is to be expected in a young nation, even if it has an ancient culture.

"As one humbly participating in the creation of a reconstructed China, I am also coming to a new understanding of the role of the early Christian missionaries in China. Being a product of that missionary movement, I never heard my parents discuss what I am now reading about the history of China. Those missionaries may have unintentionally and unknowingly been agents in the West's political domination of China. The imperialist powers forced China to accept Christian missionaries and in the nineteenth century protected 'missionary rights' with gunboats. But who protected the rights of Chinese from religious invasion? The doors to China were first kicked open by military force and then pried open again in the nineteenth and twentieth centuries by missionaries anxious for converts. I can find only a few records of missionaries who were critical of the economic and political forces that were linked to their own success. Though the missionaries brought schools and hospitals in the name of Christianity, I believe now that many ignored the social injustices that tended to keep China poor, weak, and politically disorganized.

"Because Christianity was identified with the West," Chin continued, "the violent outbursts against churches in the Cultural Revolution are not surprising. Christianity was seen as a foreign religion controlled by missionaries. Although Buddhism and Islam originated on foreign soil, they were more accepted by Chinese because there was no obvious link to external domination."

The Three-Self Movement

Chin shared with his uncle what he had discovered about the TSM through the Shanghai church and contact with its leaders. "I have recently learned that the three-self idea emerged early in the 1880s, but it did not have significant success. The modern TSM started in 1950 under the leadership of its chairman Dr. Y. T. Wu. Initially Wu had been associated with the YMCA movement and its strong emphasis on world peace and social justice.

"Due to the historical, political realities of the PRC in 1951, the word 'patriotic' was added to make it the Three-Self Patriotic Movement. A cooperative relationship was established with the Communist Party's United Front, which sought unity among religious groups in the 'New Democracy' of China. Shortly after this, Catholics established the Catholic Patriotic Association with similar self-reliant goals and relationships with the government. There were also informal groups of Christians meeting in private homes, having no formal link with either of the other two groups.

"With the beginning of the Korean War, in 1950, U.S. church support was cut off and the Chinese churches were forced to be self-supporting," Chin continued. "From 1950 to 1958 the churches decreased in membership and resources. At this time Protestant churches of different denominations began joining together at the grass-roots level. You surely remember in 1958 when the Shanghai Anglican and Baptist churches across the street from one another held a 'common service.' This happened in many places. The pastors began to work together and the churches pooled their finances. However, the churches respected denominational differences—for example, baptizing both by immersion and sprinkling. It is important to note that the TSM affirmed these unions but did not initiate their formation. This was the beginning of what Bishop Ting, current chairman of the TSM, describes as our present church. In his words, 'A new kind of Christianity is emerging before our eyes: postdenominational, deinstitutionalized, and declericalized.'

"It is my personal impression, and of course I could be mistaken," Chin confessed, "that positions the Three-Self Movement has taken are necessary conditions for the survival of the church in China. Thus, relatively free from government intervention, Chinese Christians, both Protestants and Catholics, have begun to gather again in churches for formal worship on a regular basis, though many continue to meet in the private informal setting of Christian homes. However, beyond worship, the Three-Self Movement stresses anti-imperialism and Chinese selfhood. The Three-Self Movement has sought to participate in the struggle and hopes of all the Chinese people since liberation. Bishop Ting has said, 'Chinese Christians came to realize the love and compassion of Jesus more profoundly when they identified with the weak, the poor, and hungry, and with those who for generations had been alienated, dehumanized, marginalized, and badly sinned against by unjust social, economic, and political systems.'

"Comments I read recently by Sister Chiang Pei-feng of Nanjing," Chin said, "very much support this understanding and reflect the view of a number of Christians. The sister said she was taught many years ago to oppose the communists as enemies of God. She had been taught that Christians were God's children but communists were children of the devil. The work of the TSM opened her eyes. . . . Now she understands that Christians should love their country and that Jesus welcomed all persons to come to him. In her words, 'The Bible does not say that communists are enemies of God. Only men have said this.' "

Chin added that he had seen where the sister had also said, "When I saw that the communists loved humankind, I looked anew at the Bible, which speaks not only of loving God, but also, like Moses and Paul, loving one's own people and all peoples.' The sister says that many Christians believe that witness to Christ and service of country are part of the same task. The 'Love-Country Movement' has made it possible to preach publicly and now to open churches.

"It seems to me this is a new understanding of the role of the church in China for most Christians influenced by a missionary presence. Don't you see, Uncle?" Chin asked quietly. "I am struggling to think about my faith and my country in new ways."

Need for Bibles

Chang nodded in agreement as his nephew told him of the emerging church and the role of the TSM. He then asked, "I see some of the goals of the TSM; but how does this relate to Christian groups like ours, far from centers of influence and from the churches that are reopening? For example, we have no Bibles on this commune. Will the TSM help us with this?"

"In 1980 I hear that the TSM printed about 135,000 copies of the Bible in Chinese, including whole Bibles and New Testament versions," Chin exclaimed. "And next year 250,000 copies are projected for publication. It is exciting, especially after the Cultural Revolution, to have Bibles printed in China with the support of the government's Bureau of Religious Affairs. These Bibles have now been distributed across the country where Christian groups were known to be meeting. It is not necessary for these groups to support the TSM to receive Bibles. It is estimated that in three or four years, we will have one million Bibles published."

"Why must we wait so long when I am sure there are overseas friends who would be pleased to help us?" Chang responded.

"The Chinese church could, of course, accept Bibles," Chin replied, "as gifts that are an expression of Christian love. However, Chinese Christians were given many gifts in the past that had strings attached. Han Wenzao, an associate secretary general of the Christian Council and TSM, has expressed the preference that Bibles be published in China. This provides proof of the truth of the church in China; we now have Bibles produced on Chinese paper, from Chinese printing presses, and distributed by the church in China. Han Wenzao tells the story of a member of the former Little Flock who was moved to tears when he received his first copy of a Bible published in China. I must admit that I, too, felt the greatness of this achievement when our church received its first copies.

"I must add," Chin continued, "that there appear to be those who call themselves friends of the church in China, but who do not understand the situation of our newly emerging church. Bishop K. H. Ting issued in December 1980 what has come to be called the "Fourteen Points" (see Appendix) to clarify the relationship between Christians at home and those abroad. This was done because some friends were not even consulting the leaders of the church in China about activities that would affect our church. Claiming there was 'no religious freedom' in China, some have even tried to smuggle in Bibles, some of which contain anticommunist propaganda. This activity is not only embarrassing but makes the government suspicious that the church in China may come under foreign control again and violate its own self-supporting principles."

Chang paused before asking the next question, "How would a group of Christians such as ours who meet regularly on a commune acquire these new Bibles?"

Chin responded by telling his uncle that some areas had already held provincial Christian conferences to elect representatives to the TSM. Chin would let him know if there were any representatives in his province. He could request Bibles from the representative or inquire directly at the TSM office in Shanghai. The TSM distributed Bibles to family meetings as well as to churches.

Chang shared with his nephew that he was somewhat anxious about their relationship to the commune; commune leaders who were once antagonistic to Christians now quietly tolerated them but did not support their gatherings. Some commune leaders were still convinced that all Christians were against communism. Chin reminded his uncle that the Religious Affairs Bureau had been given authority to challenge those who did not permit religious freedom. He told Chang of a specific case the past year in which leaders of a provincial capital were rebuked and ordered to recall anti-Chrisitan literature they had distributed.

As Chang remembered the conversation, he had asked for more information. "What do the leaders of the TSM see as the greatest needs of the church at this time?"

"According to Han Wenzao, nurturing is the major task of the church in China at the moment," Chin stated. "The churches must be reopened, Bibles must be published, and Christians must be trained in the use of Scripture. Just like you and your fellow Christians here on the commune, many thousands of others have been without Bibles since 1966. There is a fresh interest in Bible study and training of leaders. Our first Protestant seminary has opened in Nanjing (Nanking) this spring with forty-nine students drawn from over three hundred applicants. A Catholic seminary will soon open in Beijing. There have been over thirty thousand requests directed to the TSM for theological extension courses coming mostly from lay persons like yourself, active in the family gatherings or house churches. Requests focus on biblical studies for lay leaders. Through the efforts of the TSM and the support of the Religious Affairs Bureau, it is hoped these needs will be met."

Government Policy

"Why are you so confident that the promises of the Chinese Communist Party (CCP) are reliable?" Chang asked his nephew. "The official communist attitude toward religion has not changed, has it? The Cultural Revolution gave evidence that a government policy of freedom of religion can be temporary. Under these circumstances, how can the TSM support the government?"

"Yes, in 1966 when the Cultural Revolution began," Chin responded, "there was an antireligion policy instituted. However, since 1976 there has been open criticism of the Gang of Four who dominated that destructive period. They are now seen as having deviated from the original tenets of the constitution.

"The CCP United Front Policy initiated in 1949 established a new government political process known as the Chinese People's Political Consultative Conference (CPPCC)," Chin reminded his uncle. "These conference gatherings, ranging from a local to a national level, allowed minority perspectives, including ethnic and religious groups, to be represented. The Three-Self Movement and the CPPCC appeared to be the only routes open for Christians to participate in 'nation building.' However, through involvement, some Christians found themselves in leadership positions in China's drive toward 'selfhood and independence.' Without judging the appropriateness of the decision," Chin mused, "it may have been a necessity for the survival of an organized church in China. I am not sure what I would have felt the Lord was calling me to do if I had been active in the church at that time."

Chin added, "I know that the Cultural Revolution meant suffering for all persons associated with 'things foreign and bourgeois.' This was certainly true for our family. However, it was through this suffering and the persecution of the church that some TSM leaders believe Christians earned the right to be regarded as an integral part of the struggle to build a new China. Ironically, it was through participation in a political struggle that Christianity began to be truly 'indigenized' in China for the first time. It was possible for the first time to be a Christian and also truly Chinese."

"That is one important interpretation, and I am grateful for your involvement in the church and your sharing," Chang responded. "But we need also to ask ourselves the more basic question of the CCP's attitude toward the church. I remember even fifteen years ago some friends arguing that the whole United Front Policy was merely short-term expediency and that the patriotic religious organizations were tools of the Chinese Communist Party. Now you say that the United Front represents a long-term policy that was undermined by extremists during the Cultural Revolution. Today the reemergence of the United Front and revival of religious groups make this view more credible. From what you describe, it seems that presently the official government policy is one of religious freedom. Thus I must ask," Chang continued, "whether this technical freedom could be simply a way to use religious believers in the desperately needed push toward modernization. In past visits, you have also told me of renewed relationships with America. Is it possible that technical and limited freedom for Christians is a way to placate the predominantly Christian West?"

Chin paused and drank from the cup of hot tea his aunt had prepared. He then responded slowly, "This view is possible, and Christian friends in Shanghai frequently ask the same question in our small Bible study group that meets weekly. Recently we read Mao's 1945 statement on religious freedom, which one member of the group brought for us to see. I have a copy of one page here in my briefcase. It states: 'All religions are permitted . . . all believers . . . enjoy the protection of the people's government so long as they are abiding by its laws.' I agree that originally one motivation for religious freedom may have been based in part on encouraging law-abiding participation in the building of a new society among an extraordinarily diverse population. But in 1979 the National People's Congress passed two criminal codes making it illegal to interfere with the exercise of one's religious freedom or to use religion to exploit citizens.

"The United Front policy, which is supported by the TSM, seeks to solidify the diverse elements in our country around common national goals that vary with time. The CPPCC is a government structure formed to promote discussion and communication. The CPPCC involves not only religious organizations, as I said, but also ethnic minorities, occupational groups, and even political parties other than the Communist Party. It surprised me to learn there is a fairly large number of political parties represented in the CPPCC. Of the 1,280 delegates at the recent Shanghai conference, less than fifty were members of the Communist Party. Thus, the argument, as I understand it from the Three-Self leaders, is that it is better to have some Christian representatives on such a consultative council and risk the dangers of manipulation, rather than have no voice at all. A United Front policy is necessary for the reconstruction of the country by all who love China. We have faith in Christ. We must also have confidence in our country."

Chang asked, "How do you balance this hopeful view of the Three-Self Movement against the concern about another step toward coopting religion for the state? Perhaps the government's condoning of religion—expressed in organizations such as the Religious Affairs Bureau—is not only to have law-abiding citizens, but primarily to have productive ones and avoid trouble. I heard that CCP's vice-chairman, Deng Xiao-ping, said, 'I couldn't care less about individuals' religious beliefs as long as they observe the law and work hard.' The goal is modernization and every minority must be enlisted if possible. How do you interpret the role of the government's Religious Affairs Bureau? How does your study group consider this issue?"

Chin replied, "It is clear that the bureau's director, Xiao Xianfa, who visited Shanghai recently, reflects the Chinese leaders' pragmatic attitude toward religion when he declares that all of China's people, including religious believers, are needed for the program of modernization. Whether Xiao's position is manipulative or totally honest remains to be seen."

"I must say this troubles me," Chang responded slowly. "I can still remember almost word for word Zhou Enlai's (Chou En-lai) address to a group of religious leaders when I was still in Shanghai in 1950—some sixteen years before our churches were forcefully closed. The essence of what he said was:

So we are going to go on letting you [Christians] teach, trying to gain converts. . . . After all, we both believe that truth will prevail. We think your beliefs untrue and false; therefore, if we are right, the people will reject them, and your church will decay. If you are right, then the people will believe you, but as we are sure that you are wrong, we are prepared for the risk.

"I wonder, after the Cultural Revolution, how much of a risk the CCP is willing to take. If the church grows, will some new element in the party emerge to close us down again? Yet," Chang concluded, "in spite of the doubts of an old man, I am pleased to hear your reports on the TSM and on events in Shanghai and Nanjing. I confess that I am still confused about the church in China. Our family gatherings for worship and fellowship are meaningful and secure. Some Christians here have become model workers and members of the commune's governing council. They have gained respect through a witness of deeds rather than words. Now we need Bibles and educational support, and some would like to have a small church." Chang recalled that they then discussed the family over a meal and said goodbye, looking forward to Chin's next business trip south in about six months.

An Alternative

As Chang recalled this dialogue with his nephew, he was aware of how sharply it contrasted with his visit with James Wong. James, a good friend and former business colleague, had sent a message that he hoped to visit for a few hours his old friend Chang whom he had not seen in over thirty years. It was during this visit that Wong's offer of Bibles and money confronted Chang with a difficult decision. Chang recalled their conversation, especially Wong's final words.

"Chang, the last few hours have renewed our personal friendship from the old days in Shanghai. The Lord has allowed my business to prosper in Hong Kong. I have not suffered as you and your family did during the Cultural Revolution. You have a struggling house church on this commune and I am concerned about the future of the church on the mainland. As an evangelical Christian businessman, I should like to make a gift to you and the church. You have expressed the need for Bibles, for hymnals, and the desire to have a church building. I can provide several hundred copies of the Bible and will arrange to get these across the border with a business order I must bring to Guangzhou next month. This will be enough for Christians on this commune and enough for you to distribute to other Christians in the province. Also I want to privately give you and our brothers in Christ enough money to ease your hardships and perhaps to clear the way for a church building of your own. The Lord has given me riches in Hong Kong and I want to share them with you."

"Your offer is very generous," Chang replied, "and we do need Bibles and hymnals. However, in a recent visit with my nephew, I have learned that leaders of the TSM are against this course of action. The church in China should produce its own Bibles if we are to maintain our independence and our self-supporting principles. Also I don't want you to make an offer that might lead to any inconvenience or even danger on your own part. I must refuse your kind offer of support. What we need most are your prayers."

"Chang, I hope you will not refuse the offer until we have discussed it further and you have had time to think about it," Wong proposed. "I will be passing through here tomorrow on my way back to Guangzhou and Hong Kong. You must not be concerned about me, although I appreciate it. The border system is relatively safe. Also the opportunity to do this as an act of faith would be a privilege. The Chinese constitution is supposed to guarantee religious freedom, so I do not see this as an illegal act; those border officials who stop Bibles are clearly violating individual rights set forth in the constitution."

Individual Rights vs. Corporate Gain

Chang did not respond to his old friend's urging. Wong looked intently at him and spoke thoughtfully, "During this, my first personal visit to the PRC in many years, I am struck with the changes I find. The hunger and disease that plagued China, especially Shanghai, seem to have been eliminated. Yet what disturbs me is the enormous cost of this development in terms of personal freedom and individual choice. The government appears to control, directly or indirectly, every important organization and decision. That seems to be the case with these new patriotic churches."

Wong continued, "I have heard the argument that this central control was necessary in order to assure the basic rights of the entire population over against the individual rights of given persons who might jeopardize the welfare of the whole for the sake of personal profit. Yet the Cultural Revolution was a disaster for China and is now generally acknowledged even by Chinese leaders as a mistake. Policies designed to force a whole population to the level of the masses—ostensibly for the good of the masses—made university presidents clean the toilets in their own institutions and sent capable businessmen and bankers, like yourself, to do manual labor in factories or on farms. The real development of the country was delayed for ten years. This is a result, I believe, of the control of all institutions by government policy. Hong Kong is sometimes mismanaged and unequal in opportunity, but it is free. The young people are not assigned to an occupation but are free to make their own choice; business decisions are made on the basis of different views of the economy and the market. God created us with a diversity of skills and talents; Christ's offer of abundant life urges us to see that all have the freedom to exercise them for success or failure."

Chang looked at Wong and responded carefully. "Perhaps, my friend, you do not understand fully what it means for us as a people to have enough food. I, too, did not understand the agony of poor peasants until I lived with them. The choice of a vocation is a luxury when you and your neighbors face starvation. I was reminded by my nephew in the church in Shanghai that the gospel calls us in Matthew 25 to feed, shelter, and clothe those in need as if they were our Lord. If the PRC is now providing food and housing for everyone, perhaps they are doing the Lord's work without knowing it. Perhaps that is why the TSM and the Patriotic Catholic Association urge us to work together to build our country."

The Issue of Outside Help

Wong responded, "The TSM and the Patriotic Catholic Association, although both well-meaning, may have succumbed to government control for the sake of survival. Some Christians believe this is unintentionally reflected in Bishop Ting's 'Fourteen Points.' Why is one so afraid of genuine help from the outside unless the TSM is also concerned about losing control of religious development in China? The TSM offers too elaborate a defense of communist party policies and makes repeated statements that they are 'not forced upon the people.' The link between missionaries and imperialism in the past is probably true, but seems exaggerated by the TSM to the point that all past external religious involvement is now perceived in terms of colonial and imperialistic aggression against China. The TSM policy is seen by some overseas Christians to be dictated by a desire to protect its jurisdiction and, above all, avoid having Christianity seen as a 'foreign religion.'

"Thus, the 'Fourteen Points' explains why missionaries, donations, imported Bibles, and even Christian broadcasts beamed at the mainland are unwelcome. This sweeping condemnation of overseas friends is an affront. The document seeks to justify exclusive influence by the TSM over all religious activities. However, if Jesus is Lord of the whole world, then no plan for individual institutional church sovereignty seems justified."

Wong continued with enthusiasm. "A mandate comes to us from the gospel of Matthew when Jesus says, 'All authority in heaven and on earth has been given to me. Go, therefore, and make disciples of all nations.' If other authorities—either of one's country or the church—block the distribution of materials essential to making disciples, then the Bible says we are to obey God rather than men. Bibles and funds provided from around the world are simply one example of Christians responding to the needs of other Christians in the name of Christ's love. The TSM's refusal of outside help is an indication of its desire to dominate. I believe this is the reason why the house churches continue to thrive even in areas where churches have been opened. The people do not want to worship in churches opened by the TSM, which may have sold out to the government."

Church and House Church

Chang responded strongly, "I do not believe there is an 'official Chinese church' sponsored or controlled by the government through the TSM or through the Religious Affairs Bureau. Bishop Ting, Shen De-Rong, and other church leaders have won the respect of government officials and have been appointed and elected to national and local People's Congresses by the people. In 1949 no pastor was elected to a governing congress. Religious leaders are now working together under the sponsorship of the TSM to have the wording of the constitution changed to allow propagation of religious belief, which is now guaranteed only for atheism. I believe my nephew when he says the TSM is seeking to form a bridge between the people and the government, but the TSM is autonomous, not controlled by the government. In the same way, I see the TSM seeking to serve the church but not seeking to dominate it.

"Also, I know that it is difficult for you to understand, because you have lived so long in Hong Kong. But I believe you are exaggerating the difference between the so-called house churches and the public worship congregations of the patriotic movements. The family worship service has always been part of the Chinese tradition with close family units. My nephew in Shanghai has told me that the continuation of the family gatherings stems less from resistance to the TSM movement than from a preference for fellowship and convenience. Even where churches are open, they are often very crowded and far away for many members. Many older persons especially prefer the family gathering; here they sometimes listen to a tape recording of regular church services made for them by younger worshipers. If a church service with a pastor were available to us here on the commune, our family worship meeting would probably continue. It is natural that a few are also still afraid of exposing themselves to the danger of a possible new Cultural Revolution.

Interim Freedom?

"That is precisely my point on the Bibles," Wong declared. "You may be in a brief or even extended period that allows expression of religious belief. It is vital that you are now provided with Bibles, educational materials, and funds to nurture the church while there is time. If you refuse the offer and for some unforeseen historical circumstances the PRC policy changes, the TSM and those who cooperated with their restrictions will have deprived people of the word of God."

"One must not only have the word of God, but know what it requires of you and then do it," Chang replied. "Since I have been at the commune, I have begun to hear the Scriptures speaking to me in a way I refused to hear in Shanghai. James, how are we to understand the passage about it being more difficult for a rich man to enter the kingdom of God than for a camel to go through the eye of the needle? Hong Kong is filled with rich men. How are they to do the word of God? In the PRC that obstacle for me is removed. The question is what the Lord requires of me this day, in this place. How valuable is even temporary religious freedom if you misuse it?"

Wong responded rapidly and with enthusiasm. "You are correct when you refer to temporary religious freedom. Recent publications indicate that public worship in all the faiths may be only temporary in China. For example, the director of the Research Institute on World Religions of the National Academy of Social Sciences in Beijing, Ren Jiyu, has an article in a recent edition of the journal *Ching Feng*. I have copies of this with me as well as other material that expresses the plans of the Chinese Communist Party. I will bring more copies the next time I visit. The director justifies religious research because one must recognize it as a human phenomenon that has an impact on the people. Ren is clear that ultimately 'religious theology on the one hand and science and revolution on the other hand cannot tolerate each other . . . the abolition of religious authority has become an important responsibility. . . in the democratic revolution.' Ren's position appears to be that of recognizing the interim existence of religious belief and practice. I understand the purpose of the institute to be the development of a Marxist science of religion. The critique of theology, which is its aim, will finally reveal that religion is not only irrelevant to China's secularized society, but also potentially dangerous if the fallacious and superstitious basis for all religions is not exposed by scientific materialism.

"There appears to be now in the People's Republic," Wong explained, "a proliferation of conferences, institutes, and centers concerned with religion. One of these is the Center for Religious Studies at the University of Nanjing. The Marxist evaluation of religion as the opium of the people has not been rejected or even modified by the CCP. However, the pragmatic teaching of Mao is that the abolition of religious authority, necessitated by mutual antagonism between religion and the democratic revolution, is not best accomplished by a deliberate state policy of eradicating religion. Human beings resist such encroachment on their freedom. Rather, it is the process of history itself, not the force of government control, that will bring about this goal. In the meantime, the study of religion and the support of its institutional structures in Buddhism, Christianity, and Islam promotes unity, encourages goals of modernization, provides for critical study, and produces good will and contacts on an international as well as national level. Given these statements by their own study centers, how can you not believe that the TSM and CPA are being used as tools of the government?"

Wong continued, "I can see how some of the Christian literature coming from outside could create problems for mainland Christians. Brother Andrew of Operation Pearl and Paul Kaufman of Asian Outreach make requests for support based on strong anticommunist appeals that see atheistic communism as the anti-Christ. Yet I am not convinced that they are wrong. They certainly appear to me to be right about China's need for biblical and educational material. In connection with appeals for Bibles and funds, these groups also highlight a lack of true religious freedom on the mainland. They maintain that some Christians, both Catholics and Protestants, are still in prison. The publicity over Roman Catholic Bishop Dominic Deng, who was released after twenty-two years in Chinese prisons and labor camps, brought the issue to the world news scene."

Bishop Deng

"It is true, according to my nephew, that some Christians remain in prison," Chang responded. "However, they are there for political, not religious, offenses. Bishop Deng, so I understand from what my nephew said, was incarcerated in 1958 on charges of 'counterrevolutionary' activity. He was accused of preventing young Chinese men from joining Chinese volunteer units to fight in the Korean War. Deng also was said to have threatened excommunication for those Catholics who joined the Patriotic Catholic Association (PCA), which had been formed in 1957 as the Catholic equivalent to the Protestant TSM. My nephew said that Deng repented of his crimes and was not only released in 1980, but at age seventy-three was reappointed as bishop of Guangzhou by the PCA, although I assume he had always remained bishop in the eyes of Rome. The mistake of Bishop Deng, in my view, was to proceed from Hong Kong—where he had gone to visit relatives and have medical treatment—to Rome. There he was appointed by the pope as Archbishop in China, evidently without consultation with the PCA.

"However, my nephew states that the PCA has insisted on the right to appoint its own bishops and clergy without reference to the Vatican for a number of years, just as it has objected to the Vatican's recognition of Taiwan as the 'Republic of China.' It is hardly surprising, given the independent nature of the PCA, that both Beijing and the Catholic Church in China should have denounced the appointment. Deng was dismissed last June from his PCA appointment as bishop. This incident is only an illustration of the Vatican's misunderstanding of the Catholic Church in China. As a man of seventy-three who had spent twenty-two of his last twenty-three years in prison, it is understandable where his sympathy would lie and how little of the new China he would understand. There can be little hope of rapprochement between the Chinese church and churches overseas until our independent and autonomous role is acknowledged. Why is the attempt to control the Chinese church from the outside not seen as a denial of freedom in the same way you accuse the CCP of manipulating the church on the mainland?"

Nurture or Prophecy?

"There is need for independence," Wong conceded, "but how autonomous the patriotic churches really are has come into question in many circles. The governments described as oppressive by the PRC—those of South Korea,

Taiwan, and Argentina—have all imprisoned priests and bishops who are fighting for the rights of their flocks, especially the right to criticize the government. Each country has publicly declared that these persons are imprisoned for illegal political activity—not religious reasons. Some American and Korean pastors did what Deng was charged with—namely, urged their parishioners not to participate in the 'Korean police action,' which was called a war by their governments and which brought death to soldiers and civilians on both sides.

"Few persons, and certainly not I, question the good will of the TSM or PCA leaders," Wong continued. "The concern is about the wisdom of their judgment and the right to exclusive jurisdiction over religious activities in China with the assumption that they speak for all Christians in China because they have government recognition. It would be more convincing if there were some prophetic critique of the PRC government by the Chinese patriotic churches. A respected world organization such as Amnesty International, the 1977 winner of the Nobel Peace Prize, acts on behalf of prisoners of conscience. It lists not only Taiwan, South Korea, and Argentina, but also the PRC as a country where reports of flagrant violations of human rights occur with regularity. I realize it is both dangerous and alienating for the TSM to speak publicly on these issues, especially given the church's priority on church nurture. However, some Christians in South Korea and Taiwan are willing to be prophetic at the expense of church growth."

Chang responded to his friend thoughtfully. "From what you ask of the church in China, I assume that churches in Hong Kong speak out strongly against instances of injustice and demand equal sharing of resources, just as our government is struggling to achieve. But with no history of a Cultural Revolution and its dangers, you cannot imagine the implications of what you are asking of us."

The Choice

"My friend," Wong replied, "I know that Christ gives us strength to do his will. I see my calling as a Christian to make available the word of Christ and only to ask that the Scriptures speak for themselves. Thus I ask you again to accept my offer of help, given your needs. You have a responsibility to think about your fellow Christians. You yourself have told me of the strange beliefs surfacing among Christians who have been too long without Bibles or trustworthy commentaries. There are those who are convinced they are not truly saved unless they dream that their names are written in the 'heavenly book of life.' Still others who were physically healed by Christian laying on of hands believe that Jesus was a doctor. As you say, some do not understand the true meaning of Jesus as savior. Without Bibles, it is difficult even for a trained lay leader like yourself to convince others of the meaning of only partly remembered Scripture. You have told me your nephew will bring you a few Bibles on his next visit. I can send you enough for your entire family gathering and enough to share with other Christians, plus money to use for the needs of the church. I want to help you as a gift of Christian love and support with no strings attached. The government or the TSM need never know. Please give me a response by tomorrow. If you do not want the help, I intend to make a similar offer in Guangzhou before I return to Hong Kong. May God bless you and care for you in this place."

After seeing his friend to a waiting car, Chang went to his garden and restlessly began hoeing weeds. He was not certain about the correct response to Wong's offer of help. He saw a choice between the individual needs of his fellow believers for Bibles and religious education at a definite date versus the needs of a whole church struggling to achieve a new identity as seen through the eyes of the official leadership of the TSM. He, too, was concerned that the Chinese people see Christianity as an indigenous faith—not dominated by the West. Chang also knew that only by the suppression of some individual rights, including his own for a choice of occupation and location, was China being transformed into a society of which he was now proud. China could and did feed and care for all its people as the Lord commanded in Matthew 25. Yet Chang was struck by the notion that his own Chinese pride might be blocking a bridge to the universal church of Christ and access to God's word, both of which were certainly essential to any authentic nurture of the church.

Chang would not assume responsibility for the decision alone. It must be made together with the members of the family gathering. He knew many friends had been excited to hear from his nephew of the emerging church and the work of the TSM. Yet he also knew that some were still bitter over the communist party. A great number of the young who had been forced to work on the farms for a few years had now been allowed to return to the university and to jobs in the city. However, many of the older Chinese who had no family and no connections remained apparently forgotten on the commune. Chang was afraid they would neither support the TSM nor request its Bibles, because of its stance in support of the government. Others would be unwilling to risk alienation from the commune leaders and their neighbors by an open request for Christian literature. How would he personally respond if they urged the secret acceptance of Bibles and funds from James Wong?

By tomorrow Chang would need an answer for Wong. Tonight he would take the matter to the family gathering. His anxiety about the meeting and about reaction from the commune leaders, genuine pride in his country's achievement of the past thirty years, his concern about the TSM—all were at war within him as he bowed his head and prayed for guidance.

NOTE

1. In January 1979 the government of the People's Republic of China changed the transliteration of Chinese names for persons and places from the Wade/Giles system (its version appears in this text within parentheses the first time the name occurs) to the Pin Yin system, to approximate more closely the Chinese pronunciation.

Appendix

A CALL FOR CLARITY: FOURTEEN POINTS FROM CHRISTIANS IN THE PEOPLE'S REPUBLIC OF CHINA TO CHRISTIANS ABROAD[1]

BY BISHOP K. H. TING[2]

There has already been a good deal of reporting on the Chinese Christian situation and on our guiding principles, but there is still some confusion among fellow Christians overseas, including those in Hong Kong. I would like to present some of our views.

1. New China

We Chinese Christians take a positive attitude towards New China. It is not as it was before Liberation when we took a negative attitude towards the cause of the Chinese people's liberation—as a result of misinformation and misunderstanding. Christians cannot deny that New China has brought many good changes to the Chinese people. For over thirty years the price of our food and other necessities has basically been stable. In the past, there were many Chinese people who did not have enough to eat. Now, although special delicacies may be out of reach, our nine hundred million people have enough to eat, so that there is no longer the need for people to go scrounging for roots and tree bark. Our approximately 10 percent of the world's arable land feeds almost 25 percent of the world's people. This must certainly be regarded as an amazing accomplishment, even though it is not a miracle. In

---

Translated by Philip Wickeri

the past, many people were without adequate clothing. On the streets there were rickshaw pullers, beggars, and other poor people who often went barefoot in the rain and snow. Now there are no more rickshaws or beggars, and everyone has shoes and adequate clothing, even a cotton-padded jacket for the winter. The jacket may be patched, but it is no longer worn by several generations, as it was before. People's thinking and mental outlook have also undergone significant changes. Despite the ten-year catastrophe, the level of people's morality and self-respect is much higher than it was before Liberation.

For a poverty-stricken people deprived of their rights for thousands of years, to have made mistakes in their first attempt at governing a vast country is only natural. But mistakes cannot stifle the wisdom and character of a people which has stood up. There have been many shortcomings in the thirty-year history of New China, and more than a few mistakes. But summing up both our negative and positive experiences and learning from them, we will once again move forward. Thus, those overseas people who gloat over our misfortunes are really too short-sighted.

For us, patriotism is not just an abstract love of a nation with a long history. It is first and foremost a love for New China. Our positive attitude toward New China is genuine and based on facts. The claim of some persons overseas that our patriotism is feigned—dictated by the desire for church survival—is an insult to us. Of course our patriotism is not without a prophetic and critical character. It does not mean blind praise for everything in our homeland.

2. The Policy of Religious Freedom

We regard the policy of religious freedom in New China to be a reasonable one. Communists do not have a high regard for religion, and we harbor no illusions about the Communist Party on matters of religious faith. But the Communist Party is a good political party which aims at uniting the Chinese people. For the sake of national unity, it maintains a respect for the people's customs and special characteristics, including religious ones. It would benefit neither national unity nor socialism if this respect were neglected. The Communist Party understands this better than anyone else and, therefore, advocates the policy of "emphasizing the common ground while preserving differences." "Emphasizing the common ground" refers to the common ground of patriotism. "Preserving differences" means a recognition of and respect for the differences among people, and refraining from trying to eliminate them. Just as the difference between the national minorities and the Han Chinese cannot be eliminated, neither can those between believers and nonbelievers. Therefore, the Communist Party maintains a policy of religious freedom. We consider this to be a policy as good for religion as it is good for the country.

I am of course speaking of the Communist Party and not of the "Gang of Four." The Gang of Four is not the Communist Party and the Communist Party is not the Gang of Four. The Gang of Four wished to eradicate religion, but the Communist Party seeks to protect religious belief by adopting the policy of religious freedom. Since the smashing of the Gang of Four, we are returning to the Communist Party's original policy of religious freedom. Overseas there is the mistaken idea that the religious policy of the Communist Party itself has changed or loosened. This confuses the Communist Party with the Gang of Four and is of no help for coming to a correct understanding of New China. Today, the Communist Party is leading the people throughout China in revolution and reconstruction, and the Gang of Four has been put on trial in the people's courts. To speak of the two as one and the same really creates a lot of confusion.

3. Organizations in New China

China is a properly constituted country. Each of the organizations listed below has its own proper function and sphere of authority, and these should not be confused:

(1) The *National People's Congress* (NPC) is our supreme national legislative body. Only the NPC is empowered to approve and revise the Constitution, the Marriage Law, the Penal Code, the Civil Code, and other laws. Appointments of important officials, such as the premier, vice-premiers, and department heads, must also be approved by the NPC. Deputies to the NPC, which may be both Party and non-Party members, are elected by each province. There are deputies who are religious believers.

(2) The *Chinese People's Political Consultative Conference* (CPPCC) is our political consultative body. While NPC deputies are elected by each province, members of the CPPCC come from every corner of Chinese society. Membership is drawn from the youth, women, workers, peasants, and soldiers; from the Communist Party and democratic parties; from cultural, athletic, scientific, and religious circles; from the national minorities, overseas Chinese, and people from all walks of life. The CPPCC is an important institution for the promotion of socialist democracy and an important organ of the United Front. There is within the CPPCC a religious group, comprised of Buddhist, Islamic, Taoist, Catholic, and Protestant representatives. The 46th article of the present National Constitution stipulates: "Citizens enjoy the freedom to believe in religion and the freedom not to believe in religion and to propagate atheism." Members of the CPPCC religious group are dissatisfied with this article, which preserves a lingering influence of the Gang of Four period, and have made a proposal that it be changed. If this proposal for modifying the wording of Article 46 of the Constitution is passed by the

next session of the NPC, then we will be happy. If not, we will continue in our efforts.

(3) The *State Council* is the administrative or executive organ set up under the NPC. It is the central Government of our country.

(4) The *Religious Affairs Bureau* (RAB) of the State Council is set up expressly for the handling of the religious affairs of the State Council. It does not deal with the faith, life, and work of Buddhism, Catholicism, Protestantism, and all other religions. There are some people overseas who, consciously or not, have created confusion by saying that the RAB of the State Council supervises us and that Chinese Christian churches and organizations are parts of the RAB. This would be totally at odds with our social and political system. The bulk of the work of the RAB is to represent the state and the government in implementing the policy of religious freedom. For example, when we want to open a church, the RAB assists us by negotiating with all parties concerned. Or, when we need special paper for the printing of Bibles, the RAB helps us arrange for its purchase. In 1980, we bought eighty-two tons of paper for the printing of 135,000 Bibles. As we will be printing more Bibles in 1981, the RAB will continue to help us with the purchase of paper and arrangements for meeting our printing needs. The RAB of the State Council only handles the religious affairs of the State. As to the development of the Chinese Christian Three-Self Patriotic Movement and the administration of the Chinese Church, these are our own concerns.

(5) One important organization in the life of our country is the *Chinese Communist Party.* It is the leading force behind the Chinese revolution and national reconstruction. This leadership is not forced upon the people. After much investigation and study, the Party puts its proposals regarding principles and policies before the NPC, the CPPCC, and the people for their study, revision, approval, or adoption. Party members through their exemplary role mobilize the people for the implementation of the adopted policies.

(6) The National Committee of the *Chinese Christian Three-Self Patriotic Movement* (hereafter the Three-Self Movement) is the patriotic association of Chinese Christians ourselves, not a governmental organ. That there are friends overseas who think of the Three-Self Movement as a department of the RAB is the result of the distortions made by certain individuals. The Three-Self Movement was founded by Chinese Christians ourselves. Although there were some missionaries and Chinese church leaders who advocated Three-Self before Liberation, the Three-Self principle of the Chinese church could not be implemented full-scale under the historical conditions which prevailed at that time. When Y. T. Wu and others launched the Three-Self Movement after Liberation, they did receive appreciation and encouragement from Premier Zhou Enlai (Chou En-lai). But this certainly does not mean that the Communist Party told the Chinese Church to launch such a movement.

(7) We have also set up the *China Christian Council* for the pastoral needs

of the Chinese churches. This is the Church affairs organization of Chinese Christians.

In sum, organizations in China are properly constituted and the differences and relationships among them should be clearly noted. Our Chinese churches are independent not only of foreign churches, but also of the NPC, the CPPCC, the Government, and the Party. It is wrong for people outside China to say that the Three-Self Movement is an "official church." China has no "official church." The Chinese Church is run by Chinese Christians ourselves. It is understandable why those who adopt a hostile political attitude toward New China would call the Chinese church, which generally supports New China, an "official church." We regard the term "official church" to be a political expression with which to attack New China. Among the many churches of the world, ours is not one which can be labelled an "official church."

4. Religion and Imperialism

Religion has been exploited by colonialists and imperialists in their aggression against China. We have not denied the scientific character of this assertion. Many of our policy decisions today are related to this fact. This is not any more a question which requires much explanation inside China. Even overseas, more and more people are today recognizing this fact.

5. Our Three-Self Principle

We are resolved to uphold the reasonableness and justice of Three-Self for the Chinese Church. On the basis of past history it is necessary for the Chinese Church to follow the Three-Self road. Today for the Chinese church to bear witness to the gospel among the Chinese people, self-government, self-support, and self-propagation are also necessary. We cannot return to the old situation representing a "foreign religion." Following the ten-year catastrophe, we are returning to our guiding principle of the fifties, not that of the forties. It is wrong for those people outside China who long for a return to the past to think that we are returning to the forties. A return to the forties would mean discarding Three-Self, again making Christianity a "foreign religion." In returning to the guiding principle of the fifties, we wish to continue to uphold self-government, self-support, and self-propagation, and to make the Church one which is well governed, well supported, and well propagating too.

6. The Unity of the Chinese Church

The present unity of the Chinese Christians is unprecedented. When I first came to Nanking in the early fifties, there were still many denominations separated by deep divisions. The members of one denomination in particular would not even pray with the rest of us. Now, the brothers and sisters of this group are not only willing to pray with us, but even to share the sacraments together. The unity which has emerged in the Chinese Church is closer than ever before. We are no longer separated by denominational walls. We do experience "how good and beautiful it is for brothers and sisters to dwell in harmony."

The number of churches which have been reopened is still quite small, perhaps not more than eighty at present in the entire country. But Christians have not stopped gathering together; many meet in their homes. It is a tradition in the Chinese Church for Christians to gather in homes to pray and read the Bible. Even in the past when there were many churches, people still liked to worship in their homes in addition to going to church. When I was little, my mother used to ask friends, relatives, and neighbors over to our home once a week for a worship service. There was an increase in such gatherings in homes during the "Cultural Revolution" period. We found there were twenty-five home worship gatherings in Nanking alone. Although many Christians now go to the churches which have recently been reopened, there are in Nanking, for instance, still five such home worship gatherings. Some older people find that it is inconvenient to go to services in churches because of the distance they would have to travel. Others prefer the intimacy of the home worship gatherings, while still others attend both types of worship. Frequently, people record a church service to take back to listen to in their home worship gathering.

There are people outside China who are not thankful to God that the Chinese Church is more united now than ever before, but instead try to split the Chinese Church by dividing it into a "Three-Self Church" and a "House Church." Why should the simple question of where one worships be turned into a contradiction between the home and Three-Self? Does the fact that first-century Christians all worshipped in their homes mean that they would oppose the three-self principle and rely on support from foreign quarters? Today in China, no matter where Christians gather for worship, the vast majority are patriotic and seek to defend and implement self-government, self-support, and self-propagation. When there were twenty-five home-worship gatherings in Nanking and the local committee of the Three-Self Movement called a meeting, those who attended the home worship gatherings all came.

We are pleased to tell you that now, after these ten catastrophic years of the Cultural Revolution, the Chinese Church is even more united. Christians saw with their own eyes that many leaders of the Three-Self Movement were harassed by the Gang of Four because of the Church, and yet they did not complain or advertise it. It was also these leaders who did what they could to preserve Bibles. Such actions could not but inspire people and deepen our unity in Christ. China being a big country with many Christians, it will always be possible to find a few people who disapprove of or oppose Three-

Self. But today the center of opposition to Three-Self is not within China, but overseas.

We Chinese Christians have chosen the road of postdenominational unity, not because we are better than anyone else, but because we live in our particular historical situation. In retrospect, we can only say that this has been a result of the leading of the Holy Spirit, who has allowed us to bathe in the ocean of God's grace.

7. The Work We Have Before Us

The Chinese Church does not only want to be self-governing, self-supporting, and self-propagating, but well governed, well supported, and well propagating. We must make up for lost time and do our pastoral work well. Each day we receive many letters asking us to send pastoral workers, and requesting Bibles, hymnals, devotional materials, and theological literature. These are the calls of Macedonia to which we must give heed. Chinese Church workers have a great deal of work ahead. Our churches must have good worship services; there must be better spiritual nurture for lay people; we must witness faithfully to the people around us; and we must be deeply concerned for the welfare of the Chinese people. To do all this we have set up the China Christian Council. It is not a Church, but an ecclesial organization for the service of Christians. We cannot proceed at a faster pace than one permitted by the present capacity of the Chinese Church. There are some questions, the sacraments and orders, for example, over which we are unable to arrive at a unanimity of opinion all at once. But there are many other matters which do await our common initiative. We have begun to print Bibles and have republished the *Tian Feng* periodical. The seminary has published teaching materials for nationwide theological education by extension courses, and it is also in the process of recruiting students. A newly edited hymnal has also come out for temporary use. Books for the training of lay people are now being edited. So the China Christian Council and the Three-Self Movement both have a great deal that they would like to do.

8. Evangelistic Work in China is the Responsibility of the Chinese Church

We do not approve of those people overseas who try to mold public opinion into thinking that they should send missionaries back to China. No matter how large the population of China is and how small our Church is, the responsibility for spreading the gospel and building up the Church in China is the mission of Chinese Christians. We will not invite missionaries to China from overseas. We wish to declare that no group or individual overseas should engage in evangelical activity in China without the expressed consent of Chinese Church authorities, who retain responsibility and jurisdiction in this area.

There recently was the case of an American passing out religious tracts on the streets of Guangzhou, who drew the attention and intervention of the police. Then he got angry and said that China had no religious freedom nor freedom for missionary work, and he threatened to telegraph President-elect Reagan requesting that America cut off its "financial aid" to China. We believe this person was in the wrong. If a large number of foreigners all acted in a similar fashion, then what would become of the image of Christianity in China? Would it not once again be regarded as a "foreign religion"? Would that not wipe away Chinese Christians' thirty-year effort in promoting Three-Self? Therefore we feel sensitive over the question of missionary work in China.

All missionary and church activities, including radio broadcasts beamed at China, which are carried on willfully and unmindful of Chinese Church authorities are expressions of disrespect and unfriendliness. It is not we who are closing the door of the Gospel in China. We are but learning the lessons of history. We uphold self-government, self-support, and self-propagation as the road of an independent and self-administered church in order to guarantee that the door of the Gospel may be open and remain open in China. It would simply be self-destructive for the Chinese Church to return to a colonial status, and that in the long run is to shut the door to the gospel. And for this American to speak of mutually beneficial trade as "financial aid" is just arrogance and lack of education.

9. Overseas Church Group's Activities with Non-Christian Chinese Enterprises

Some Church-related groups overseas are now in the process of negotiating with Chinese schools, hospitals, factories, communes, and other enterprises for cooperative investment and exchange programs. We would not have any opinion if these groups were not Church-affiliated, providing that they were not injurious to our national sovereignty. But we are concerned when Church-related groups are so involved. For example, can those church groups which are engaged in activity of a technical nature in China honestly say that they have no goal of bearing witness or doing mission work? Insofar as it is in the nature of a church to be involved in things, how can their people deny having that goal, even if it is not explicitly stated in the contract? This has serious implications for a whole series of questions. One is a question of Christian ethics on the relationship between means and ends. Another is the harm which could be done to the Three-Self principle of the Chinese Church if our jurisdiction is violated. There are priests, ministers, and nuns who came to China to teach English who have said that English teaching is their method and means but that their real purpose is evangelism. Is it honest for them to conceal their identity? Is it right that they should not consult the Chinese Church and in some cases should have even attacked us?

We cannot rely on foreigners for the preaching of the gospel and the building up of the Church among the nine-hundred million Chinese people. Let the church take root today in Chinese soil, so that tomorrow it may blossom and bear fruit. By doing missionary work in China in unauthorized ways, foreign churches will be going against the direction chosen by Chinese Christians thirty years ago and will have a damaging effect on Three-Self. We are deeply concerned and must study the matter more carefully.

10. No Return to Denominationalism

We feel that the Chinese Church can only go forward and not backward. The denominational consciousness of Chinese Christians has been quite weak. I myself am an Anglican, and there are many Christians and church workers in China who are also Anglican. But I do not know of any who want to restore the Anglican Church.

There are a small number of people overseas who have worked to restore their particular denominations in China, but they have not found popular support among Chinese Christians. We would like them to stop working to that end.

When former missionaries come to China, it is natural for them to seek out people they have known who belonged to their particular denominations. This is something we can understand. But let them not go so far as to attempt to revive denominational feelings and loyalties, thus inviting misunderstanding and unpleasantness.

11. International Relationships

We are a small Church with many responsibilities within China. We think our major efforts must be devoted to our domestic work. We wish to immerse ourselves in our work so as to push this experiment of ours forward. Then, perhaps sometime in the future, we will be able to speak of some contribution to the international Christian community. But for now, our international commitments must be limited, meaning that we must differentiate and be selective.

We want to have contacts and exchange for the purpose of mutual learning with church groups and individuals overseas who have a friendly attitude towards New China and who respect the Three-Self principle of the Chinese Christians. But we will adopt a different attitude to those individuals and groups who are unfriendly toward New China and oppose our Three-Self principle. Today we are making observations which will enable us to accurately differentiate one from the other. We are by no means suggesting that we regard only those who approve of everything that New China does as friendly. What we are looking at is their basic attitude in recent years. People can change, and we will not dwell on the past or try to settle old scores. We like our friends to grow more and more numerous.

12. Our Participation in International Organizations and Conferences

Here we must differentiate too, and, because of our limited resources, be selective. There are a number of organizations and conferences which have

taken a friendly attitude toward us in which we have not been able to participate. We have also not been able to invite many friendly church groups from
overseas for visits in China. We ask for our overseas friends' understanding
in these matters.

13. Material or Financial Contributions from Abroad

Ours is a very small church with limited financial resources, but we are able
to support ourselves. The strength of our position lies in the fact that we will
not do anything beyond our ability and thus be forced to become parasitic.
But because our Chinese Church is now already self-supporting and independent, there is probably no longer the need to maintain a simple "closed-door
policy" on the question of receiving contributions. We are pondering over the
wisdom of accepting certain contributions from friendly church groups and
persons overseas, with no strings attached and with due respect for the independent stance of our Church, simply as an expression of the universality of
our Christian fellowship. This may stop the slander of our enemies and dispel
the misunderstanding of our friends too.

Contributions would have to be from groups and individuals friendly towards New China and our Church, and there could be no strings attached. I
think we can open the door a little to allow people to make contributions to
our local churches. But larger amounts should generally be handled by the
China Christian Council, perhaps for its pastoral work fund, because we
could not allow foreign contributions to create or restore disparities between
rich and poor churches. This tentative idea will be discussed by the leaders of
the Three-Self Committee and the China Christian Council. If it is put into
effect, it would certainly be carried out with extreme care, and we hope our
friends overseas will be able to understand.

There are people overseas who presumptuously speak of financial contributions in the name of saving the Chinese Church, playing up their own role
by going so far as to solicit contributions for this purpose. We want to declare
that we have not and will not entrust anyone overseas to solicit contributions
for the Chinese Church. We basically believe that our Church should be content with what it has, enjoying its poverty and thriftiness. It should live within
its means by relying primarily upon contributions from Chinese Christians.
We are opposed to making a big thing out of the financial problems of the
Church, which would obscure its true character and witness.

14. Differentiation among China Programs in Overseas Churches

There are many "China programs" in churches overseas which seem to
take quite different attitudes towards China. We are observing and studying
these programs so that we may differentiate among them. We are very grateful for the good work which some of them are doing. But there are also others
which in name are engaged in research, in the promotion of prayer for China,

and in the work of Christian fellowship, but in actuality are collecting intelligence, spreading hate-China propaganda, and seeking to infiltrate China and violate our Church's jurisdiction. This tells us that we must not only listen to what they say, but also watch their actions. We must be careful observers and draw the necessary line of demarcation.

We will not disappoint those who are friendly toward us, and we will treat them in a friendly manner. Together with them in true Christian fellowship, we can more deeply enter into Christ's abundance and grace.

NOTES

1. "Fourteen Points" was published in *China Talk* (Ewing W. Carroll, Jr., ed.), a publication of the Board of Global Ministries of the United Methodist Church, Hong Kong, 1981, and in *China and Ourselves; Newsletter of the Canada China Programme*, Canadian Council of Churches, Toronto, No. 24, February 1981.

2. Bishop Ting is chairman of the Chinese Christian Three-Self Patriotic Movement Committee and president of the China Christian Council. The fourteen points discussed here were originally presented in a conversation with Rev. Andrew Chiu and Rev. Arthur Wu of Hong Kong on December 23, 1980.

TEACHING NOTE ON "CHINA AND THE CHURCH"

In responding to the offer of James Wong, Chang Yao-chung and his Christian community are faced with a choice that has far-reaching implications not only for the church in China but for the church universal. A discussion of this case could focus on several categories.

A. The relationship between church and state.
B. Communal rights versus individual rights.
C. The meaning of a postdenominational, deinstitutionalized, and declericized church.
D. The mandate of the church universal to evangelize versus the right of the Chinese church to national self-determination.

CASE PLAN
1. Trace the development of the Chinese Church before and after the Cultural Revolution. Discuss the role of the Western missionary presence as perceived by Chin. How did the TSM and CPA emerge? What changes did the Cultural Revolution bring? What is the official position of the Chinese constitution on religious freedom? What are the central components of Bishop Ting's "Fourteen Points"? What is the basis for his initital rejection of financial support from the West?

2. Discuss Chang's personal story. Over the past twenty years how have his views changed concerning: (a) the role of the government in the lives of its citizens and the subjugation of individual rights to the rights of the community as a whole; and (b) the relationship between the state and the church?

3. Wong criticizes the TSM and PCA for not risking "prophetic critique of the PRC government" for the violation of individual human rights. He further implies that these bodies have compromised the gospel and become tools of a government which needs their support for nation building. Chang, Chin, and Bishop Ting acknowledge the acceptance of continued government restrictions, and agree that the government officially dismisses the value of the church. However, they point to the fact that Chinese government policies have indeed brought about the mandates of Matthew 25: one quarter of the world's population now has adequate food, housing, and medical care. Develop the implications of these differing positions. Discuss how any

church keeps its integrity as it balances between its own mandates and the mandates of its cultural setting.

4. Following a discussion of the development of the Chinese Church, analyze the meaning of a postdenominational, deinstitutionalized, and declericized church. How are the Chinese Catholic and Protestant churches different from the church in most other parts of the world?

Develop James Wong's argument for the right of the church universal to evangelize. Consider a role play between Wong and Chin as they discuss Bishop Ting's declaration that "the responsibility for spreading the gospel and building up the church in China is the mission of Chinese Christians" (Point 8).

5. Following a discussion of the historical development of the Chinese church and a discussion of the issues raised by the case, move to a role play between Chang and his Christian community on the commune as they debate acceptance of James Wong's offer. Urge participants to be themselves and to develop the reasoning behind their statements of position.

SUGGESTIONS FOR ADDITIONAL READING

China Reconstructs. A montly publication distributed by the China Publications Center (Guoji Shudian), P.O. Box 399, Beijing, China, and published by China Reconstructs, Wai Wen Building, Beijing (37) China.

Carroll, Ewing W., Jr., ed. *China Talk.* A regular publication of the United Methodist Church available from China Liaison Office, World Division, Board of Global Ministries, 2 Man Wan Road, C-17, Hong Kong.

Chu, Theresa Mei-Fen and Christopher Lind, eds. *China and Ourselves; Newsletter of the Canada China Programme.* Distributed by the Canadian Council of Churches, 40 St. Clair East, Toronto, Canada M4T 1M9.

Lee, Peter, ed. *Ching Feng: Quarterly Notes on Christianity and Chinese Religion and Culture.* Available from the Christian Study Centre on Chinese Religion and Culture, Tao Fong Shan, Shatin, N.T., Hong Kong.

Meisner, Maurice. *Mao's China: A History of the People's Republic.* New York: Free Press, 1977.

Munro, Donald. *The Concept of Man in Contemporary China.* Ann Arbor: University of Michigan, 1977.

Terrill, Ross. *The China Difference.* New York: Harper & Row, 1979.

THERESA MEI-FEN CHU

COMMENTARY ON
"CHINA AND THE CHURCH"

In responding to Chang's dilemma, the first question to be addressed concerns the nature of the decision facing him. How much of his difficulty is grounded in a limited perception of reality? Speaking theologically, how much of his antipathy is derived from his own creed as he understands it? How much of his indecision is a carry-over from past history and, therefore, something that can be cleared up, provided Chang is willing to expand his understanding and confront present reality?

Chang has greatly changed in the course of thirty years. He has not been broken by the trials: loss of his only son, move to a life in the countryside where hardships abound, not to mention the work of tilling the earth and doing without the comforts of city life, which he had enjoyed for years as a bank manager. Striking is the fact that he and Lin have little desire to go back to the big city. That in itself speaks for the quality of his life. He delights in communicating his Christian beliefs and values and, inasmuch as he can do that very well in the commune, he is not anxious to return to the city. He and Lin are probably very virtuous persons. They seem to be patient, hardworking, kind to all, helpful to those in trouble. Along with the actual witness he is giving, however, Chang will discover greater possibilities of serving God and witnessing to Christ if he finds new insights for interpreting his faith.

For one thing, Chang really appreciates what his government has done and is doing for the people: fighting hunger and disease and trying to improve their life. But his antipathy, his lingering fear of and distrust for the Communist Party, complicates what would be a simple choice. The confusion he experiences is likely to be reflected by the commune group of Christians when the moment comes to discuss with them the issue of the gifts offered by Wong. But if Chang sees the positive aspects of the social change brought about under the leadership of the Communist Party, how much more so will those other commune members who previously lived in impoverished rural areas. For the latter, the revolution will have meant a change for the better in

230

terms of access to food, education, and health care. The issue, then, even for Chang, would not be complex if he had a clearer perception of reality.

However, if the choice is difficult for Chang, this may be due to a linkage vacuum between the positive, secular experience of progress and a faith interpretation that drove him toward a negative attitude about the very government that made the secular progress possible.

Chang must first identify the real issue. Is it a question of vowing loyalty to a government unconditionally and once and for all? If that is the case, Chang could understandably refuse to do so. However, no one is asking him to make that kind of commitment.

Given Chang's Christian beliefs and values, he would be the first one to obey the pertinent laws of his government. However, if he considers breaking the law by accepting smuggled goods, then he must ask himself seriously the reason for such inconsistency.

Chang's nephew, Chin, has been clear that the Bible is not a forbidden book in China. Chang now knows that it is not against the law to have a Bible. He knows that China has already begun to print Bibles. He also knows that it is against the law to import large numbers of Bibles without previous consent from the customs. Yet Chang does not need to break the laws of his country to receive Bibles.

Chang appears to perceive the issue as a choice between China and the church: "Chang was struck by the notion that his own Chinese pride might be blocking a bridge to the universal church of Christ and access to God's word, both of which were certainly essential to any authentic nurture of the church."

The real issue posed by the case seems to be: either ask the TSM for Bibles and run the risk of not getting enough copies for everyone all at once, or break the law and get the Bibles from the outside. For Chang to see the issue as one between the "universal church" and "national pride" is a false premise to start with. On the ground of such a premise, the choice would be between a universal Christ without the slightest political dimension on the one hand, and a godless nation on the other. Such an implicit view is indicated by another passage further on: "Chang was afraid they [the members of his Christian gathering] would neither support the TSM nor request its Bibles, because of its stance in support of the government."

The issue involves a certain attitude and worldview. The attitude is obviously one of distrust of the Chinese government to begin with, and of the TSM as a consequence. Many questions are raised by such an attitude: Is the freedom of religion guaranteed to the people a strategic move on the part of the government—that is, a move destined to create a good impression in the Western world, but not seriously meant? If this is so, would the policy not be subject to sudden, unforeseen, and irrational changes? Is the TSM an arm of the government despite the ministries it actually carries out in the service of the Christian people? His nephew could not convince Chang that the policy of freedom of religion is real and would last. This attitude in turn influences

Chang's worldview. He is split between a thankful, positive outlook on an ordered Chinese society achieved through government actions, and an overall refusal to endorse the government as other Chinese citizens do.

The confusion in Chang's worldview is further complicated by the fact that James Wong offers him money to help maintain the Christian community, probably with a view to seeing membership grow. The split between the spiritual and the material has its ironic consequences here as well.

The Bible, which ought to stand for the spiritual on the ground of Wong's own perspective, ends up linked with money of foreign origination. This money could mean greater purchasing power for more and better consumer goods made in China, and even the possibility for Chang eventually to leave China to settle abroad.

Wong's offer of money could have been an occasion for Chang to enter more deeply into the intermingling of the spiritual and the material aspects of life. In Wong's logic, the TSM lacks spiritual wealth. Yet it is Wong who offers him a monetary gift. The TSM, on the contrary, urges self-support. That means a more austere life shared with millions upon millions of Chinese who, to improve their own lives and the lives of their children, must work against enormous odds to build a better nation for all. Again, Chang would apparently defend these values of self-support. However, he seems to have a hard time sorting out the real from the apparent: the materialism linked to the "universal church" theory and the spiritual quality of the church in China at this point of history.

Wong does not tell Chang the source of the money he is offering, although the implication is profit from his own business. However, similar gifts offered recently to church leaders in China have been connected with fund-raising campaigns in many parts of the world. These campaigns could not have been successful without the explicit or implicit support of various governments around the world. Neither Wong nor Chang has given any thought to the difficulty of supporting those governments. Both seem prepared to accept these other governments without questioning what might be happening in the countries involved. Neither Wong nor Chang expresses any difficulty with supporting nonsocialist countries regardless of their practices.

Here, perhaps, we touch upon the crux of the matter: Can a Christian support an atheistic government? If the answer is in the negative, then the next question is naturally: Why? But, as long as the answer is in the negative, with or without reason, no matter what the Chinese government does or does not do, the so-called Christian perspective will always basically reject it. The same Christian perspective will also be in the vulnerable position of being manipulated by political powers that are hostile to the country.

If Chang's present worldview falls in this category, then it is easy to understand why he sees the issue as a choice between China and the church. Given his hesitation, however, perhaps he is called to ask the second question: Why? A series of related questions would be: Is it useful and necessary to make a distinction between what a government does and what it says? If so, which is more important? Chang might find some help in the parable of Jesus on the two sons: one who said yes to his father but did not act, and the other who said no but finished by doing the father's will. Chang will be assisted in his decision if he is able to expand his worldview.

A second central question raised by the case concerns the relationship between the faith one professes and the concrete, everyday life one leads. Can faith really be colorless—that is, above and beyond the social, economic, and political spheres of life? Chang's personal experience does not seem to affirm this kind of neutrality. Is Wong's offer beyond the economic and the political? Is the choice between an apolitical and a political faith? Or is the choice one between faith related to one kind of economics and politics, and faith related to another kind of economics and politics? Many Christians in the world live through life without having to confront such questions, but Chang is forced to do so because of the world situation, as well as his own situation in the world.

A third question emerges: Why does one think it necessary to doubt a government because it professes atheism but allows believers to practice and propagate their faith? Chang reiterates his fear that religious freedom might be disallowed later on. If this is the only reason for his fear, then it seems logical that he would seize the chance to practice his faith freely as long as he could do so. He would wish to consolidate his community and expand it as much as he could. His nephew offers him an opening to do so—through an avenue acceptable to the government—but he is reluctant. Would a hungry person refuse to accept food that is offered for fear that one day the food might be taken away?

Christians the world over have a choice of the particular form of Christianity that appeals to them. Chinese Christians are no exception. Postdenominational Christianity in China still respects denominational differences in approaches to faith and life. Conservative evangelism, which Wong, Chang, and the family gathering seem to profess, has its contributions to make. There is no sign of any reluctance by the Chinese church in accepting evangelicals as true fellow Christians. But conservative evangelism in China faces a privileged position of self-examination and of deepening its faith. It is time to move to a wider perception of reality.

What can possibly prevent Chang's community from living a life of more universal love? If it is not the freedom of religion that is in question here, what is the critical issue in the final analysis? In my judgment, unless Chang faces these questions, he will not be happy, whatever decision he makes regarding Wong's offer of money and Bibles. Perhaps what ultimately concerns Wong—and Chang, to some degree—is not so much Christ, but the particular form of Christianity and its ramifications in the social, economic, and political spheres of life. Instead of the living Christ, Wong appears to have bound himself to a set of institutions, styles, and methods, all of which have economic and political implications. He seems unable to distinguish between this type of faith and the "pure," apolitical, economically disinterested

Christianity he thinks he professes. Ironically, Wong binds himself to human institutions contrary to his profession of freedom from those institutions.

If Chang did not share some of Wong's attitudes, the choice would be simple for him. He could point out to his commune members that this is not purely a choice between law-abiding citizenship versus disobeying human law in favor of a higher loyalty to God. Chang could then point out to his friends that Bibles do exist in China and that more and more copies will be available to them, that the choice is not one between God, Christ, and the Bible on the one hand, and a patriotism not blessed by God on the other. He could explain to them that the choice is between upholding Christian values connected with the particular law and the particular style of nation-building in China at this moment, and seeking an easier, but illegal, way of obtaining copies of the Bible. He could also point out that the agency offering them money and Bibles might be supported by a philosophy hostile to their government; otherwise that agency would show more respect toward their government.

From a pastoral point of view, Chang could invite the commune members to think about the freedom of religion they presently enjoy—the freedom from materialistic enticement in society, and the encouragement to be virtuous, which they daily receive from the public realm, as well as from their Christian communal sharing. By introducing his fellow Christians to a realization of the presence of God in history, Chang could perhaps prepare them for a more authentic transcendence. Then their implicit concern will not be for self-preservation as a group, but for a life lived for Christ.

SELECT BIBLIOGRAPHY

Documents of the Three-Self Movement: Source Materials for the Study of the Protestant Church in Communist China. New York: Far Eastern Office, Division of Foreign Missions, N.C.C. of U.S.A., 1963.

Fairbank, John K. *The Missionary Enterprise in China and America.* Cambridge, Mass.: Harvard University Press, 1974.

Orr, Robert G. *Religion in China.* New York: Friendship Press, 1980.

Wei, Tsin-sing. *Le Saint-Siége et la Chine, 1922-1966.* Paris: Edition Allais, 1968.

GORDON DICKER

COMMENTARY ON "CHINA AND THE CHURCH"

The decision with which Chang Yao-chung is faced may appear relatively straightforward to an outsider, but to a person in Chang's position it is not easy. On the one hand, he is impressed with what his nephew has told him about the new religious freedom in China, the re-emergence of the church and the role that the TSM leaders are playing. He is impressed with what he sees taking place in the New China. In spite of the loss of his son and his own suffering, he is proud of the fact that as a people the Chinese at last have enough food. He accepts the fact that to achieve that goal it was reasonable that persons like himself had to give up their privileged lifestyle.

On the other hand his Christian faith is very important to him. It is this that has sustained him through the commune years. It is a joy to him that at last he is able to meet with fellow Christians with some degree of freedom. However, he cannot be certain how long this situation will continue. He has witnessed many changes of policy in China, some of them quite abrupt. The point made by James Wong will not be lost on him. This period in which expression of religious belief is permitted may be brief. The period allowed to Christians to replenish their supply of Bibles may be short. Can they afford to wait until sufficient copies come off the presses in China? Should he and the Christians of his commune not accept the offer of supplies from Hong Kong while they can? And after the special hardships inflicted on Christians in China, is it inappropriate that they should now receive some special assistance to relieve their hardships?

The significance of the case study for most persons, however, will lie in the fact that it poses serious questions about how Christians in other countries should now seek to relate to Christians in China. Beyond that, it raises in a quite concrete way important theological and missiological issues of much wider application. There are issues of the relationship of Christianity and culture, church and state, God and Caesar. These are as old as the New Testament itself and have always been a subject of debate, but this case study gives

235

a new twist to them. It is one thing to wrestle with these issues as they apply to our own situation; it is something else to try to resolve the questions that arise when we, in the midst of our wrestling, try to relate to another group of Christians who are struggling with the same issues in a totally different national, political, and cultural situation. This is what the case challenges us to do. There are a great many persons like James Wong in many countries who are eager to resume missionary contacts with China without thinking these issues through, and before the Chinese church has had time to think them through, and the result could well be disastrous for Christianity in China.

One of the issues with which Christians in China have been struggling for the past thirty years is the question, What does it mean to be both Chinese and Christian? This has been a major concern of the TSM, but clearly Chang has also been seeking an answer to that question. It would seem that many Chinese Christians, perhaps most, are now at the point where they can be wholeheartedly both Chinese and Christian. With the new openness of China to the West goes the danger that once again a Christianity heavily laden with Western cultural trappings will be pressed upon the Chinese. Even where it is not expressly intended, those who contribute to that lading give the impression that it is not possible to be truly Chinese and truly Christian at the same time. They broadcast the implication that to be a Christian one must first become a Westerner, just as in the early church it was sometimes implied that to become a Christian one must first become a Jew. To that implication the Scriptures respond with a firm no. Yet it continues to be a view widely held in the West that there is a Christian *culture* that must be adopted along with the Christian *faith,* and that it is *Western* culture. When Bishop K. H. Ting spoke at Trinity College, Toronto, in October 1979, he cited and criticized a paper by Fr. Joseph Spae in which this view found clear expression.[1]

H. Richard Niebuhr's work *Christ and Culture* has demonstrated that even in Western Christianity there have been widely differing views on the relationship between Christianity and culture. One of the extreme views is that which Niebuhr characterizes as "Christ against Culture." According to this view, loyalty to Christ is believed to require rejection of the culture of any society. Though some Christians have taken this view, it has not been widely held. At the other extreme is the "Christ of Culture" view in which Christianity and culture are accommodated to one another. This view has many more supporters, but it has not been the predominant understanding of the relationship between Christ and culture. Niebuhr identified three other positions on this relationship: Christ above Culture, Christ and Culture in Paradox, and Christ the Transformer of Culture. Each of these views, which between them would probably represent the majority opinion, in some sense affirms human culture but at the same time offers a Christian critique of it.

Niebuhr's analysis is instructive. Most Western Christians cannot simply affirm their culture; they view their culture critically and look to Christ to transform it and supply what is lacking. They cannot expect persons of other cultures to adopt it uncritically as part of what it means to be Christian.

At the same time missionary thinking has come to recognize that other cultures stand in a very similar position with respect to Christ. A critical assessment is necessary, but not outright rejection. Christ has clearly been a major factor in the shaping of Western culture through Christian tradition, but it is possible to speak of the cosmic Christ as a shaping influence in all cultures. Balinese are no longer expected to give up their rich culture when they become Christians. Instead, their culture serves and illuminates the gospel, and Christ illumines and transforms their culture. Australian Aborigines are encouraged to remain Aborigines when they become Christian, their own culture serving as a kind of Old Testament to the gospel.

Chinese Christians have a right and a need to be wary of cultural imperialism in the guise of Christian mission. The offer of Bibles is not in itself a threat; but the offer of money is a threat: it constitutes a temptation to break solidarity with the rest of Chinese society at a crucial point, which helps to increase susceptibility to other influences from outside Chinese society and culture.

It should be observed, in passing, that leaders of the Christian community in China have an excellent opportunity to rethink the matter of church order. Which aspects of church order belong to the gospel and which are purely cultural accretions and unessential traditions? One outcome of the recent history of the church in China is that it has been declericalized. The church must now consider whether it needs a clerical office and, if so, what kind. Christian leaders, especially those of the TSM, should seize the opportunity to think this issue through before they precipitately open seminaries and develop a clergy in the Western pattern. Christians in family gatherings—house churches such as Chang's—may not be eager to see such a development, and the TSM will need to listen to their voice.

Similarly, there has been some rejoicing that a deinstitutionalized Christianity has emerged in China. But already there are signs, in the report that Chang's nephew gives, that reinstitutionalization may be taking place. Again, the house churches may act as a brake on such a development. The TSM and the house church movement need to be in creative dialogue for the sake of the continuing indigenization of the church in China. The danger is that dialogue will break down because of suspicion and disunity. James Wong's offer of money, if accepted, is bound to promote both.

The issue of church-state relationships is raised by Chang's questioning of TSM support for the government. Many Christians in the West are likely to be suspicious of this also, though they support their own governments, often in quite un-Christian policies. In part this is due to the communist bogey. It is assumed quite uncritically that no Christian could support a communist government in any policy. In part, too, this is the result of parochialism. In the West we assume that the form of church-state relationships with which we are familiar is the only one that genuine Christians can accept. The pattern of relationships with which North Americans are most familiar is that characterized by the phrase "separation of church and state." According to this pattern, church and state both exist legitimately alongside each other, each with its own sphere of influence, and they interact in ways regulated by a long tradition of what is acceptable and what is not. The state does not enact laws with respect to religion, and the church has no direct voice in government. According to this understanding, the only way the church should influence legislation is through moral persuasion of lawmakers or by influencing the voters to change their lawmakers. In this process the use of the mass media to give publicity to criticism and prophetic statements is very important.

This, however, is not the only possible pattern of relationships between church and state, nor is it even necessarily the most effective or the most satisfactory. In medieval Europe a quite different pattern of church-state relationships prevailed. The church attempted to subordinate the state to itself and to some extent succeeded. Orthodox Islam still attempts to maintain this pattern. The results of this pattern have seldom been very impressive, though that is not to say that it cannot work well.

Yet another form of the relationship is that in which the church is subordinated to the state. Paul V. Martinson has argued that this is the form of relationship between religion and the state that traditional Chinese political philosophy requires.[2] He argues that if the church in China is ever to be accepted as indigenous, it must conform to this philosophy. It can be argued that it is not simply in China that this philosophy might apply, but in other Asian countries as well.

If this is the appropriate form of the relationship in China (and perhaps elsewhere also), it is not helpful for Christians who live under other systems to require of the Chinese church forms of action that are not congruent with that kind of relationship. For example, to expect of the church in China the kind of public criticism of government policy that one finds in the U.S.A. or in South Korea is unreasonable. This is not to say that the church does not know where it differs from the philosophy of the Communist Party or that it will not be critical where injustices or errors of judgment occur, but it will have its say in the Chinese People's Political Consultative Conference and will make its representations through personal contacts. That the church must operate in this way does not in the least imply that it has "sold out" to an ideology or is unfaithful to its own calling. Chang should understand this and so should those who live in nations where another pattern of church-state relationships exists.

It needs to be emphasized that it is not inappropriate for the church to go about its mission in a situation of subordination. It can be argued that this was the position of the early church within the Roman Empire when the gospel spread most spectacularly. St. Paul found a virtue in the fact that he had to speak out of a situation of weakness and vulnerability (1 Cor. 1:17–2:5). It was precisely his weakness, foolishness, and poverty that permitted the power and wisdom of God to be manifest through the message of the cross. By contrast, most missionaries over the past century have sought to commend the gospel from a position of strength. Even when they did not directly exercise political power, their alliance with colonial rulers gave them a position of privilege and superiority. Nowhere was the connection between missionary activity and political influence more obvious than in China during the century before World War II. To be sure, the way of strength was not without its achievements, but the way of weakness may be more effective and is certainly more in keeping with the Scriptures.

"God or Caesar" might be considered just another way of posing the church-state issue, but I take the phrase to refer to a number of questions at once more general and more personal. How far is patriotism compatible with Christianity? How far should Christian citizens comply with the laws of their country and in what circumstances may they conscientiously break them? These are not easy questions to answer, and Christians often take different attitudes with equal conscientiousness. In Australia and the U.S.A. there are some Christians—even bishops—who advocate withholding a portion of income tax equal to the proportion of tax money that the government spends on defense. Not all Christians agree on this, and many would argue that Christians are bound to pay their tax, whatever use the government makes of it (Rom. 13:6–7). In this area it is generally easier to say what others should do than to see what we should do ourselves. We may question the patriotism of others while taking it as axiomatic that all Christians in our own country should be patriotic. We may incite others to break the laws of their land while remaining very timid about doing likewise in our own country.

In the case before us Chang has to decide whether he is justified in being party to breaking the laws of his country by receiving Bibles smuggled in from Hong Kong. Wong argues that "if one's country blocks the distribution of materials essential to making disciples, then the Bible says we are to obey God rather than men." His argument would have some force if the government denied citizens the right to have Bibles or to read them, but that is not the case. It is in fact assisting in the production and distribution of Bibles. It has only placed an embargo on their import for reasons that have some substance to them. In these circumstances it can hardly be argued that God and Caesar are in such opposition that a true Christian is faced with choosing God rather than Caesar.

Looking at the issues the case raises, we should not neglect pragmatic considerations. We must always keep before us the question: What is best for the long-term mission of Christ in China? Chang must ponder that question in making his particular decision. He cannot simply think of himself, the Christian group in his commune and their need for Bibles. Having a good supply of Bibles soon may be a short-term benefit to Chang's house church. Even the acceptance of financial help may not seem difficult for him to justify. It is inconceivable, however, that other members of the commune will not eventually discover (probably sooner than later) what has happened, and then once again suspicions will be aroused that Christians are fundamentally disloyal to their country and Christianity unalterably foreign. If this sort of incident is repeated here and there throughout China, Christian mission will be set back another generation.

Similar considerations must guide mission bodies eager to embrace the new openness of China for evangelistic purposes. Broadcasts, materials, and evangelists from abroad may quickly gain some converts, but the burden of evangelization and nurture rests upon the church in China. Whatever embarrasses the Chinese church must, in the long term, hinder the Christian mission in China.

That is not to say that fellowship and dialogue between Chinese Christians and Christians from other countries is not to be earnestly encouraged. Christianity is fundamentally ecumenical, in the sense of belonging to the whole world and uniting persons of every race and nation. Prolonged isolation of any group of Christians cannot be beneficial. Chinese Christians need fellowship with Christians who look at the world from different perspectives, and other Christians need to be enriched by what Chinese Christians have learned and the wisdom they have gained through the experiences of the past thirty years.

For the sake of the Christian mission in China in the long term, Chang Yao-chung should support the objectives of self-government, self-support, and self-propagation. There is no reason why he should reject the general direction that the Three-Self Patriotic Movement is taking. That is not to say that he should uncritically accept everything the leaders of the TSM may say or decide. As a movement with institutional and worldly aspects, it will not be free from errors. Thus, although appreciating the initiative the leaders of the movement have taken, Chang and other Christians in similar situations might well plan to take a more active role in helping to determine the forms Christian community and mission will take in China in the years ahead. He will not be able to do that if he compromises his position by accepting Wong's offer. He must help his house church to see why they should say no.

NOTES

1. "Facing the Future or Restoring the Past?," in *Mission Review*, April/June 1980, reprinted from *China Notes*, Autumn-Winter 1979–1980. The paper by Fr. Joseph Spae that Bishop Ting criticized was contained in *Western Christianity and the People's Republic of China: Exploring New Possibilities*, James A. Scherer, ed. Ting quoted the following sentences from the paper: "All American values have Christian overtones. . . . America is a country which is a model of rational and humane government. . . . Its national ethos cannot be explained, let alone imitated, without reference to Christianity. . . . It reminds the Chinese of the best in the Confucianist tradition. . . . There was no greater loss for China than the loss of America in 1949."

2. Paul V. Martinson, "Musings on Church and State in China, 1979," in *Ching Feng*, vol. 13, no. 2, 1980.

Conclusion

ROBERT A. EVANS

FROM REFLECTION TO ACTION

Three Needs in the Rights Debate

Analysis of our research leads us to three conclusions that can be phrased in terms of three basic "needs," if all are to have access to the biblical promise of abundant life:

(1) The "rights perspectives" of the three worlds could be complementary rather than competitive. Thus, we need to nurture a broader, more global perspective on human rights. This calls for greater understanding of the legitimate variety and diversity of claims for human rights.

(2) Human rights need to be understood as interdependent and as forming the basis for a positive vision of human cooperation. As it is, human rights are all too often seen as restricted by the negative boundaries that lead to litigation or violence against any group or person who threatens to trespass upon the territory of our personal or national rights.

(3) In the midst of presently competing perspectives on human rights, issues of survival and liberation require that the global village to move toward some agreement on the priority of rights. An agreed upon priority list of rights is crucial where there are conflicts among nations or individuals about their claims for human rights. Guidelines must be such that they can be supported and gradually implemented through dialogue and action. However, this call for an international community prepared to make some sacrifices for the sake of the human dignity, liberty, and equality that stand behind any sound covenant on human rights.

In order for those who support one of the three world perspectives to be willing to relinquish some rights for others, we need to be able to understand the imperative before us. The case studies in this book and the commentaries that follow them have been offered to further this understanding. It is especially important to see the struggle over rights as one involving concrete human encounters, one that takes place in a global context, and one that can be illumined by education and dialogue.

In order to respond to the three components listed above, it is also imperative that we are reminded again and again of the human tragedy that can result when human rights are ignored, dismissed, or violated. The statistics on a global perspective are readily available in such documents as the *Report of the Club of Rome,* the *Brandt Commission Report,* and the *Global 2000 Report to the President.* All picture a world that, if it makes it to the turn of the century, and if present trends and national policies continue, "will be more crowded, more polluted, less stable ecologically," and perhaps—most frightening of all—will be more vulnerable to disruption by natural and human causes, including a nuclear war.[1] The hundreds of millions of poor will be even poorer, and the huge gap between the rich and the poor in every continent will widen.

This enormous disparity may not be communicated as well by statistics as by an analogy of the world population reduced proportionately to a village numbering one hundred residents. This analogy, using data from several sources, begins to make the problem graspable especially for those of us with a First World perspective.[2]

If the world were a village of one hundred persons, thirty would be white and seventy from other racial groups. One-third would be rich or of moderate income, and two-thirds would be poor. About thirty-five would suffer from hunger and malnutrition. At least half would be homeless or living in inadequate housing. In the village, forty-seven would be unable to read and write, and only one would have a college education. Six of the one hundred would be Americans and would have over one-third of the village's entire income, whereas the other ninety-four would subsist on the remaining two-thirds. The Americans would produce 16 percent of the village's food supply and consume most of it themselves, except what they would store for future use or even destroy to raise its value in the village market. Over half of the remaining ninety-four would be hungry most of the time and would consider the six to be enormously wealthy, disproportionately well fed, with three of them on a diet. Of the ninety-four, forty-two would eventually die of diseases such as malaria, or cholera. Another fifteen would die of starvation within a year; ten of these would be children. Yet the Americans would never get any of these diseases, nor would they be worried by starvation or malnutrition.

How would the wealthy six live "in peace" with their neighbors? Perhaps they would be driven to arm themselves to protect their possessions and privileges, perhaps even spending, as America now does, over twice as much per person annually for military defense as two-thirds of the villagers receive in total income.

There is of course in that village—even in the midst of such enormous inequality—laughter, music, dancing, and love. However, such a world village would not survive long without unrest and disturbance. Any illusion that it is appropriate to cry "Peace! Peace!" when there is no peace would be shattered. Ultimately, there can be no peace until we begin as a global community to do something about the wide-ranging disparities.

This analogy may also help explain the hostility and envy that was expressed by many of the knowledgeable persons in the Third World who were interviewed for this study. Poverty and illness are not a matter of accident or fate, but rather the result of a world order that denies not only hope but life to many of the globe's inhabitants. As both Pope John XXIII and Rheinhold Niebuhr, two of the moral leaders of our era, have said, "The path to peace is found in the struggle for justice."[3]

C.G. Weeramantry has written: "Taking a long-term view, the world village can do no better unless its citizens can see with unclouded eyes how idle it is in such a world village for some of the inhabitants to talk about freedom and equality for all."[4] This Third World voice reminds us that the struggle for human rights is critical in the perspectives of all three worlds.

Every case study in this book represents the human agony of violated integrity and dignity. Each should be analyzed for the impact it bears, the symbolism it purveys, to a world in which some issues of human rights are a matter of life or death, and frequently both. Perhaps most important, however, each contains seeds of hope, and the possibility of responses that can lead to a more just world.

The material is not divided into tidy categories of "worlds" or "rights," although the authors were originally tempted to do so. Such a division would belie the essential interdependency of each basic human right with others. Such a division would also belie the interconnectedness of the world community—what some have called the "global connection." Human rights cannot be pursued satisfactorily apart from this wider perspective.

Access to the "fullness of life" is the promise that stands behind the guarantee of human rights. The perspective must be not only more global geographically but also more affirmative in terms of human worth and dignity. At the heart of each of the international declarations of human rights is a vision of the human person in the context of a human community that has as its goal fullness of life. The life-sustaining conditions for that vision of fullness of life will vary from location to location. The need is to move from a predominantly negative and protective view of human rights, characterized by all three world views, to a more positive and visionary perspective implicit in all three. This vision sees the human community as one world, one fold, in which the protection of the human dignity of each person is ultimately the responsibility of all. If we are drawn to this vision, we must be prepared to make some adjustments and sacrifices for the sake of our neighbors in the global village. In the Christian perspective we are bound together as a human community by one who laid down his life for the sake of the fullness of our lives. Thus, some are called to bear the burdens of others in love, to take up their cross, and in ways small and large to lay down their lives for the sake of brothers and sisters in the global community.

Human Rights and the Church

"What were you arguing about on the way?" They were silent, because on the way they had been discussing who was the greatest. [Jesus] sat down, called the Twelve, and said to them, "If anyone wants to be first, he must make himself last of all and servant of all." Then he took a child, set him in front of them, and put his arm around him. "Whoever receives one of these children in my name," he said, "receives me; and whoever receives me, receives not me but the One who sent me." . . .
They brought children for him to touch. The disciples rebuked them, but when Jesus saw this he was indignant and said to them, "Let the children come to me; do not try to stop them; for the kingdom of God belongs to such as these. I tell you, whoever does not accept the kingdom of God like a child will never enter it." And he put his arms round them, laid his hands upon them, and blessed them [Mark 9:33–37, 10:13–16].

The children crowded around the young man, a Maryknoll priest, as he entered the room. They hugged his legs and he rubbed their heads; the affection between them was obvious, even to a visitor such as myself. He introduced me to the Nepalese staff of this small, experimental educational program for mentally retarded children in Katmandu, Nepal. I remembered our discussion a little earlier. "We came to listen and learn and serve," he had said. He did not have the traditional look of a priest as he swung off his motorbike following our trip to the outskirts of the capital of this tiny Hindu Kingdom in Asia. As I had been reminded earlier, Nepal was the second most needy nation, according to the U.N. Hunger, malnutrition, and disease stalk the nation to the extent that infant mortality ranges from 17 percent to over 50 percent in some parts of the country.

The young priest continued to share his understanding of his mission: "The mandate of Pope Paul VI—'we earnestly exhort everyone to strive by united planning and joint action for the full development of each individual and the common progress of all peoples'—became the basis of our work. Being present in Nepal in 1979 and 1980 for the International Year of the Child had an impact on me. Do you realize that conservative figures place the number of mentally retarded persons in Nepal at 10 percent of the population—over a million persons, most of them children? The children who escape death by starvation are shaped by malnutrition and years of living in hiding. They are being hidden and ignored by communities and the government because their plight is seen as 'part of their karma.' We listened and heard a cry for help."

He continued, "I asked how those kids were to have any hope and dignity and the answer wasn't very clear; except that somehow I bear some responsibility for their plight. Now we have a simple operation doing research, applying new models of education, working with parents. This is all with a nonprofessional Nepalese staff. A lay couple living on subsistence wages has joined us and so we begin to respond to our 'look and see' quest with a program we call 'HANDS.' It is a beginning and has become a model for the government not only here but in other places. I have friends in Nepal, Catholic and Protestant, working on hunger, health, education. You ask me why. Because the gospel is about liberation. It is the liberation of every person and community for their own humanity, as Jesus promised. It makes no difference if they are Hindu or Buddhist or nothing religious, but they are something in human terms. Christ cares about them and so must we."

Encounters like this occurred wherever I conducted the research: in the Korean ghetto of Kyoto, Japan; in war-torn Uganda; in the wretched shacks that make up the hillside *favelas* of Rio de Janeiro; in an Aborigine urban settlement in Sydney, Australia; in company-owned houses for migrant workers in Switzerland; and in the shelters for poor and displaced Blacks and Hispanics of "Springfield," U.S.A. Here, simple, humble, magnificent human beings of all ages, races, and religions are serving and laying down their lives for others in greater need. They are, for the most part, seldom demoralized or depressed. Perhaps, because they are risking their future for the sake of others, they offer one of the most hopeful signs I have encountered in all the segments of the societies we studied. There is a pervasive belief, as one Brazilian put it, that "Not only must things change but, by God, they will change."

It was my opportunity to experience, in isolated places on the globe, the response to the question of Catholic theologian Richard A. McCormick, S.J.:

What is the Church's proper mission in the sphere of the defense and promotion of human rights? . . . human dignity as we know it from the Christ-event and the Church's commission to spread the good news. . . . Unless the Church at all levels is an outstanding promoter of the rights of human beings in word and deed, her proclamation will be literally falsified.[5]

The basis for this proclamation of good news is recorded in Luke 4 as Jesus declares: "God appointed me to preach good news to the poor. . . release to the captives . . . and to set at liberty those who are oppressed." Unfortunately, in light of the full range of our interviews, one would be forced to conclude that the proclamation, in McCormick's terms, is indeed falsified. Sensitive, courageous, and committed persons, such as the Maryknoll priest in Nepal, laboring in the name of human rights on every continent are the exception, not the rule.

The working hypothesis I held when the project was initiated in 1979 was that the Christian churches in the parts of the world to be visited contain a small minority of strong advocates for the church's role in promoting human rights and a small minority of opponents who believe the church should not be engaged in any activity that could be construed as political and thus were opposed to the advocacy of human rights. It was also my working assumption that the majority of Christians were relatively neutral on human rights as a priority matter for their congregations. I also believed that our interviews would confirm these assumptions. On the first part of the premise I was correct; the two minority opinions were confirmed. However, the distressing judgment that emerged in interviews conducted over a broad denominational and theological base was that the institutional church does not function as a neutral force in the struggle for human rights.

The Christian church was generally perceived by those interviewed in all six continents as predominantly a negative or inhibiting factor in the genuine promotion of human rights. By the support and defense given to present patterns that tend to violate the civil, political, economic, social, survival, or liberation rights of given persons or groups (often representing minorities), the institutional church denies the importance of human rights. Further, the preoccupation of individual congregations with their own survival causes them to be silent about, if not cooperative with, the policies of the agencies, governments, or international structures that perpetrate acts or conditions of injustice dehumanizing to fellow human beings.

The silence of the church often comes under the guise of ignorance or inability to effect change. This is frequently the plea in the face of authoritarian regimes or complex global economic and social conditions against which any word or action seems futile or might jeopardize the life of the church itself. As a whole, the proclamation of the church is falsified. I believe this evaluation employing McCormick's criterion is valid—and tragic.

This conclusion does not deny for a moment the courageous and painful struggle of the church in specific places or parts of the world. Nor does it deny the proclamations, confessions, and covenants enunciated by church bodies on human rights. The Roman Catholic position is carefully and systematically developed through papal encyclicals, councils, and synods of bishops. Hollenbach's work cited earlier, *Claims in Conflict,* is subtitled "Retrieving and Renewing the Catholic Human Rights Tradition." A Protestant Reformed position is reflected in a theological study noted previously, *Christian Declaration on Human Rights,* sponsored by the World Alliance of Reformed Churches. This document notes the pronouncements of both the World Council of Churches and National Councils of Churches. The Declaration has a number of contributors, as the diversity of Protestant traditions would demand. It begins with a working paper by Jürgen Moltmann, one of the commentators in our investigation of human rights.

In both the Catholic and the Protestant studies there is a basic agreement about the foundation for a Christian mandate on human rights. There is also a declaration of the urgent need for the renewal of the concern for human rights in the specific policies and actions of church bodies and individual Christians. This strong consensus is also confirmed in our field research that calls for setting clearer priorities among conflicting claims for rights and establishing an ecumenical and international "common ground" for a broader and more positive perspective on human rights. To move from a falsified gospel, the church must look again to the core of the Christian message.

Human dignity is the foundation for nurturing and protecting human rights. It is rooted in the vision of the "fullness of life" promised in the incarnation of Jesus Christ and his identification with all humankind. We must be reminded that human dignity is something persons have, not something they must earn or be granted. Dignity is not a quality bestowed on others by the family, by society, or by a government. Rather, dignity is a reality as a consequence of God's good creation and never-ending love. This reality requires acknowledgement and respect. As Hollenbach puts it:

> Human dignity. . . is more fundamental than any specific human right. It is the source of all moral principles, not a moral principle itself. Dignity is the norm by which the adequacy of all forms of human behavior. . . . [is] to be judged.[6]

From the Christian perspective it is also necessary to emphasize the social nature of human dignity. The ultimate meaning of human community becomes the basis of any adequate understanding of human rights. Recognition of God-given human dignity results in an ultimate human solidarity that resists being infringed upon by national boundaries, or racial or ethnic prejudices. The church is called in God's name to join Christ "in breaking down every dividing wall" to our human wholeness and the fullness of life. There is but one flock.

The core of the Christian consensus bonds human dignity to human solidarity by the seal of love. The foundational commandment to love God and neighbor makes any attack on the dignity or community of another human being a violation not only of the commandment to love the neighbor but also the commandment to love God. The appeal to love comes from a positive vision of the quality of human community held out to the whole world. It is because of this appeal to love, because of God's "right" to, or claim on, human beings, that we are able to respond in reconciling love to one another.

God's free gift of grace has made this interdependent human community not only desired as a vision but also sought as a human reality. In the midst of our research we discovered glimpses of such solidarity everywhere. Often it was found in small, anticipatory communities with faith in God's grace. Members of these communities are moving with courage, love, and sacrifice toward the fulfillment of the positive vision upon which human rights are founded.

The trilogy of dignity, solidarity, and love is founded, motivated, and guided by Christian conviction, but it is obviously not limited to Christians. The degree to which others who do not share the Christian faith become persuaded in a pluralistic and secular context will be the test of our declarations. It is the living out of confessions that wins credibility. Changes in priorities and lifestyles of individuals, institutions, and nations are eventually required if the life-fulfilling conditions of the vision of human rights are to take place. It is in the belief in human interrelatedness, human reciprocity, that the key for solving the problems of human rights is to be found.

Christopher Jencks makes this point central in his book *Inequality*. Our research confirms his investigation in the U.S.A. He finds that Americans simply refuse to acknowledge that inequality is a real problem if it does not impinge upon their own lives. The way to move toward equality, according to Jencks, is by altering persons' "basic assumptions about the extent to which they are responsible for their neighbors and their neighbors for them."[7] The Judeo-Christian tradition puts this global dilemma in the context of all the disputes in human history between persons and groups and nations about which will be the greatest. " 'Where is Abel your brother?' Cain said, 'I do not know; am I my brother's keeper?' " (Gen. 4:8). With the recognition that we are so linked together in human dignity and community that we must embrace our responsibility for one another, we cross onto the bridge of global human rights.

The Child and the Future

As the plane left the runway in Washington, D.C., after a two-hour delay due to the air controllers' strike, I settled back in the seat to read my notes on the two workshops I had just conducted for Air Force chaplains on family life and peace education. The gentleman in the seat next to me was studying complicated scientific drawings. I inquired about his reading material and learned that he was returning home after two days of consulting as a weapons designer and had been meeting with another group of military officers.

"These are not classified documents and will be widely known when we have a nuclear war," he said.

"You mean to say *if* we have a nuclear war, I trust," came my quick reply.

"No, the technology is in place and every scenario asks not if, only *when* and *where*," replied the arms advisor. "Every weapon we have developed so far has eventually been used. I am convinced that the nuclear holocaust will be upon us within this decade *unless* we change radically, and I doubt that we have the will to do so."

Having overheard an earlier comment to another passenger about his children, I asked, "How do you feel about your children when you say that?"

"I weep for them," he whispered, "and for me. Few will survive to live anything like a full or even humane life when the chain reaction of retaliation we have assembled is triggered."

"How," I asked, "do you live with that knowledge?"

"I usually try not to think about it," my new friend replied. "But when I do, I wish that someone could discover a way to release us from this madness. I would give up my job tomorrow and put my technical skills to more constructive uses. Yet I sincerely believe we are producing a military deterrent that holds off the horror a little longer. For the sake of our children we have to find an alternative to this constant confrontation." We shared and dreamed and were even misty-eyed together as we thought about the future, especially the future our children might never experience.

The seeds of hope throughout these two years of research seem always to point to children. Indeed, children may hold the key to the future and to the quest for human rights. The powerless children of the world starve and are deformed by malnutrition and war in appalling numbers. Their plight may motivate the adult world to explore alternatives more diligently, for their sake as well as ours. It is not only our own children but those of other peoples and nations who evoke our response. Perhaps it is not as strange as it must have appeared to the disciples—and ourselves—for Jesus to place a child in the midst of the disciples who were arguing about who should be the greatest; Jesus declared the child to be first. He spoke of the kingdom of God that promises wholeness and fullness of life, and declared that it belongs to children and those who accept it as children. The standard of dignity and solidarity and love rests with the child in weakness, humility, and innocence. To point to such powerlessness as the symbol of hope must surely be foolishness. But "The foolishness of God is wiser than men, and the weakness of God is stronger than men" (1 Cor. 1:25 RSV).

Robert McAfee Brown has helped me recognize the underlying principle that informs reflection and action. I had found it embedded in the gospels and intertwined in my research. Yet I refused to accept it. Only when I looked from the underside of history, from the side of the weak and powerless, who are most often children, did I begin to hear and respond. The concrete expression of this principle came to Brown from a friend in Chile who had been forced underground by the oppressive regime of Pinochet: "The only privileged ones will be the children." Every human strategy, to say nothing of theology, should take as its norm the dignity of children. Whatever conditions "provide for the creative growth of children," Brown suggests, "will make it on all other scores."[8] This is a simple, but perhaps profound formula that supplies the measure, the angle of vision, from which to view human rights. It will move us from reflection about the issues to actions that address them. The formula is, of course, not new. Its passionate pronouncement runs through history from Jesus to Dostoevski. However, a determined effort to apply this principle of the "privileged place of children" as a criterion for the kingdom of God would indeed be new.

"Children of War," the series for *Time* magazine done by Roger Rosenblatt, captures the beauty and strength of the human spirit in an extraordinary way. Our own research took us to three of the five war zones visited by Rosenblatt. Although we also visited a wider area, and our visits were longer and not limited to interviews with children, our conclusions are similar to Rosenblatt's. The very children who have sustained devastating losses still nurture incredible optimism. We saw children suffering from war in the refugee camps of Thailand, Pakistan, Hong Kong, and in the direct combat of Uganda and Nicaragua; others suffered from hunger, deprivation, and suppression in an Aboriginal settlement in Australia, the *favelas* of Brazil, the villages of Nepal and India and in the slums of Tokyo, Geneva, and

"Springfield." Yet there is a "copability quotient" that allows children who have suffered the most to have what Rosenblatt describes as "an essential good-heartedness . . . a generosity of nature that transcends and diminishes anything they have suffered."

The children, especially the Cambodians, who may have suffered the most, demonstrated enormous charity toward others, including their enemies. Rosenblatt's exchange with a child who had lost both parents to the genocide of Pol Pot's Khmer Rouge reveals the tone of the whole dialogue:

"Does your spirit tell you to get revenge?"

"Yes," solemnly [the child responds].

"So, you will go back to Cambodia one day and fight the Khmer Rouge?"

"No. That is not what I mean by revenge. To me revenge means that I must make the most of my life."[9]

The amazing conversion of the meaning of revenge is only a sign of why children become the model for a new standard of human rights. The majority of these children of war and deprivation respond apparently out of their own basic dignity and desire for solidarity with the rest of the human family— "kindness for cruelty, generosity for spite. In short their goodness may be a means of survival."[10] I would add: "not only for them but for all humankind." Would that we could only begin to understand and counteract the diminishing of the human spirit that occurs as we proceed from childhood to adulthood, a process that often appears to be regressive. The symbol of the kingdom is a child who, in weakness and humility, seeks to be "last of all and servant of all."

Setting Priorities

Meaningful dialogue on human rights that takes place in a global perspective needs to set priorities. An appeal to "love" has often covered over conflicting claims. These claims cannot be resolved simply by agreeing that human rights are crucial or by acknowledging that different sets of values are emphasized in different "worlds." Emphasis on the value systems already in place may lead to further isolation and hostility. Priorities must be established. We need clear directives that point to the basis not only for adjudicating claims in conflict but also for shaping a vision of the quality of relationships in the human community. That vision holds such respect for dignity and solidarity that the only privileged ones are children. The present intellectual war over human rights appears to result not simply in a series of "trade-offs," but also in a series of "stand-offs" in the global confrontation on human rights. Disputes between those nations or groups that favor *political and civil rights* versus *economic and social rights* versus those that advocate *survival and liberation rights* will not be resolved by more appeals to different declarations or covenants on human rights. Nor dare the church, if it is to be faithful to its own calling and role, simply develop different theories and articulate more clearly the moral and theological grounds for appeals. Both are important but insufficient in face of the concrete human suffering that surrounds us.

The Christian church bears special responsibility in this crisis of human rights. Renewal of the human rights commitment of the church is urgent. The call for renewal is based on God's gifts of human dignity, community, and love, and on the mutual obligation and responsibility to God and one another that we bear as persons and communities of faith. The Old Testament scholar Walter Harrelson reminds us of this in his insightful study *The Ten Commandments and Human Rights:*

> The Bible knows little or nothing about human rights in our sense of the term. It does know and say a great deal about the obligations of individuals and of the human community to the Lord the Giver of Life and to fellow human beings. But one's obligations to others are in fact the realities that the others have a right to expect. . . . God has a right to expect such faithfulness! In that sense, the Bible has much to say about human rights. It is possible to see in the basic understanding of human rights . . . a large measure of the biblical understanding of human obligation under God.[11]

This investigation of human rights on a global scale confirmed for me that the credibility of the church's mission in this decade depends on a conversion or transformation of its present and perceived stand on human rights. Based on McCormick's criterion, the predominantly protective and inhibiting role played by most religious bodies bolsters the judgment by most of the world that the gospel proclamation is a lie. The present stance of most congregations is not seen as "good news" by the poor, captives, and oppressed who are singled out by Jesus as the focus of his ministry (Luke 4:18) as he cites the prophet Isaiah (61:1).

It is my conviction that the protective role of the church is *not* a result of self-conscious malice. Rather, it results from ignorance, apathy, and inability to take the first steps and pay the human price for transformation. Most Christians in all three worlds do not recognize or have been unable to acknowledge the interdependence of the global connection between all God's children. We seek to respond to the needs in our immediate communities but find it difficult to widen our vision. The problems linked to the violation of human rights in other parts of the world or even in our own nations often seem overwhelming and unapproachable, even symbolically. Hope rests in believing that this is not true and that, with God, all things are possible.

The commentators responding to the eight case studies that follow have addressed dilemmas faced by members of their own geographic communities. Most, however, have also risked a response to issues faced by a totally different culture. They have stepped beyond their "territorial boundaries" and applied their perspectives—illuminated by the Christian faith—to specific

problems in another "world." Their venture, their insights, and their willingness to be in dialogue model for us the first step.

Renewal of the church's gospel proclamation must begin with just this kind
of risk. We must learn to feed one another. Only then can disparity begin to
diminish and the global village move closer to becoming one flock.

We must also begin with gradual agreement on priorities. The process is
complicated and often we must live with enormous levels of ambiguity. For
example, Kosuke Koyama notes that our modern technology can be used for
humanization and the enhancement of life as evidenced by advancements in
medicine, education, communication, and transportation. However, the
brilliant gifts of technology are also threatening the meaning of human life.
Dr. Koyama uses an illustration from Ruth L. Sivard's *World Military and
Social Expenditures 1981*:

> The World War II submarine could sink only passing ships; now a single
> sub can destroy 160 cities as far away as 4000 miles.
> A nuclear war which could snuff out 800 million lives in a few hours
> could be launched on the decision of a single individual.[12]

"The world spends," Koyama declares, "$550 billion annually for weapons.
. . . This staggering sum means about one million a minute! We might wonder whether we must not call this a Global Military Installation rather than a
village. . . ." It is clear that if technology is to enhance human meaning, it
must not be used "for one's own self aggrandizement. The world has become
too small a place for such self aggrandizement."[13]

Ambiguity must be lived with and through, not used as an escape for failing to set priorities. Again, it is dialogue between the First and Third Worlds
that points the way. The "strategic moral priorities" that Hollenbach suggests
as the basis for the renewal of the Catholic human rights tradition coincide
with the pleas of those such as Weeramantry from the Third World. Hollenbach declares that the basic human *needs* of food, housing, work, and health
"can be met only in community."[14] The social right to fulfill these needs can be
honored only "through participation in the economic and productive life of
society."[15] The exercise of personal *freedoms,* such as religious belief or political activity, are secured by political and civil rights that also depend on participation in structures of the community. There is also a group of rights
that guarantee the *relationships* that bind persons together, such as the
right to assemble, form associations, and found a family. These rights are
all "basic forms of human interaction and interdependence" that provide
the ultimate societal support for the "group bonds necessary for human dignity."[16]

For Hollenbach, these three areas—need, freedom, and relationship—
form the basis for his suggested priorities. The primary area must be the right
to meaningful participation. This is in contrast to the dehumanizing trend
toward the marginalization of persons and groups. This marginalization dis-
honors the right to free oneself from situations that deny human dignity. The

words of the National Conference of Brazilian Bishops capture what I have heard again and again in cities and villages throughout the world:

> To be marginalized . . . is to receive an unjust salary. It is to be deprived of education, medical attention, and credit; it is to be hungry and live in sordid huts; it is to be deprived of land by inadequate, unjust . . . structures.[17]

Convictions about community, solidarity, and participation lead Hollenbach and others—myself included—to give primacy to social rights. Such a conclusion demands that those of us who *benefit* from unjust structures must seriously reconsider our own priorities.

The whole range of human rights emphasized by all three worlds is to be honored; and to a degree this occurs in all three worlds. The intention of priorities is not arbitrarily to side with the emphasis of one world over another. Rather, it is to take with ultimate seriousness the human encounters of our field research and the resources of an ecumenical community of Christian faith to respond to the overwhelming needs in our global village. It is not enough, even in light of the interconnectedness of all human rights, simply to declare the need to respect, protect, and promote all human rights. When conflicts between rights occur, as they inevitably do, there must be guidelines with some specificity to initiate meaningful negotiations.

It is ironic that one of the predominant characteristics of contemporary society evidenced again in our research is the conflict between "the *needs* of some and the *wants* of others." Hollenbach suggests, in this context, not a set of policies or programs but three principles, which he describes as "three strategic moral priorities":

> (1) The needs of the poor take priority over the wants of the rich.
> (2) The freedom of the dominated takes priority over the liberty of the powerful.
> (3) The participation of marginalized groups takes priority over the preservation of an order which excludes them.[18]

There are no solutions to the case studies on human rights that are contained in this book; however, one can find therein the seeds of realistic alternatives. The application of Hollenbach's principles to specific cases may broaden our vision for the global village. We would then urge the application of these principles to personal cases and to decisions we and our nations face on a daily basis.

One of the most exciting and fruitful learning experiences for the authors near the conclusion of the research project was to teach many of these case studies in the national setting where they were developed and to teach them to international and cross-cultural gatherings as well. The creativity that emerged, the alternatives recommended (which went beyond the case data), the sensitivity demonstrated, the faith and hope confessed, made these dialogical encounters a gift of God's grace to the authors. What we learned became resources of grace to us for which we can never adequately express our gratitude. In the same way, we hope that the commentaries will open to readers new avenues of grace, new insights, and new sensitivity to the issues facing our world. As we "try on" other world perspectives, we must stretch. We may also grow.

Beyond the criteria for case selection given in the Preface, these real but disguised cases and the often intensely personal commentaries should be self-explanatory. They witness to the hope that a dialogue between those we presently describe as belonging to the First, Second, and Third Worlds will contribute to our becoming more aware of our one-worldness. The conclusions from the research, shared in this final chapter, are, of course, personal to a degree. The guidelines and priorities outlined will perhaps be of some assistance as one reflects on the human drama within each case study. However, overemphasis on dignity, solidarity, love and childlikeness contains the danger of missing the full spectrum of Christ's message. The strategic moral priorities of Hollenbach may also need revision. The challenge, however, is to continue—or perhaps begin—dialogue as the basis for continual conversion and progress toward global transformation.

As a French colleague told a First World group returning from an "enacted case" of living three weeks in rural areas of East Africa, "The test upon your return will not be what you say, or even what you do, but rather what you become." So it is with all of us—our challenge is in becoming.

Plowshares Institute: Beginning with Simple Steps

Convinced that such research was revealing and that education is a critical step toward global wholeness, one unanticipated result of this project was the formation, with several colleagues, of Plowshares Institute, a nonprofit educational corporation in the service of the church. Plowshares Institute seeks to contribute to a more just, sustainable, and peaceful world community through research, education, and dialogue. The Institute takes its name and its inspiration from Micah 4:3 and Isaiah:

> They shall beat their swords into plowshares,
>   and their spears into pruning hooks;
> nation shall not lift up sword against nation,
>   neither shall they learn war anymore. [Isa. 2:4 RSV].

The vision of Plowshares is that of a world where the conditions for the fullness of life may be possible for all. By God's grace, we seek to move, however slowly, toward the reality of human dignity, solidarity, and transforming love promised in the gospel. Christ's presence with us is one of the few lights in this darkness of suffering, restrictions, and failure in a global village that is still frantically beating plowshares into swords. Our task is to discover ways to abandon the study of war and violence in every form, whether military, economic, or social, and then commit ourselves to concrete strategy and action. The dream is for us as one people, as a global community, to put our hands on the double handles of a plowshare, and recognize the earth and every neighbor as gifts from God.

Plowshares Institute joins other persons and organizations in this journey convinced there are three important tasks ahead. First, basic research on what factors induce persons and institutions to *change* their priorities and lifestyles in the light of global needs (currently, this kind of research appears almost totally lacking). Secondly, consultation on which new models of education including cross-cultural dialogue are most faithful and effective in facilitating such change. Thirdly, application of these models to initiate concrete individual and institutional change that reflects global priorities.

Plowshares Institute seeks to engage churches, judicatories, and other institutions in projects of research, education, and model application toward greater global awareness. The goal is human transformation based on new levels of understanding. The staff of the Institute has witnessed such transformation of institutional priorities and personal patterns of life that are more just and faithful to the gospel proclamation. The reasons for such changes, apart from God's grace, are not always clear. There are some clues in the human stories contained in the case studies: First, hope for change is linked with face-to-face encounters between persons in various parts of the world; second, a community of support and accountability that allows meaningful change to begin and to be sustained is essential.

The International Advisory Committee and staff of Plowshares Institute are made up of persons whose places of birth span the globe but who now serve as educators, primarily in the First World. In all our diversity of experience with, and approach to, issues of global justice and peace, which I celebrate, I also believe we share the common vision of Plowshares. This book becomes the first published contribution of Plowshares Institute to this quest for global wholeness. The authors take responsibility for all errors and presumptions contained herein. We express gratitude for those who have shared their lives and hopes through the case studies and commentaries. Now we invite dialogue with our readers, and with participants in case discussions that may emerge from contact with this research and educational project.

The richness and diversity of the highly confessional commentaries on the case studies confirm the judgment that the cases have no solution, no one answer. These personal reflections, we trust, will have made it easier for readers to seek their own appropriate response for themselves and their communities. Liberation is the aim of the experiment. We seek to liberate ourselves in the process of this dialogue; we seek to move from rhetoric to response, from reflection to action.

Those of us now involved with Plowshares Institute have witnessed the transformation of individuals and institutions. Our initial observation is that change in priorities and life patterns, when they occur, appear linked with one or more of the following components: (1) relatively nonthreatening education based on the connection between the mandates of the gospel and global awareness; (2) the support of a community of faith that makes a covenant to take simple beginning steps; and (3) person-to-person dialogue and exchange on a cross-cultural basis beyond the boundaries of the First, Second, or Third Worlds. Empirical research has been initiated by Plowshares Institute in an attempt to test these preliminary observations and to develop educational resources and experiential opportunities to build on these learnings for the sake of the human rights of all of God's children.

Perhaps a few vignettes will provide a glimpse into the process of human transformation and reconciliation—a process that is small and anticipatory but profoundly hopeful. Each person in his or her own way has embodied what we believe is a central theme for ministry in this decade—Micah's call to do justice, love mercy, and walk humbly with one's God. This theme undergirds lay theologian Jacques Ellul's call to "think globally and act locally."

A midwest suburban congregation held a weekend retreat on the "Future of Mission in a Global Context." Those in attendance comprised a broad-based representation of the church officers and youth leaders. They explored—through case studies, group Bible study, and assessment of patterns of living—the issues raised in a book co-authored by Larry Rasmussen, a member of the Plowshares Advisory Council: *Predicament of the Prosperous*.[19] The results of this intensive weekend were culminated by relating elements of this experience to the congregation during the Sunday morning worship. The first step by the weekend participants was a covenant of support for those persons and families moving gradually toward a more simplified and freer lifestyle in terms of food, transportation, and energy consumption. With philosophy and resources of a Mennonite cookbook, *More With Less*,[20] they agreed to model new forms of satisfying but ecologically responsible meals for future fellowship dinners for the congregation. The proceeds of these events were to be used as the basis for sharing time, presence, and resources with those economically deprived in the urban community where most of the members of the congregation were employed. Finally, the seminar members gave fresh scrutiny to the distribution of the congregation's resources of time and talent. They then set a goal of equal dollar-for-dollar sharing of their funds in the awareness of a global village requiring more just and equitable distribution of resources. Several lay members and the pastor will have engaged in a cross-cultural exchange experience by the time this book is released. One involved lay leader said, "We have begun—with God's grace, the help of Plowshares, and the support of the congregation of Christ. We may even have the courage to persevere."

A black pastor of an urban New England mainline congregation accepted an invitation to participate in a traveling seminar to Africa in order, he declared, "to get in touch with my African roots." As part of a community of twenty other persons, both laity and clergy, he studied and prepared to learn about new forms of the church in Africa and share his own struggles in ministry with his African hosts. By his own testimony this three-week immersion in the ordinary life of the people in the villages and cities of East Africa—linked with a prior covenant to live simply and directly with the people and to interpret the experience within his own constituency for one year—was "life-changing." "I was startled to find myself seen not primarily as a Black but as an American who was part of an economically developed, colonizing nation. Those weeks, especially when I was in African homes separated from the group, were almost overwhelming. It is not so much what I learned about Africans, although their vitality and cultural identity were impressive. It was what I learned about myself. I could never again see my own parish with the same eyes. Ours is a middle class church that basically ignored the poverty of Blacks and Hispanics in our parish. Upon my return we moved toward change that was often resisted by the congregation and even by me. But now, five years later, our priorities are on "good news to the poor" in programs and presence. We even have an Hispanic associate pastor, which would have been unheard of five years ago."

A Roman Catholic archbishop in Brazil spoke in a humble and moving way with the members of a joint Catholic and Protestant traveling seminar about the transformation of his church. The move had been from identification with the privileged classes of a society oppressive to the poor to a voluntary stance of identification with the disenfranchised. The bishop shared that he had just agreed to set the new priorities of the diocese around the needs expressed by a consensus of the base communities of the church. These priorities were aligned almost directly with the demands for justice by the labor unions opposed by the current government. Our host joked that this was quite a change in the decision-making process for the bishop and the diocese.

The group had presented to the bishop a gift of a hand-worked stole. In concluding his remarks, the bishop placed the stole around the shoulders of the Brazilian Protestant pastor standing next to him. The bishop fondly referred to him as his "ally in the struggle for the kingdom." When group members asked the bishop if he had any advice for them to take home, he responded, "No, I have enough difficulty trying to do justice in my own country, as I assume you do in yours."

The message of the bishop was clear—to focus priorities on issues of justice and liberation, taking actions urged by the grass-roots communities of faith.

During dinner the chairman of the investment committee of a large multinational corporation shared his reflections with the local coordinator of a visiting African delegation of church and civic leaders. "The events of this morning, especially the frank dialogue between members of my investment committee and the African delegation concerning our investment policies in the Third World, influenced me. I see more clearly the potential negative impact of some of our international policies. In the next few weeks I must vote on a number of resolutions concerning international issues which come before the annual meetings of companies for which we are major stockholders. I intend to change my vote on the corporation's position on several issues. I also intend to accept the delegation's invitation to visit them in Africa."

A rural parish in Nicaragua, located near the capital, faced a request of the new Sandinista government, in which several Roman Catholic priests served as principal officials. Following the devastating civil war with the Somoza regime, one of the first acts of the new administration was a literacy campaign to address isolated rural areas where illiteracy was as high as 70 percent. The government argued that the democratic process depended on a literate populace. More important, the long-term relief of extensive human suffering depended on basic knowledge of nutrition, health, and agriculture. Each of these concerns could be addressed by a campaign that would send all available literate persons to spend several months teaching on a volunteer basis in these isolated areas.

The cost of the plan in this particular village would be great, for it was fortunate enough to have a high percentage of literate citizens. Those who remained would have additional responsibilities in the fields, in the town, and in the schools. The local priest supported the plan; the bishop was silent. Members of the community gathered to vote on accepting or rejecting the government proposals. They argued for several hours. Suddenly the discussion came to a close when an elderly man stood and paraphrased Matthew 25:40: "If you do this to the least of these, you have done it unto me." He then called for the vote.

The program was overwhelmingly approved. Other villages joined in and together sent out volunteers who finally numbered in the thousands. Months later a foundation study of the literacy volunteers indicated that the educational impact on the volunteers may have been as great as that on the rural villages. As one young woman volunteer stated, "Now I understand what the struggle for liberation was about and what proclaiming 'release to the captives' really means. Being unable to read is clearly a form of imprisonment."

These five, true pictures of global villagers faced with changing perceptions appear to indicate that simple beginning steps require: (1) conviction about the need; (2) a vision of where it is possible to start; (3) a community of support; and (4) God's grace and forgiveness when we fall short of our covenants.

Toward a Theology of Letting-Go

Each response will take a distinctive form, depending on the location, history, and condition of the respondent. Our reflection and our actions will be shaped by those to whom we listen and on whose behalf we act. The authors had their cultural shackles at least loosened through gifts offered by and lessons learned from new friends while living briefly in parts of the Third World in the U.S.A., in Africa, and in the South Pacific. Our response is guided by these brothers and sisters. They challenge us to convert the rhythms of our living that belie what we confess. We fail more frequently than we succeed, but by God's forgiveness and grace we are revived, held accountable, and sent on our way again.

Those times in our lives when our family lived in the Third World prepared us for the turning point that occurred in the midst of this project. It is now clear that the task to which we are called is what one member of the Plowshares Council, Sister Marie Augusta Neal, describes as a "theology of letting-go."[21] We have come to see the application of Christ's mandate and Hollenbach's "strategic moral principles" in concrete terms as we seek to give priority to the needs of the poor and the oppressed. To relinquish the firm grasp on our possessions, on our power, and on our pride is a condition for solidarity with the sisters and brothers of the globe we have come to know. The door of our prison is only ajar and colleagues from the Third World urge us to have the courage to come out.

However, we also know that means embracing what is called "an indigenous theology of the cross."[22] We must go with women and men into the darkness of our world to suffer with them—and we are afraid—afraid to give up the answers we have cherished, the glory we crave, the security we desire, in order to opt for voluntary servanthood. We are afraid to come as little children. Yet we also know in our hearts there is no dawn without the night, no resurrection without the cross. We seek premature resurrection and painless liberation. Only a community of the cross with the innocence and hope of children will bear us through that prison door and onto that path of justice. One cannot replenish the earth or push the plowshare alone. This path to peace is the struggle for justice; it is our conviction that we are accompanied by a community of faith and a God of inexhaustible mercy.

The responses and actions each of us takes may be quite different. They depend on individual situations. We invite our readers to be in dialogue with us and to share with others their own case studies as gifts of grace. The present address of Plowshares Institute is P.O. Box 243, Simsbury, Connecticut 06070.

NOTES

1. *The Global 2000 Report to the President,* vol. 1, *Entering the Twenty-First Century* (Washington, D.C.: U.S. Government Printing Office, 1980).

2. Sources for the analogy were drawn from work of Dr. Alvin Leipers cited in Weeramantry, *Equality,* p. 159, and from D. L. Shettel, *Life-Style Change for Children* (New York: United Presbyterian Program Agency, 1981), p. 17.

3. Cited from Robert McAfee Brown, *Making Peace in the Global Village* (Philadelphia: Westminster, 1981), p. 15.

4. Weeramantry, *Equality,* p. 160.

5. Richard A. McCormick, "Human Rights and the Mission of the Church," *Mission Trends No. 4,* G. H. Anderson and T. F. Stransky, eds. (New York: Paulist, 1979), p. 37.

6. David Hollenbach, *Claims in Conflict: Retrieving and Renewing the Catholic Human Tradition* (New York: Paulist Press, 1979), p. 90.

7. Christopher Jencks, *Inequality* (New York: Basic Books, 1972).

8. Robert McAfee Brown, *Creative Dislocation—The Movement of Grace* (Philadelphia: Abingdon, 1980), p. 128.

9. *Time,* January 22, 1982, p. 52.

10. Ibid., p. 51.

11. Walter Harrelson, *The Ten Commandments and Human Rights* (Philadelphia: Fortress, 1980).

12. Kosuke Koyama, "Religion in the Global Village," quotes taken from an unpublished address delivered on April 26, 1982 at the University of Charleston.

13. Ibid.

14. Hollenbach, *Claims,* p. 203.

15. Ibid.

16. Ibid.

17. Ibid., p. 199.

18. Ibid., p. 204.

19. B. C. Birch and Larry Rasmussen, (Philadelphia: Westminster, 1978).

20. Doris Janzen Longacre, (Scottsdale, Pa.: Herald, 1976).

21. Marie Augusta Neal, *A Socio-theology of Letting-Go* (New York: Paulist, 1977).

22. See Douglass John Hall, *Lighten Our Darkness* (Philadelphia: Westminster, 1976).

SUGGESTIONS FOR ADDITIONAL READING

Brown, Robert McAfee, *Making Peace in the Global Village.* Philadelphia: Westminster, 1981.

Hall, Douglas John. *Lighten Our Darkness: Toward an Indigenous Theology of the Cross.* Philadelphia: Westminster, 1976.

Harrelson, Walter. *The Ten Commandments and Human Rights.* Philadelphia: Fortress, 1980.

Hollenbach, David. *Claims in Conflict: Retrieving and Renewing the Catholic Human Rights Traditon.* New York: Paulist, 1979.

Miller, A. O. *Christian Declaration on Human Rights.* Grand Rapids: Eerdmans, 1977.

Neal, Marie Augusta. *A Socio-Theology of Letting-Go.* New York: Paulist, 1977.

Rasmussen, Larry L. *Economic Anxiety and the Christian Faith.* Minneapolis: Augsburg, 1981.

Sider, Ronald J. *Rich Christians in an Age of Hunger.* New York: Paulist, 1977.

Simon, Arthur. *Bread for the World.* New York: Paulist, 1975.

Stivers, Robert. *The Sustainable Society: Ethics and Economic Growth.* Philadelphia: Westminster, 1976.

Taylor, John V. *Enough is Enough.* Minneapolis: Augsburg, 1977.

Weeramantry, C. G. *Equality and Freedom: Some Third World Perspectives.* Columbo: Lake House Pub., 1976.

CONTRIBUTORS

Rubem Alves was born in Bôa Esperança, Minas Gerais, Brazil. He was educated at the Campinas Presbyterian Seminary (São Paulo), Union Theological Seminary (New York), and Princeton Theological Seminary. In his own words: "I do theology for sheer pleasure, as a hobby, because my church reacted with horror at the possibility that I should in any way teach theology. I make my living as a professor of philosophy in the Teacher's College of the State University of Campinas. I have written a few books: *A Theology of Human Hope; Tomorrow's Child; The Enigma of Religion; What is Religion?; Protestantism and Repression;* and *Variations on Life and Death.*"

Wesley N. Campbell is a doctoral student under the supervision of Professor Jürgen Moltmann at the University of Tübingen. His dissertation is entitled "Christian Theology in the Context of Historical Relativity: A Critical Examination of the Contribution of Ernst Troeltsch." He studied at the University of Western Australia, Barclay Theological Hall in Perth, and the United Faculty of Theology in Melbourne. He is an ordained pastor in the Uniting Church in Australia and served four years in the parish ministry.

Don Carrington is a lecturer in theological studies at Nungalinya College, Casuarina (Darwin), Northern Territory, Australia. The college is a combined church training and research center, with a special ministry to the Aboriginal peoples of Australia. He received his bachelor of divinity degree from the Melbourne College of Divinity. He is a minister in the Uniting Church of Australia. He has served as a fraternal worker in the South Pacific and has been a strong advocate for Aboriginal peoples and their causes. He is the author of *Jesus Dreaming: Studies of Gospel Stories out of which the Community of God Lives.*

Theresa Mei-Fen Chu was born in Shanghai and was educated there in the Jesuit Aurora University. She joined the Society of the Sacred Heart and left China in 1949, on the eve of Liberation. She continued her religious life with studies at Manhattanville College and received her doctorate in philosophy from the University of Chicago Divinity School. Her dissertation focused on the religious dimension of Mao Tse-tung's thought. She has taught in Japan, France, and the U.S.A. She was for many years principal of the Sacred Heart School and president of Sacred Heart Women's College, both in Korea. She currently serves as the director of the China Program for the Canadian Council of Churches, in Toronto.

Orlando E. Costas was born in Ponce, Puerto Rico. Prior to earning his doctorate in theology at the Free University of Amsterdam, the Netherlands, he studied at the Inter-American University of Puerto Rico, Winona Lake School of Theology, and Garrett Theological Seminary. He is currently the Thornly B. Wood Professor of Missiology and director of Hispanic studies at Eastern Baptist Theological Seminary in Philadelphia. He has pastored churches both in Puerto Rico and the U.S.A. and was founder and director of the Latin American Evangelical Center for Pastoral Studies in Costa Rica. His numerous publications in Spanish and English include: *The Church and Its Mission: A Shattering Critique from the Third World; The Integrity of Mission: The Inner Life and Outreach of the Church;* and *Christ Outside the Gate: A New Place of Salvation.* He is an ordained minister in both the American Baptist Church and the United Church of Christ.

Marjorie Hall Davis is a member of the adjunct faculty at Hartford Seminary and serves on the Council of the Institute on Religion in an Age of Science. She is a fellow of the Case Study Institute and a board member of the Association for Case Teaching. She studied at Smith College and Cornell University and is presently studying at the Yale Divinity School. She has published case studies through the Intercollegiate Case Clearing House and is author of *Explorations in Faith.* When researching "To Bear Arms," she conducted first-hand interviews in Nicaragua.

Gordon Dicker is Lecturer in Historical Theology at United Theological College, Sydney, and in the Divinity School of Sydney University. He was educated at Sydney University, received his master's degree in theology from the Melbourne College of Divinity and his doctorate in theology from Union Theological Seminary, New York. He has served pastorates in Australia and the U.S.A., and for six years was a fraternal worker in Indonesia. He is the author of *Faith with Understanding.*

Terry Djiniyini is a minister of the Uniting Church of Australia. He was educated at Alcorn College, Brisbane, and at Rarongo Theological College in Rabaul in Papua New Guinea. He is minister of the Galwinky parish on Elcho Island and visiting lecturer at Nungalinya College in Casuarina (Darwin). He is a leading spokesperson for the Aborigine Christian community.

Alice Frazer Evans is director of research and writing for Plowshares Institute and co-director of the Association for Case Teaching. She was educated at Agnes Scott College, the University of Edinburgh, and the University of Wisconsin. She has published numerous case studies and has been on the faculty of case institutes in Australia, Asia, India, Latin America, and the U.S.A. She is the co-author of *Introduction to Christianity* and *Casebook for Christian Living: Value Formation for Families and Congregations.* She is an ordained lay elder in the United Presbyterian Church, U.S.A.

Robert A. Evans is the executive director of Plowshares Institute and co-director of the Association for Case Teaching. He was educated at Yale University, the University of Edinburgh, the University of Basel, Yale Divinity School, and received his doctorate in philosophy from Union Theological Seminary, New York. He has been a professor of theology at McCormick Seminary, Makerere University in Uganda, Pacific Theological College in Fiji, and Hartford Seminary. His publications include *Christian Theology: A Case Method Approach; The Future of Philosophical Theology;* and *Intelligible and Responsible Talk about God.* He is general editor of the Harper & Row series Experience and Reflection: Theological Casebooks. A pastor in the United Presbyterian Church, U.S.A., he has served churches in the U.S.A. and overseas.

Eileen Fitzsimons studied languages at St. Olaf College, Aarhus, Denmark, and the Universities of Marburg and Münster, West Germany. She received her master of arts degree and doctorate in German from the University of Chicago. She has taught German at the College of the University of Chicago and at Indiana University Northwest, in Gary. She is currently acting Jesuit librarian at the Jesuit-Krauss-McCormick Library, Chicago.

Kosuke Koyama is Professor of Ecumenics and World Christianity at Union Theological Seminary, New York. He was educated at Tokyo Union Theological Seminary and Drew University, and received his master of theology and doctorate in philosophy from Princeton Theological Seminary. An ordained minister in the Church of Christ in Thailand, he has served at the Thailand Theological Seminary (Chiengmai), the Southeast Asia Graduate School of Theology (Singapore), and the University of Otago (Dunedin, New Zealand). He has also held various posts with the World Council of Churches. His publications include *Waterbuffalo Theology; No Handle on the Cross;* and *Three Mile an Hour God.*

John Mbiti, an African theologian and an Anglican priest, is currently pastor of a Swiss Reformed congregation in Burgdorf, Switzerland. Prior to this appointment, he served as the director of the World Council of Churches Ecumenical Institute at Bossey and as professor of theology and comparative religion at Makerere University, Kampala, Uganda. A Kenyan by birth, he was educated at Makerere University, Barrington College, Rhode Island, and obtained his doctorate in theology at Cambridge University. He has written numerous books and articles, poems, and short stories. His books include *Concepts of God in Africa, African Religions and Philosophy, New Testament Eschatology in an African Background, Introduction to African Religion, The Prayers of African Religion, African and Asian Contributions to Contemporary Theology* (ed.), and *Confessing Christ in Different Cultures* (ed.).

Johann Baptist Metz is professor of fundamental theology at the University of Münster. Born in Welluck, Germany, he studied at the Universities of Innsbruck and Munich, where he received his doctorate in theology. He was ordained as a Roman Catholic priest in 1954. Among his numerous books translated into English are *Theology of the World, Followers of Christ, Poverty of Spirit, Faith in History and Society, The Courage to Pray* (with Karl Rahner), and most recently, *The Emergent Church.*

Jürgen Moltmann, born in Hamburg, began studying Protestant theology as a prisoner of war in England. After his return to Germany in 1948, he continued his studies at the University of Göttingen. Following several years in pastoral work, he served as professor at the Church Seminary in Wuppertal and at the University of Bonn. At present he is Professor of Systematic Theology at the University of Tübingen. He has been involved in Jewish-Christian dialogue in Germany and through the World Council of Churches has been active in ecumenical conferences. He serves as the editor of the journal *Evangelische Theologie.* His most important books have been translated into the major world languages. These include *Theology of Hope; Man, The Future of Creation;* and *Trinity and Kingdom of God.*

Heinrich Ott holds the chair of systematic theology at the University of Basel. He studied at the Universities of Marburg and Basel, where he received his doctorate in theology. His publications in English translation include *Theology and Preaching; God;* and *Reality and Faith: The Theological Legacy of Dietrich Bonhoeffer.* He is an ordained pastor in the Reformed Church in Switzerland and has served in the pastoral ministry. Currently he is serving as an elected representative in the Swiss Parliament.

J. Deotis Roberts is professor of philosophical theology and is the president of the Interdenominational Theological Center in Atlanta, Georgia. Born in Spindale, North Carolina, he was educated at Johnson C. Smith University and Hartford Seminary. He received his doctorate in philosophical theology from the University of Edinburgh. Before assuming his present position, he served as a Baptist pastor, was dean of the School of Theology at Virginia Union University, and professor of theology and editor of the *Journal of Religious Thought* at Howard University. His books include *From Puritanism to Platonism in 17th Century England; Liberation and Reconciliation: A Black Theology;* and *Roots of a Black Future: Family and Church.*

Philip Wickeri currently lives in China as a "Foreign Expert" and teaches in the Department of Foreign Languages at Nanjing University. He is a candidate for a doctorate in philosophy at Princeton Theological Seminary and is on leave as a fraternal worker for the United Presbyterian Church in the U.S.A. His dissertation deals with the Protestant experience in China's United Front.